HOW TO WRITE MANGA

Your Complete Guide to Manga Storytelling

R.A. Paterson

(Revised Edition)

Robyn Paterson
Visit my website at www.robynpaterson.com

First Printing: July 2019
Second Printing: January 2021
Kung Fu Action Theatre

ISBN-978-1-989357-03-3

Image Credits:
Cover Image:
Agungsugiarto

Character Images
#78878664 | © utako068 - Fotolia.com
#78878086 | © utako068 - Fotolia.com
#132940241 | © utako068 - Fotolia.com

For Charlotte, and the manga and anime writers of the future.

AUTHOR NOTES

Two years ago, I released a book called *Write! Shonen Manga* which was very well received, and so I began working on a second edition of that book. However, after collecting a huge amount of new research materials and notes, what was intended to be a second edition of a book on writing shonen manga turned into a book on writing manga in general.

There is very little left of that original book in this one, except for some of the better parts of the previous book that I thought were worth keeping. Most of the book is completely new material which covers a far greater number of manga genres and adds new things like common plots to the mix. I also did away with the IDEA system and replaced it with the proper *ki-sho-ten-ketsu* form, since I decided that the Japanese had it right the first time, and I was trying to improve on perfection.

Most of the basic writing materials were revised and moved to another book called *All the Write Moves*, since many people who weren't interested in manga wanted a copy of those. In their place is a primer to help writers get off on the right foot, and hopefully give them a head start on making their own manga.

So, if you enjoyed *Write! Shonen Manga*, then now you have a (almost) whole new book to explore that will expand your manga writing abilities even further. And, if you're a new reader, welcome to the even better *How to Write Manga*. Now get out there and start creating comics!

Robyn Paterson- July 2019

This version you're reading is the first revised edition which was made because I had some things I wanted to fix and update from the previous version. In addition to various small changes, I have added a new section about the Four Essential Stories, a section about how Japanese storytellers see the world, and a new chapter on Exploratory Manga. I hope these make your manga writing even easier.

Robyn Paterson – January 2021

CONTENTS

HOW TO USE THIS BOOK

This book is divided up into three sections:

- Making Manga
- Genres and Meta-Genres
- Getting Published

The first section on Making Manga is all about what makes manga stories different from the other stories you might see in non-Japanese books or movies. It covers what makes manga (and by association- anime) different from other kinds of storytelling. How you make manga characters. What your target audience expects. The differences between Shonen and Shoujo manga. And, what extra tricks you can use to keep your audience reading until the end.

The second section is about the different manga Genres and Meta-Genres, and leads you through the ins and outs of the different kinds of popular manga. From Battle Manga to Romance and Slice-of-Life manga, this section breaks down what you need to know to write each of them, from characters and plots, to setting and tone. And then, it covers the winning plots manga readers can't seem to get enough of, leading you step by step through how to write manga-style duels, romantic comedies, and more.

Last, in the final section, you'll find important information about how the manga industry works, and what your options are if you want to get published in Japan or the English-speaking world. The comics industry is always changing, but this section will help you in getting your work out there and into the hands of your audience.

Naturally, you can read these sections in any order, and just skip to the parts you need for your own work. This is your book, and it is here to help you any way you need it to. However, they're organized this way to lead you through your manga journey, from a beginning storyteller to a master of their craft who is ready to show the world what they can do. So, you might want to read it through in order the first time around.

Now, what are you waiting for? Get in there and find your manga path!

Your own amazing journey is only beginning

R.A. Paterson

MAKING MANGA

CREATING CHARACTERS

"Manga is characters." − *Kazuo Koike, creator of* Lone Wolf and Cub.

Stories are made of five elements- controlling ideas, character, plot, setting, and audience. However, when it comes to manga, the most important of these is character. Manga (and manga-type stories) live or die based on their characters, and are almost always character driven.

Think about it this way, would you read a story with...
- Poor art but interesting characters?
- A weak story but interesting characters?
- A poorly developed setting but interesting characters?
- Characters who were very different from you, but still interesting and engaging?

Most people would answer yes to all of these, but if you flip it around...
- Amazing art but boring characters?
- An amazing story but boring characters?
- A well-developed setting but boring characters?
- Characters who were the same as you, but boring and dull?

For many readers, this would be a hard no. People will forgive poor art, story, setting, and even unrelatable characters, just so long as the characters themselves are interesting and presented in an interesting way.

So, in this chapter, we'll look at ways to create interesting characters and the traits they need to be successful with readers.

MAIN CHARACTERS

For the most part, main characters in manga tend to come in two types- the main character, and everybody else. This isn't so different from any genre fiction, but how this division applies to manga is important to understand.

THE TRAITS OF A MANGA MAIN CHARACTER

In manga, lead characters generally have a few common traits that keep popping up. Since these are qualities the audience wants to have, it makes the character instantly relatable to most of the audience who also want to be like this.

Manga lead characters are often...

1. Exaggerated
2. Surprising
3. Sympathetic
4. Motivated
5. Heroic
6. Uniquely Strong
7. Have a Cheat
8. The Right Person for the Job
9. Memorable
10. The Ideal Man/Woman

You will find that almost all successful manga lead characters have these ten traits, and manga editors encourage creators to focus on them when making characters for manga. Let's look at each in turn.

1) They are Exaggerated

Lead characters in manga are not real people- they are larger than life figures who do things that the audience only wishes they could do. Even the more realistic characters have traits or attributes that are outside normal because that makes them livelier and more interesting to read and write about.

This is what exaggeration does with characters:

- Quickly simplifies characters into their most essential basic form
- Saves time when introducing characters
- Makes them story worthy

By exaggerating characters, you find the essence of that character and what makes a character special right away. By making someone the "best _____," "worst _____," "biggest _____," (or another exaggerated person of a certain type) you automatically zero in on their most important traits and the things that make them special.

It's a great technique because it does away with all the cluttered thinking about details that usually trap writers when first creating characters. It gives them a big picture view of the most important parts of the character, and then lets them begin developing that character from that central idea instead of having to build them up from different parts. Like planning a story, you're starting at the end and working backwards to figure out why this character is who they are, and since you already know their core idea from the start, it keeps everything on track.

Next, having an exaggerated view of the character gives both you and your audience a clear idea of who the character is right from the start- saving a whole lot of time. This helps in both story development and presentation. Since you're using an already-existing mental picture which is in your head (and the heads of the audience), that includes a whole world of details you don't have to explain or think about. If a character is a police officer, teacher, doctor, company president, or any other job, you already know how that person acts, reacts, dresses, behaves, smells and a million other details from your own experiences with people like them. You just need to customize them to your version of that person, and you're good to go!

Meanwhile, this exaggerated clarity also helps the audience because it works with their ideas of that type of person and lets them fill in lots of smaller details so that you (the storyteller) don't have to! Once the audience knows that this character is a "athlete," then they just need to be told what makes this athlete different from other athletes they already know. They have an instant picture in their heads, and then will use how that character behaves and other details the storyteller gives them to customize that image. But, and this is the best part, the version they come up with of that character in their heads will always be their own version of that character, since they put some of their own ideas into it as they enjoy the story.

In addition, exaggerating characters also saves time by telling you how the characters will act and react. They make storytelling easier, since you already know what that type of person will do in a particular situation. You just need to figure out what your version of that person will do (or not do) that is different from what the standard one would do.

And lastly, exaggerated characters are story-worthy! While normal everyday people can be interesting, when you add exaggeration you end up with a character worth telling a story about. Extreme characters are naturally special and attractive to readers, and audiences naturally want to know more about them. If you think about the characters from fiction you love, you're likely going to realize they're all exaggerated versions of people. Whether they're the bravest adventurer, the strongest knight, the wittiest socialite, the loneliest billionaire, the laziest detective, or the best starfighter pilot in the galaxy, they're always greater than normal in some area. That's what makes them people worth writing about.

Therefore, as you can see, exaggeration is a powerful tool for writers when making characters because it clarifies who the character is, makes them instantly recognizable, and attracts audiences to them. Of course, this isn't enough, you also have to add even more to the characters- you need to add surprise!

2) They are Surprising

When it comes to characters, just being the best isn't enough, and there has to be something intriguing about them that drives the audience to want to know more. The easiest way to create this sensation is to offer the audience character paradoxes- where the characters have two parts which don't fit together.

- She's the best computer tech you ever met, but she hates machines.
- He's the biggest loser in the world, but women love him.
- She can't cook to save her life, but she runs a catering business.

See how each of these (extremely simple) examples comes to life when you pair one thing which is true, but another which is also true that doesn't seem to match the first thing? You automatically end up with an intriguing character which can generate story ideas and situations that the audience hasn't seen before, and will want to know more about.

Surprise doesn't just create drama, it creates interesting characters. The more unexpected things you add to a character, the deeper and more interesting that character becomes. Just remember not to overdo it because it can quickly turn very silly.

- He's a rock star, who is also a nuclear physicist, but also runs a secret society of crime fighters and moonlights as a celebrity chef. When he's not working as a heart surgeon, that is.

Keep yourself down to one or two paradoxes, just to keep the character simple and focused, and see how far you can go before adding more.

3) They are Sympathetic

Next, your characters must connect with the audience if you're going to keep their attention. Audiences naturally bond with sympathetic characters, and that sympathy can come from who the character is or how they act.

When creating characters, you want to give them traits which will make the audience feel they can understand them. The best way to do this is to add flaws or quirks that most people have or know others who do, which makes the character more human. The more basic or common the flaw or trait, the better, and you can occasionally exaggerate them a little as well.

Using the above examples:

- She's the best computer tech you ever met, but she hates machines. Also, she's really shy.
- He's the biggest loser in the world, but women love him. Also, he's been divorced six times.
- She can't cook to save her life, but she runs a catering business. Also, she's super greedy.

By adding these little human extras, the characters not only become more relatable, but also easier to understand and write. Often the trait will also be something which doesn't fit, or complicates the character's situation even further, and might even be what motivates them in the story. Like the woman who suddenly found herself running a catering business which she's unsuited to run, but won't give it up because she's greedy and doesn't want to lose the chance to make money.

You can, of course, add other traits as well to make them more sympathetic, but having a major one which shapes the character is a must. This can also include the character's background and past experiences, as in the poor fellow who has been divorced six times and is now too scared of relationships to connect with the women who keep chasing him. Orphans or people with personal tragedies are very common exactly because that heartbreaking background makes them instantly sympathetic to audiences who know what it's like to be alone or hurt.

Like surprises, keep your sympathetic traits simple, though. Each flaw or quirk you add makes the character more distinct and less universal, so they become harder to relate to. A few key flaws that any audience member can remember off the top of their head is enough to hang the character on and make them relatable without weighing them down.

4) They are Motivated

Lead characters should be determined to succeed in accomplishing some goal, whatever it may be, and willing to do whatever is necessary to make it happen. They should have some reason they don't just give up, and it should be a clear primal reason they can't escape- they MUST do this thing to feel satisfied and fulfilled in their lives. And, it must be something which drives them to keep going when others would have given up or failed, even through their darkest hours.

Human beings want comfort and happiness, but your character needs something which makes them willing to give up all that for a greater goal. A motivation so strong it can't be avoided and affects not only what they do, but how they do it. They must be willing to do things that are unpleasant to them, and take actions they really don't want to do because they know the alternative (to them) is worse. Even when the going gets tough (and it will), this determination keeps them from quitting and keeps the character (and story) moving forward.

Where this determination comes from is up to you, and it will depend on the story and characters involved. However, storytellers are advised to keep this motivation primal, as it makes it easier for audiences to connect with. Everyone understands the need for food, sex, money, family, trust, love, revenge, pride, and the other basic human motivations, and your characters should be driven by them as well.

Also, don't be afraid to throw in the Three Key Principles (see *Engaging your Audience*) when developing motivations.

"He wants everyone to know he's a hard worker." Is okay.

"He wants to show he's the hardest worker they've ever seen because his ex-girlfriend called him a lazy slob and he wants to show her how wrong she is!" (Exaggeration, Surprise, Sympathy) This not only gives you a clear picture of his motivations, but also an interesting and sympathetic set of plot points you can work with.

Just remember, the more your audience can empathize and sympathize with a character's actions, the closer to that character they will become and more they will like them. Connecting that with their motivations will only make this stronger.

5) They are Heroic

Especially in Shonen and Shoujo manga, the lead characters are heroes, and they need to act like it.

What are the attributes of a hero? A hero is someone who...

1. Puts others before themselves.
2. Has the courage to do the right thing.
3. Fights for something they believe in.
4. Stands on their own two feet.

So, to go into more detail, a hero is someone who puts others before themselves- in other words, instead of being selfish like most people are, a hero works for the benefit of others. They take their role in society and the world seriously, and thus want to make it a better place. This makes us naturally like them because we like people who do things to help others, and admire selfless people like soldiers, police officers, teachers, and doctors who work tirelessly to make life better for those around them.

Of course, wanting to help others doesn't matter if you don't actually **do** it. And, a hero is someone who has the courage to step forward and do what needs to be done to fix and solve problems. They might be nervous about it, or even afraid, but they still do it because in spite of their fears they know it has to be done and are willing to take the risks and responsibility that comes with taking action.

And the reason they take action is because they believe in something so strongly that they're willing to fight for it. They might believe in justice, honesty, responsibility, duty, honor, revenge, or any number other things, but that principal motivates them to leap in and do things while others sit on the sidelines. This strong belief should also be something which is sympathetic to the audience, and which the audience also believes in (although maybe not enough to act on it). We are all raised to believe in responsibility, justice, hard work, telling the truth, and other things which make us good members of society, and your characters should believe in something "good" too.

And lastly, when the going gets tough, a heroic character is willing to stand alone.

There is nothing more heroic than someone who stands up for what they believe in, but doesn't rely on others while doing it. They don't question, they don't need support- they act, and are willing to take the whole world on their shoulders to get the job done. That doesn't mean they don't work with other people, but it does mean that the audience needs to be able to feel that this character would do it even if they were alone, no matter how hard it got. They are determined to be that lone figure that leads the way to change and fight for what's "right," no matter what.

6) They are Uniquely Strong

This is something which is particular to shonen manga characters, but can work for characters in other genres and stories as well. The key here is that the character has a special strength or an attribute which is so strong that it gives them the edge over others and helps them solve their problems. This is a unique way of solving problems that only they can do- a strength which makes them the hero of the story and which will come out to affect the climax of each tale.

Usually, this ability is a relatable trait that many people have (or could have), but theirs is exaggerated so they are abnormally good at it. A few examples are:

- Being able to understand the pain of others
- Getting people to trust you
- Being an exceptionally hard worker
- Having an indomitable will
- Being exceptionally caring about others
- Bringing out the best in other people
- Being incredibly observant
- Having an encyclopedic knowledge of a specific topic
- Having a superior memory
- Being amazingly talented in an art or craft
- Being incredibility optimistic or cheerful

This is an incredible talent they can use to solve problems, and it may be something they do unconsciously or that comes out when they're following their "true" path. Anyone can make a character that can transform into a powerful hero and win by being the strongest, but your character's special strength should be something which makes them stand out while reflecting the themes or ideals of the story. So, if the theme is "doing your best", then the character's special strength will be "hard worker" or maybe "super determined." If the theme is about the power of knowledge, then the special strength will be "learns fast" or maybe "exceptional at researching." Of if the story is about making friends, maybe they have the ability to "see into the hearts of others" or

The key is that their special unique strength is the "right" way to solve problems for them, and it is only by using it that they overcome their challenges. Often, they (or those around them) will try other ways first, preferring to go the direct route, but when that doesn't work, the hero will finally commit to doing it the way they're best at, and this will be the path to their success. This reinforces the idea that this way is the way for winning at life, as their special strength is usually an exaggerated version of something the audience can do, if they only tried.

One thing to remember is that special strengths are something the character can usually control or make full use of when they really try. If they have special abilities which are often outside their control, especially powerful ones, those are probably really cheats...

7) They Have a Cheat

This is another thing which is particular to shonen manga characters, but you can also find it in stories targeted at other audiences. Shonen characters almost always have some built-in cheat ability that helps them to win when things get extremely difficult.

Cheats are useful because they...
- Allow characters to get out of situations they wouldn't normally get out of.
- Help give a reason why that character is special and the main character.
- Can create surprising dramatic situations.
- Let the story flow more smoothly over some rough spots.
- Give that character a cool ability the audience wishes they had as well.

In fact, they're so useful, it's hard to find a shonen character who doesn't have at least one cheat that helps them when the going gets tough.

A few examples of cheats are:
- Having a magical demon inside you – *Naruto*
- Having a berserker mode – *Inu-Yasha*
- Having a superpower that changes and evolves – *One Piece*
- Having a magic item with a mind of its own – *Black Clover*
- Having knowledge that nobody else could have – *Dr. Stone*
- Having a mysterious power you can't entirely control – *My Hero Academia*
- Having a special background – *Bakuman*
- Having a mysterious backer – *Glass Mask*
- Having an innate but not understood talent – *Master of the Sea*

As you can see from the examples, usually cheats are things which are a) slightly mysterious (to the character and audience) and b) not entirely under the control of the main character. *Naruto*'s Kyuubi (Fox Demon) is a perfect example of a cheat- a demon which gives the main character advantages and could step in when needed, but isn't likely to because the cheat doesn't have any special reason to help the main character. Similarly, Moritaka Mashiro from *Bakuman* is an aspiring manga artist, but his late uncle was once also a famous manga artist and his connection to his uncle aides him in many unexpected ways throughout the story. And finally, in the story about ocean salvage called *Master of the Sea*, the main character Nanba Rintarou, has the ability to read the "Heart of the Sea" which lets him predict how the ocean will behave in advance. This instinctual ability (which not even he realizes he has), saves him and his comrades more than once in difficult situations.

In each case, the cheat is something that kicks in when it's most dramatically appropriate to save the hero's butt while also acting as a mysterious element to the character which the audience will want to know more about. On top of that, the "cheat" allows the storyteller to avoid critics claiming the main character only succeeds because they have "plot armor" or the author interfered. After all, the cheat was established as being there from the start (or at least hinted at), and the storyteller can just say that it was a planned part of the story all along.

8) The Right Person for the Job

Since your story is about how **this** particular character solves this particular problem, then they must be the right character to be the lead in this story. The story and the characters must match and suit each other, otherwise the story isn't going to work, much to the frustration of the storyteller and their audience.

For example, a fantasy adventure story about marching off to defeat the great evil overlord isn't likely to be successful if the main character is a bedridden ninety-year-old grandmother. Nor is a detective story going to be very interesting if the main character isn't interested in solving mysteries or restoring justice, but instead just wants to sit and play video games. Both of these characters could be made to do the job, but they'll require a lot of thinking by the storyteller to make them suitable.

The simple truth is that the less suitable the lead character is to the story, the harder the storyteller's job is going to be to make them fit. For creators who love a challenge, this is fine, but for most people the reward may not be worth the effort. Characters need to be able to solve the problems they're faced with in the story, and if they're unable to do so (through their own abilities or those of allies) then they're not the right person for this role.

Similarly, the main character should reflect the themes and ideas behind the story as well. If the story is about learning bravery, and the character is already brave at the beginning, then that character isn't going to learn anything or change much at all. (Unless of course, the character loses that bravery shortly after the story begins and regains it later on.) And, the if the story is about standing up for your ideals, but the character has no ideals to speak of, they're not going to be very effective at conveying that idea to the audience either.

So, like a craftsperson who chooses the right tool for the job, a storyteller must also find the right characters to fit their story and the themes and events that play out within it.

9) Memorable

There is nothing that kills a manga faster than a boring lead character. Lead characters in manga must always stick in the minds of the audience. They must have something about them that makes them unique and special in the way they appear or act. In manga, there's the advantage of visual design, so the creator can easily make a character unique through their appearance, but just having a unique appearance isn't enough. They also need to have their own way of acting or doing things that makes them stand out to the audience as something special.

Much of what makes a character unique comes from their creator- lead characters are reflections of their makers, after all. However, a good storyteller is always trying to think of ways of making their characters (lead and otherwise) stand out to their audience. The best way to do this is by putting yourself in the mind of your character and asking how they see the world. How they look and act needs to make sense from both the character and audience's points of view, and not just be a collection of random quirks.

If they're a character who doesn't smile, then ask yourself why they don't smile. If they wear a strange hat, then ask why that hat is so important to them. If they're afraid of cats, then why is that? The more you think your characters through, the more memorable they will be for both you and the audience. You need your characters to stand out and be special.

However, be careful not to make them too special. Lead characters need to leave space for the audience to insert their own ideas and feelings onto the character. They need to be just special enough to stand out, but not special enough that they become completely alien to the audience. Finding the right balance is a tricky thing, and takes skill and experience, but when you do, characters the audience can't get enough of appear.

10) The Ideal Man or Woman

Lastly, the character should have a few additional different attributes depending on whether the lead character is intended to appeal to a male audience or a female one. Men and women in our society have different sets of traits they admire and there seems to be something primal about these traits that gives them universal appeal.

The ideal male lead has the following traits: he is trustworthy, he's brave, and he's a leader. These three key male traits pop up in the majority of leads in manga, and fiction in general. Not all lead characters are this way, or show these traits to the same degree, but in general the majority of male main characters will display these three traits.

Looking at each of them together, it isn't hard to understand why. The character must be trustworthy for other people to support them and to be a successful member of society. If they weren't trustworthy to some degree, it would be hard for other characters to accept them, much less the audience. In addition, they must be brave because that willingness to take risks is what helps to make them into a lead character who does the things the audience wishes they could do. If the character wasn't brave, they'd be a secondary character who supported someone who was brave enough to be the lead.

Finally, the character must be a leader, which means that other people respect and gravitate to this character. This is what makes them the center of the story, not just the main character but a figure that their setting revolves around. They need to be someone other people are attracted to and want to work with, and who shows traits that justify that position. This is also why they need to be trustworthy and brave, because those two traits are the foundation of someone being considered a leader in our society.

The ideal female lead, similarly, also has three key traits: <u>she is attractive, she is independent, and she is intelligent.</u> These are the three traits that keep popping up in female leads across manga and genre fiction (especially romance), and you can find them in most female lead characters to one degree or another.

Again, there are reasons in these traits. Female audience members all imagine themselves as physically attractive (or want to be attractive), and the lead character is meant to be a stand-in for the audience so they must have this trait. Also, research has shown that we rate attractive people much more highly in competence and trustworthiness than we rate unattractive people, so in this case beauty is also a marker of the character's positive social status. And finally, the female lead will almost inevitably end up with a love interest, who is usually also going to be attractive in some way, and if she wasn't attractive the audience wouldn't be able to accept them getting together.

Of course, she must also be independent, because if she wasn't, she wouldn't be the lead character in the story, or be the one taking a leadership role in the situations that come up. And, also to be successful with both the audience and in the story, she needs to be intelligent, as this will often be her strongest weapon in overcoming the challenges which come up in the story.

Naturally, not all male or female lead characters have all of these traits at the start of the story, but eventually they will develop them as the story goes on, and they will usually show the potential for them right from the beginning. Very often, stories are about a character learning to develop some or all of these traits, especially in stories about young characters learning their place in the world. This both gives the character room to grow, and lets the audience see ways they can develop these traits in their own lives (which is always popular because most audience members feel they are lacking in these areas).

Also, these traits are pretty basic, and you can build on them and use them in a lot of different ways. Characters can have any number of other traits as well, as long as those traits don't cancel out the big three the character is trying to show. A loner character can still show leadership traits when the situation calls for it, they just might not like taking that role unless they have to. Similarly, a very naïve character may show great intelligence when it comes to things that aren't about society or the greater world. But a cowardly character won't show bravery easily, and the author will have to work hard to bring out that trait in them during the story to make it work.

In addition, these should be taken less as the traits that male or female leads must have, but as the traits that make male or female audiences connect with a character. The "ideal male" traits will get a male audience to like that character, and the "ideal female" traits will get a female audience to like a character, but these traits can actually be shown by members of any sex, or even species in a story. Yes, they seem to work best when shown by a character of that gender, but you could do a story about robots that show these traits and get a similar audience reaction.

ANTI-HEROES AND VILLAINOUS LEADS

One type of lead which sometimes pops up in manga is the anti-hero (or occasionally villain) lead. These are leads which go against society's rules, and seem to break all the conventional wisdom that the main character should be a "good" person and liked by the audience. They are often murderers, psychopaths, and sometimes cruel and vicious characters that do everything that should make an audience hate them- and yet the audience loves them anyways.

Why is this? And how do you write such a character?

The first thing to understand about writing this type of character is that everything is relative. A character is good or bad based on the setting they're in and the people around them. Just like people think about whether they're rich by comparing themselves to their neighbors, or students judge their marks based on their classmates' scores, whether someone is good or evil can all depend on what their environment is.

Thus, in a story where the character lives in a world filled with bad people, the least bad person will look heroic by comparison. For example, in a happy and stable society filled with loving and caring people that look out for each other, characters like Batman, Wolverine, and The Punisher are angry psychopaths who dress up in weird costumes and beat up other mentally ill people. But, in a crime-filled hard place like Gotham City (or 1980s New York), they're avenging angels of justice fighting the good fight in a world gone mad. In a stable world, they're villains, but in a chaotic world, they become cool anti-heroes. Just so long as your main character has more relatable traits than their enemies, the audience will accept them as being "heroic" even when they're actually not by the standards of the real world.

Anti-heroes are characters that reject the conventional heroic mold, but the truth is that there still needs to something heroic or noble about them for the audience to bond or connect with them. A character without any redeeming traits will be viewed as a villain, and not accepted by most audiences unless the author is extremely skilled.

This is why most anti-hero stories are built up around the Righteous Avenger plot (see *Common Manga Plots*), where an innocent is tortured by someone worse than the hero, and then the hero swoops in to inflict a little justice on the "bad" guy. Sure, the hero is a terrible person too, but at least they don't stoop to torturing innocents, and in a relative way this makes them the "good" guy in this story that the audience can root for. The storyteller just needs to take time building up the villain's evil reputation, and it's all good!

And this leads to the other major thing for writers of anti-heroes to consider- anti-hero lead characters are almost always OP power fantasy characters. They're acting out the audience's anti-social dreams, and doing the things that audiences wish they could do free of social constraints. The anti-hero or villain lead can blow up that annoying woman's car, or shove that rich CEO through the window of his office, or engage in massive property damage, and it's all okay! They're a wild character who exists to do the things the audience dreams of, and do it without the consequences that a real-life person might face. (All while saying witty one-liners like- "No, after you!")

Just so long as the author doesn't do anything to kill the audience's "fun," they will laugh and enjoy the ride as the anti-hero does horrible thing after horrible thing. They will revel in the mayhem, and feel satisfied that the anti-hero gets away with doing whatever they like, just so long as it's done in an entertaining way.

And this all applies to full villains too. A villainous lead is really just a more extreme anti-hero who happens to crush villains who are worse than they are while trying to achieve their goals. For some great examples, check out Tanya (from *The Saga of Tanya the Evil*), Ains Ooal Gown (from *Overlord*) and Dantalian (from *Dungeon Defense*), well written stories about characters who cross the line from being anti-heros into full-blown villains, but audiences love them anyways.

SUPPORTING CHARACTERS

Manga are dramas, which means they're about characters interacting with other characters. As a result, there are two supporting roles that most manga stories should have:

1. Someone for the main character to talk to/interact with.
2. Someone to oppose the main character.

These two roles can be played by the same person or different people, but both are very important to have in most stories.

The first is important because your main character needs someone to talk with to get them to present their thoughts, ideas and perspectives. Dialogues are much more interesting than monologues, and watching two characters interact is much livelier and more entertaining than watching one person talk to themselves or the audience. Interaction- action and reaction, is the heart of drama, and the audience is there to see drama, not read an essay on a topic.

The second role is important because (at least in more conflict-based stories), the main character needs someone to push back against them and present them with challenges to keep things interesting. Opponents are there to add surprise and suspense to the story- will the main character succeed in their goals? How will they succeed? How will they overcome the opposition, and why is the main character right and the opponent wrong? These are all dramatic questions that opponents create and which must be answered by the end of the story.

With both a dramatic partner and someone to voice opposition, a story then comes to life. Without these character roles, a story will be flat and won't be appealing to audiences, who are there to see drama and interaction. These can be a lead, a victim, and a villain; a lead, a mentor, and a rival; or even just a lead and villain/rival (with the latter playing both roles). But however you do it, at minimum, the drama will include these three roles, and everyone else involved in the story is just there to support or expand on these roles.

One simple way of thinking about these is as what are called "role pairs"- which are two people who have a defined relationship with each other. In our own lives, we have many role pairs – mother-son, father-daughter, friend-friend, teacher-student, boss-worker, lover-lover, husband-wife, and so on. These are each a unique relationship that defines how we interact with that person, and how they interact with us. Characters are no different.

Each character has a relationship with other characters in your story which is unique to that role pair, and it can involve all kinds of feelings and connections.

Sometimes these connections and feelings are positive, like feelings of deep admiration, trust, or love. Other times, these feelings are negative, like feelings of contempt, mistrust, or hate. Sometimes they are about power, like parent-child, boss-employee, or mentor-learner. Other times, they are based on social roles: clerk-customer, police officer-thief, judge-defendant. And lastly, they can be based on situations: faithful partner-cheating partner, criminal-victim, spy-target.

When trying to come up with supporting cast members, try to think of interesting and unusual role pairs you can put together to generate surprise and interest on the part of the audience. Some role pairs are natural drama generators because they have goals or positions which are opposed to each other (spy-target) or make it hard for one person to oppose the other (boss-employee). Putting characters into these role pairs makes stories and generates interesting situations that almost write themselves, so try to come up with the most thought-provoking pairs you can.

Also, don't forget to include the three key principles of storytelling as you create and flesh out these characters. The principal which the student needs help from should have touches of exaggeration (they're the meanest principal, ever), surprise (but they love music) and sympathy (and also love their grandkids), to help bring them to life in more interesting ways than just a generic principal character might be. (And, it also gives you weak points the main character might focus on to get what they want in the story.)

Just remember that the more unique the other characters are, the more they will distract from your main character. And, this is supposed to be your main character's story, so don't create a bunch of other characters who steal their spotlight unless your goal is to have an ensemble cast of equal characters who all get their own stories and screen time.

Generally speaking, the more you want your main character to stand out, the less unique their supporting cast should be. Although, there are some creators who flip this and have a very bland main character surrounded by a very unique supporting cast. (Usually in stories where the main character is just a window in the lives of the more interesting people around them.)

Lastly, always keep in mind that the supporting cast, especially the opponents, are there to reflect the themes and ideas of the story. The opponents especially are usually funhouse mirror versions of the main character who are twisted and warped because they took a bad path to try to get to the same goals that the main character did.

Typically in manga, the main villain is doing the same thing the hero does, but they do it in the wrong way. For example, the hero might be trying to become the top warrior-mage in the land, and does this by working with other characters who learn from each other in the spirit of friendship. The villain, then, will be trying to become the greatest-warrior mage by conquering and controlling others- manipulating them and stealing their secrets. One is using the power of teamwork, the other domination, but both have the same goals and are mirrors of each other.

The hero's allies and rivals can also reflect the themes of the story, but usually do them in more positive ways, or start on the wrong path and are brought over to the hero's way of thinking as the story goes on.

MAIN OPPONENTS

In stories, there are two kinds of opponents who stand in the way of the characters accomplishing their goals- main opponents and story opponents. In simplest terms, main opponents are the character that the main character must defeat to accomplish their major story goal, whereas other (story) opponents are there to get in the main character's way during a story but overcoming them only accomplishes the goal of that story, not the overall plot.

In manga, we rarely see main opponents, and the main reason for this comes down to the nature of these as long-form serialized stories.

Major Opponents, especially main villains, represent the end of a story. They're the final thing the hero needs to defeat to win and show that they've conquered their enemies and become the true savior of the nation. (Or whatever winning means for that story.) However, manga are designed to keep running for as long as they're popular and the author is interested in them, so having a character around who represents the end of the story is a bit of a problem.

If you have a clear villain, you have to keep coming up with reasons why the main character isn't focused on marching toward defeating that villain. And, not only that, the villain character needs to steal story-time from the main character to be developed as a real threat that the hero must face, but every time you focus on the main villain you're leading the story toward an ending you're trying to avoid until you absolutely have to face it, since you don't want the story to end.

So, in order to solve this problem, manga have come up with a few solutions.

1. Vague Organizations
2. Endless Enemies
3. Story Arc Villains
4. Situational Opponents

Vague Organizations: As the name suggests, instead of having an actual villain who must be faced and defeated, the story will instead have an organization (clan, gang, secret society, club, pirate fleet, etc) whose members progressively cause problems for the heroes. The structure of that organization is purposely left unclear, and so is their power and membership, so that the storyteller can make it up as they go along. They presumably have a boss, king, head, or an elite council, but that's something that will only come into the story when it's time to wrap things up. Until then, the heroes can fight endless members of the organization and the story can go on for as long as needed. The storyteller just needs to occasionally throw in a reference to indicate that the hero is getting closer to the heart of the organization, whether they really are or not.

Endless Enemies: There is an old saying that no matter how good you are, there is always someone better. In this case, while the hero may have a clear opponent to defeat today, once they're done the hero will learn that their opponent wasn't the top of the food chain, and that now the hero must face a whole new enemy threat. Today you defeat a kingdom, tomorrow you need to defeat an empire, the day after that there's a whole continent to conquer, then a world, a galaxy, a universe, a dimension, and so on. There is always someone better, and each new accomplishment brings new challenges and problems for our hero until the author or audience decides enough is enough.

Arc Opponents: Similar to Endless Enemies, the story is broken down into Story Arcs (usually lasting exactly the length of one or two printed volumes), and each Story Arc introduces an opponent who must be dealt with by the hero. If the main character is active, then the arc opponent is usually someone who stands between them and achieving their goals. While if they're a passive lead, the Arc Opponent is attacking them or something they consider to be precious and they must defeat the Arc Opponent to restore the balance of their life.

Situational Opponents: These are a special type of Arc Opponent, where the character is actually an ally (or potential ally) who is brought into conflict with the lead due to the situation or circumstances of the story. Usually this is a method for introducing a character who will eventually become part of the main character's group or allies, and in romantic comedy manga is a common method of introducing the members of the main character's harem. (The main character must defeat each harem member to show them how cool they are and get them to fall in love with the main character.)

THE THREE SUPPORT CHARACTERS

Since manga can be of any genre, it's hard to say what support characters should be present in any given story; however, general best practice is to make sure that somewhere in the story the character has a best friend character who they can talk to about their inner feelings (thus sharing them with the audience as well), a resource character who gives them the information/support they need to succeed, and a love interest character who helps to inspire them and represents the reward the character gets when they finally win. These three characters can be the same person, or some combination, but the first two will generally need to be there in some form.

This doesn't mean these three characters have the stay the same for the entire story, or that they will always be there, but in any longer story characters playing these three roles will almost always be present in the character's life. If they're not there, the character will seek out people to play the friend role and resource role because they need them to succeed, and fate will always be putting (potential) love interest characters in their way to keep them motivated. (And provide eye candy for the audience...)

BACKGROUND CHARACTERS

Each background character is a representative of some part of the setting the character lives in. And, how that character speaks, acts, and behaves are all clues that the audience will use to build their own mental picture of the setting and its culture. If everyone the character meets is nice, then the audience will assume that this is a peaceful and happy place where most people's basic needs are being met. However, if most of the background characters are unfriendly, businesslike and anxious, then it will be clear this setting is out of balance and people are worried about their futures.

So, think about each character the leads encounter carefully because they are the living representatives of your world, and the main way you will bring the setting to life.

FINAL THOUGHTS

There is old storyteller's wisdom that states that the best characters write themselves, and this is very true. If you have a strongly defined lead character who has their own voice and own clear story direction, then the rest of the story will pretty much fall into place by itself. One of the most important things you can do as a storyteller is to keep trying until you have a character that naturally comes alive in your head and on the page. That's the golden character that will interest audiences and make writing the story fun and interesting.

Having that golden character who comes alive on the page is the single most important factor in whether a manga story will succeed or not. Manga are about following interactions between interesting characters who bring out the best (and worst) in each other. Characters who keep the audience entertained with their emotional actions and reactions. So, you need a strong lead character and supporting cast which attracts the audience and gives the story a clear, unique direction.

In the best manga, story and setting are secondary, and the characters and the audience's emotional connections with them are what keep them glued to the story and reading on.

Audiences follow characters, not events, and want to see stories which are unique to that character, and which only that character can give them. This is why so many manga characters are exaggerated into extremes of "the most..." conceptually, because it automatically makes them unique and gives them a strong flavor. The exaggerated character on the page is that creator's idea of "the most...", and each of us has a different idea of what that means, so the characters become special through exaggeration.

Not only that, they also have their own special ways to solve problems because they are so unique. You only need to ask yourself- "How does the world's most _____ solve this problem?" and you automatically get a result that's special to that character. The character's own quirks, style, strengths, and weaknesses that you imagine will come together to give you a unique approach to different situations that only that character can give. This creates both an element of surprise (finding out how this unique person solves this problem in their own unique way), and expectation (once we know how they solve problems, we can see when it's coming in the story), that audiences enjoy in their manga stories.

So always remember, strong and clear characters build their own solutions to their own stories, and the storyteller only needs to sit down and think the situation through from the character's special point of view to know what needs to happen. This is also where the principle of surprise comes in, because the storyteller should also be thinking of ways to emphasize how the character acts in different situations that are special to that character. Don't just have them solve their problems in a normal way, but look for unusual ways that reflect the character's personality, abilities, and style.

Every action the character takes should reflect the character, and every character's essence should be reflected in their actions.

You show character through actions, and if those actions are also ones that the reader understands and agrees with, it will generate empathy between the character and audience. This creates a strong bond between the two, and makes the audience feel like the character is an extension of themselves- they feel what the character feels and react to the events the character faces in a deep and personal way. They become immersed in the story, and this is always the storyteller's ultimate goal.

Therefore, strong and clearly presented characters with their own way of facing the world are the key to writing successful manga stories. Through exaggeration, surprise, and sympathy, these characters write their own stories and connect with audiences in a way which makes the reader a part of the story and carries them along on a unique journey. Everything else is just expanding on those simple, central core ideas.

THE AUDIENCE FOR MANGA

Manga is a way of telling stories, not a type of story. There is no single audience for manga because there can't be- it would be like saying there is a single audience for the television, books, movies, music or theatre. Those are all ways of communicating stories, and because they don't decide the content of the stories, they also don't control who the audience is. There are as many kinds of movie, book, and television stories as there are types of people who watch them because the point is the story, not the way you watch it.

As a result, there are manga for every age group, gender, religion, hobby, and background you can name, and probably a few that you can't. Manga have been a central part of Japanese life since just after the Second World War, and so every Japanese has read manga at one time, and many people still do in different ways. This means it's hard to say there is only one type of manga reader, or that manga appeal to a certain type of person.

But, while it's true that there are as many kinds of readers as there are manga, there are some audiences that read more manga, and some types of manga that are more popular than others.

Most manga are read by people between the ages of 6 and 25- from the time they learn to read, to the time they graduate university and start to build their families and careers. At that point, they don't have time to read manga anymore, and so most people stop reading as other things begin to take priority. They only keep reading their long-running favorites, usually online or standing in bookstores.

This means that the majority of manga are written, drawn and produced for young audiences, and not just young people, but teenagers who have the money to buy manga anthology magazines and are looking for lively and interesting entertainment. The most popular of these is *Shonen JUMP*, which has a distribution of around two million copies a week, and is targeted at 8-14-year-old boys, but read by both sexes. It is hardly alone, as *shonen* (lit. "boys") manga rules the charts, with the majority of best-selling manga in Japan being ones for younger and older male teens.

This might seem similar to America, where most Marvel and DC comics are read by teenaged boys, but in Japan there is also a strong girl's comic market. While *CIAO* magazine, the top selling *shoujo* (lit. "girls") manga anthology only sells around a half a million copies a month, it still has far more female readers than any American comic does. It isn't alone, either, as competing girl's comic anthologies like *Margaret* sell around 50,000 copies a week. (By comparison, the average American comic book sells 20-40,000 copies a month.)

So, even in Japan, comics are youth-oriented, and this means that the types of stories they tell are ones that also appeal to younger audiences. Many manga are filled with coming-of-age stories, where young heroes start out on their journeys and overcome obstacles to achieve some greater goal. This is what the young audience wants, and so that's what they get. The audience of these comics wants to learn about the world and their place in it, and do it through lively and fun fictional heroes that face challenges head-on and win the day in interesting ways.

That doesn't mean that manga can't tell other kinds of stories, but those are the most popular among all audiences, and that's why those are the ones usually chosen to become anime as well. With more serious and thoughtful stories being pushed back to manga targeted at older teens and adults that have much smaller audiences and rarely getting anime adaptations.

In any case, let's look at the different age groups in more detail to see what each wants from their manga, and how best to reach them...

WRITING FOR YOUNG MANGA AUDIENCES

The audience for youth-oriented manga are a very tricky thing. Officially, most manga are targeted at 8-14-year-olds, which in the English book market is called Middle Grade (MG) fiction. Children at this age are trying to find a way to fit into the world around them, and learning their place in society. Their main focus is fitting in and trying to become a positive member of the social order, and so fiction aimed at this group is about young people learning to integrate and find their place in the world. This age is where in English you'll find the early *Harry Potter* books, books by Rick Riordan like *Percy Jackson and the Olympians*, the *Artemis Fowl series*, *Diary of a Wimpy Kid* series, and many others.

Middle grade is also the traditional target audience of American superhero comic books, which makes sense because one of the important things to remember about MG readers is that they're trying to fit into society. Part of fitting in is finding your place, and so MG stories tend to be about characters working to earn a place in society and protecting society.

From Harry Potter to Naruto, heroes for the middle grade set are there to learn the way the world works, become an important part of it, and protect it. Unconsciously, they want a society which is stable and orderly. A society which they don't understand is scary, so they want a world where everything has a place and they can fit themselves into that order. Their efforts might not always be appreciated, but they keep fighting because society and the people they love are worth protecting.

However, while officially shonen and shoujo comics are for 8-14-year-olds, they have a very large demographic of older readers in their mid to late teens. (And a fair number of adults, too.) This teen demographic is called Young Adult (YA) fiction in the English publishing world, and runs from 12-18 years of age. These are young people who have discovered that the world isn't a black and white place you can easily fit into and who are trying to figure out who they are and how they're going to deal with the world.

Young adults like stories about change, big change, and love to see society torn apart and rebuilt in different ways. Young adults feel like their emotions and lives are chaotic, and they like stories that reflect the inner chaos they feel. They also want to feel powerful, like they can reach out and reshape society to make the world appreciate them and their ways of thinking. Thus, almost all YA stories are about characters who are exceptional and use that power to change their story worlds in small or big ways.

So, you can see that most manga are actually split between two audiences- the middle grade kids who are all about protecting and working together, and the young adults who want their power fantasies and characters who feel out-of-place in society like they do. Add to this that the young people in question are also Japanese, not American, and have a completely different worldview, and things get even more messy.

It's a difficult mix to get right, and the editors at JUMP, CIAO, and the other publications fail more than they succeed at it. Every year new titles come and go, failing to find their audiences, and then there are also surprise hits that nobody except an editor who believed in a manga creator's work saw coming. (Then again, every editor believes in their artist's work, or else it wouldn't have gotten in the magazine.)

The most common way they deal with the different audiences, at least at JUMP, is that they split the difference. The typical shonen hero is actually targeted at a middle grade (8-14) audience, with a lead character who is barely older than the target readers. The character will have a goal or dream which is compatible with the idea of becoming part of something greater and protecting things that are important to them, and they'll be working hard to find their place in some larger group. The comic will be written and drawn in a lively way which will appeal to younger reader, and usually have a fair amount of lively humor in it.

However, the comic will also include some more mature elements to keep the older audience happy, like fan service sexuality, interesting characters, interesting settings, slightly complex morals, and relatable relationships. Also, as the manga story (and its audience) ages, then the style and presentation of the story will also go up in maturity as well, until its main audience becomes YA, which is a nice spot where older and younger readers will both enjoy it.

A perfect example of this is *Naruto*, which started as a classic middle grade manga targeted at a young audience, and then (once the author and audience were ready) transitioned to *Naruto: Shippudden*, a solidly YA book filled with teenaged versions of the characters and much more mature themes. Just as J.K. Rowling transitioned her boy wizard books as he grew, manga that last tend to start younger and grow with their audiences into their teens.

They also tend to have an ending where their world is metaphorically (or literally) destroyed and remade, which is how teens like it- leaving the heroes as powerful figures who will guide and reshape a new society in their image. This is a powerful fanservice message that resonates across cultures, as can be seen in books like *The Hunger Games*, *Divergent*, *The Maze Runner*, *Twilight*, and other hit young adult English novels.

Of course, not all shonen or shoujo manga titles follow this formula. They all have young protagonists, but some of them like *Death Note* or *NANA* do the opposite and go directly for the teen market by having leads in their mid to late teens. They start with a lead who is 15 or 16, and who has teen problems and whose story involves older teen situations, stories, and attitudes, and hope that between the teen audience and the older readers it will get enough of a fanbase to be a hit. However, content-wise, they're still limited to general audience material- so no graphic sex, gore, drug use, heavy swearing, or other things that would be inappropriate for a younger audience. (Those go in proper *Seinen* and *Josei* (young adult) magazines.)

Once upon a time, titles *Shonen JUMP* and *Margaret* even had adult main characters, just like American superhero comics, and titles like *Fist of the North Star*, *City Hunter*, and *Rose of Versailles* could become popular series with a large following. However, after the 80's those faded out of favor, and now the main characters in youth manga are almost always teens, with the only adults being aged-up characters who started their stories are teens and have gotten older. (And even then, most series will stop before the characters ever stop being teens.)

So, how should you write your comics?

The truth is, you're not beholden to a manga editorial board, so you can write and make comics however you like and include whatever content you wish. That said, if you're targeting the youth manga market, then you'll probably want to stick close to the standards that those magazines follow. Pick either a middle grade, or young adult (not both) target audience, figure out what they'll find appealing, and figure out what you'll find appealing to write- and then find a happy sweet spot between the two.

Content-wise, things are a little more difficult. Japanese standards of content are different than those of North America, and they tolerate a lot more violence and sexuality in their young adult stories than North Americans do. (Which is why so much anime ends up with content warnings, despite it being for a young teen audience in Japan.) However, you're not writing for a Japanese audience, you're writing for an English-speaking one (or whatever audience you're writing to), so take some time and figure out what your audience will and won't find acceptable.

As a general rule, if it won't be shown in prime-time television or general audience movies in your country, then you probably shouldn't include it in a shonen manga-type story. In North America, this would mean everything should fall under a Parental Guidance (PG) rating, although many actual youth manga and anime would really be rated PG-13 (Parental Guidance for those under 13 years of age) due to their levels of violence.

If you're targeting the MG audience, then you probably want to look up the rules for G-rated (General Audience) or F-rated (Family) and stay close to those. The last thing you need is a bunch of angry parents leaving bad reviews because you threw some more mature content into a story that was otherwise for middle grade readers. That can cost you an audience very quickly, and will make it harder to grow your fanbase.

On the other hand, if your target audience is people who grew up reading youth-targeted comics but are looking for something more mature, then go nuts and have fun doing the kinds of stories you want to write. Just be aware that this audience is probably a lot smaller than the teen market, and it may be harder to find success in it unless you're really, really good.

THE AUDIENCE FOR SHONEN MANGA

Shonen Manga are manga for boys 8-14, and includes titles like *Naruto, One Piece, My Hero Academia, Dr. Stone, Dragonball, Full Metal Alchemist, Death Note, Prince of Tennis,* and many others. It is also read by older teens, adults and many others who enjoy the lively stories and interesting characters.

Shonen JUMP, the most popular manga anthology magazine of all time, famously has the motto "Friendship. Effort. Victory." that they use to describe their winning formula. And, while not all shonen manga subscribe to *JUMP*'s philosophy, there is a lot to be learned about the thinking of shonen manga in general by understanding the deeper thinking behind this motto.

Friendship

Given *JUMP*'s audience, it's no surprise that friendship is a pretty much standard part of shonen manga. For young people at the target age of shonen comics, there is nothing more important to them than their friends/peer group. They're at an age where they're rejecting their families and parents to find out who they really are, and they're doing it alongside their friends. Nothing has more influence on teenagers than their friends, and their worldview is built on what their friends believe and tell them is important. As a result, they want stories which tell them about what friendship means and how to navigate the world of friends and social relationships.

Not only that, but shonen stories are all about showing young readers just how powerful and necessary friendships are to succeed in life. The Japanese are a group-oriented culture, and in their way of thinking teamwork is the ultimate tool for success. Shonen manga pass this philosophy on to their young readers by showing heroes who struggle against great odds, and by working with others are able to achieve their dreams.

And finally, nothing makes a character more endearing to readers than someone who works not for themselves, but for others. We admire and respect those who sacrifice or fight for someone else, and that draws the audience in even more, making shonen characters incredibly appealing as they lead their audience by example.

Effort

Shonen editors believe that nothing worth having is gained easily, and characters in shonen manga live lives that are built around struggling against insurmountable odds. Characters like *One Piece*'s Luffy and Naruto dream big, and with big dreams comes a long hard road to success. But, if there's one thing shonen characters never do- it's give up. Shonen manga characters never get anything handed to them, and never stop working hard to achieve their goals.

If there's one word that can describe shonen heroes, it's "tenacity." They never quit, and they never stop trying to achieve their goals- not the big ones, and not the small ones. They also don't take shortcuts in trying to make these goals into reality, and if they do take shortcuts, it will usually come back to haunt them later. The message these comics are trying to teach is that hard work is something that's worthwhile in itself, and there's pride it doing it right and not stopping until the job is done.

Writing stories based around effort is a longtime winning formula, and writers like Horatio Alger were doing it over a century ago to inspire poor youth to make something better of themselves. These stories are there to inspire the young and give them the mental tools they need to strive towards their goals and build their futures with their own two hands.

Victory

You can't ask people to work hard without a reward, and you can't tell young people they should give everything for dreams they have no hope of achieving. Shonen heroes are there to tell the readers that they can win, and that despite all the challenges and odds, everything they put into achieving their goals is worth it.

Heroes don't lose. Not in shonen manga. Those who follow the right path of staying true to their friends and working hard always achieve victory. They might experience setbacks, and they might sometimes lose their way, but with a little help from those around them, they will cross the finish line every time. This message reassures readers and gives them a sense of hope and optimism about the future, and this in turn keeps them marching forward.

For young men (and women) who are unsure about their path in life, and are unsure about their futures, this positive message that their dreams are in their grasp, and that it will all work out in the end, is an important one. It makes them feel the world will reward them if they give it their best, which is what always happens in shonen manga.

Thus, shonen manga are built on giving readers a sense of hope, and reminding them that the tools they need to build their futures are in their hands. Through working together and not giving up, they can achieve great things and make their place in the world ahead of them.

This is an aspirational message that resonates clearly with audiences, and has turned *Shonen JUMP* into the powerhouse it is today. In fact, despite being a comic magazine written and focused on boys, a 2012 survey found that roughly half of *Shonen JUMP*'s readership was girls and women. That's part of the reason why so many *JUMP* manga end up becoming anime, because they know that their best stories have global appeal and aren't just limited to young men.

In fact, when many people think of manga, they're actually thinking of *JUMP*-style manga, and it's almost become the default idea for what manga is. Which isn't true, of course, since manga is many things, but for most of the world, manga means *Naruto, One Piece, Dragonball, BLEACH!* and those are all *Shonen JUMP* manga.

TOP 10 THINGS SHONEN MANGA AUDIENCES EXPECT

Knowing your audience is the single biggest thing that will determine the success of any story you write. You can't reach an audience unless you know who they are and what they want. Luckily, in your case, you can probably find your audience by looking in the mirror. If you're reading this book, then there's a good chance you are a lover of shonen manga and anime, and so your tastes probably match the tastes of your target audience.

When planning your stories, think about what you want to see, what would make you react emotionally, what would shock or surprise you, and then use that in the story because it will probably work on your audience as well. If you're not sure, tell your friends about your ideas (if they're into shonen-type stories) and see what they think. They are going to be members of your audience, after all, so use them for figuring things out.

That said, there's ten things that are definitely expected by the reader of a typical shonen manga book.

1) Action

Action doesn't (just) mean fighting, it means characters doing something. Characters in shonen manga aren't bystanders or dreamers, they're doers who leap right in and get the job done. They have goals they pursue, and the manga focuses on the activities they do in pursuit of those goals. They don't sit around and talk about what they're going to do- they do it and get right in the thick of things as quickly as possible. That's what the audience is there for- characters taking action. Give it to them.

2) Humor

With rare exceptions, shonen manga is expected to have some humor mixed in. Even stories as serious as *Death Note* and *Fist of the North Star* made an effort to mix in visual humor and lighter moments from time to time to relieve the incredible tension the stories built up. More typical shonen comics like *One Piece* and *The Seven Deadly Sins* have a lot of visual humor going on, even when the stories themselves are deadly serious at times. A comedy manga is going to be filled with humor, and a serious one will have dashes of it, but somewhere in any shonen comic's visuals or characters are going to be humor elements. Characters who you can both laugh and cry with are often more endearing, and have a wider audience appeal as well.

3) Conflict

Nothing brings out the best in characters like conflict with others, and shonen heroes must face a long line of rivals and enemies if they want to reach their goals. Just like friends are important in shonen stories, so are enemies. A hero isn't rated by how strong they are, but by the quality of their opposition, and shonen heroes have some of the most strange and devious enemies there are. In fact, the villains in shonen stories are often more popular than the heroes because they do and say the things the heroes can't, and are usually fallen heroes themselves.

4) Strategy

When you hear strategy, you might be thinking of manga like *Hikaru no Go*, *Death Note*, or maybe even *Haikyuu-* comics which are about characters playing games and using their heads to win. However, even the most blockheaded shonen heroes are actually masters of strategy, and coming up with a constant stream of surprise tactics and methods for beating their opponents. Part of this is about surprising the audience, but an equal part is about showing that most problems can be overcome with a little brain power. Shonen comics aren't just about working hard to achieve goals- they're about working smart. Whether heroes or villains, both sides are filled with clever characters using their brains, and audiences expect to see some brains behind the brawn, even if it's just presented as raw cunning.

5) Relatability

Audiences of shonen comics want characters they can relate to and sympathize with. They want characters close to their own age who are dealing with problems that are in some way similar to their own lives. They want lead characters who are similar to people they know, or who have attributes they can relate to and understand, and to see these characters struggle with life issues just like they do. Saving the world is entertaining, but watching someone save the world while also having to deal with life issues makes them a lot easier to connect with. This is why one of the basic three principles of manga is sympathy, and why shonen lead characters are almost always teens 14-16 years of age- old enough to get involved with the adult world, but young enough to struggle with it.

6) No Sex

While you will find lots of sexuality (sexy outfits and images, characters trying to get sex, etc) in shonen comics, the truth is you will only rarely actually find characters who have sex. And, even when characters do have sex, it's almost always implied rather than explicitly told to the audience. Some of this is because of the target age group- 8-to-14-year-old boys don't understand sex and feel uncomfortable about it. But, mostly this is because of a simple truism: *sex isn't entertaining, but people trying to have sex is.* People who have sex, have sex, and then deal with emotional and relationship issues around it. People who are trying to have sex do all kinds of stupid things, and make lots of funny, interesting, and embarrassing mistakes. One of them fits in a shonen comic, the other does not. Save the sex for after the credits roll or between time jumps.

7) Surprise

If you know what's coming- why read a story? Audiences of shonen comics read them to see how interesting characters overcome interesting obstacles in interesting ways. Sometimes it's giving the audience what they want, but with a twist, and other times it's giving them something they don't know they want but will love. Being boring is the kiss of death for shonen comics, and the audience wants to go on an emotional roller-coaster with twist and turns and loops.

8) Goals

Whether it's Naruto trying to become *Hokage*, or *Dr. Stone*'s Senku trying to reboot civilization, characters in shonen comics always have a clear and difficult goal they're aiming for. Audiences read shonen comics because they're aspirational- someone has a lofty dream or goal and they're trying to make it happen. Seeing how the lead characters reach for the stars is a big part of the appeal with shonen comics, and audiences are there to learn how to tackle the big challenges in their own lives by seeing how others tackle equally big tasks. The goal might be very specific like defeating a demon lord, or it might be more general like making the world a better place, but there must always be a clear and defining goal for it to be a shonen comic.

9) Challenges

Shonen audiences don't want to read about characters with easy lives or easy choices- they want difficult situations with hard choices and tough obstacles to overcome. A shonen comic can't just be about a character deciding whether to have ham or egg salad for lunch, there has to be a major life-changing choice or challenge they need to face to get to where they want to go. In a shonen comic, a walk isn't a walk, it's a journey of 1000 kilometers, and a test isn't a test, it's an exam that will determine the course of your whole future. Their opponents are the best at what they do, and shonen heroes need to give it their all to defeat them. The bigger the goal the character has, the greater the challenges they need to face to make it reality.

10) Emotion

Audiences don't read shonen comics- they need to feel them. Manga in general are about representing emotion through art, or what Hirohiko Araki (creator of *Jojo's Bizarre Adventure*) calls "making the invisible, visible." Shonen comics especially are for pre-teens and teens who are filled with strong emotion, and they want stories that reflect those strong feelings. Shonen manga are an emotional roller-coaster ride that take their readers in many different directions before depositing them back where they started, but happier and satisfied. Don't be afraid to exaggerate emotions, and try to make your audience react- because that's what they're there for.

THE AUDIENCE FOR SEINEN MANGA

Seinen, which means "youth" or "young men," is the term used to describe the audience of manga aimed roughly at an audience between the ages of 15-25. Older high school students, university students, and general audiences are the target of seinen manga like *Ghost in the Shell, Berserk, Vinland Saga, Liar Game, Out, Banana Fish, Monster*, and many more.

For the most part, they're very similar to shonen manga, and you can expect to find many of the same themes and ideas in both. Where they diverge is in terms of tone and content. Seinen manga are much more serious, and focus on characters making harder choices than shonen heroes would ever have to deal with. Gone are the happy days of youth, and in their place seinen stories have cold hard reality where the good guys don't always win and the bad guys aren't always wrong. Since the audience aren't children, the authors don't treat them like children, and these manga often explore the difficult grey areas of life their audiences will have to deal with.

That said, the audience for seinen stories is still young. So, while they might have things like sex, drugs and gore that you won't see in a shonen manga, they still tend to be optimistic in tone and aren't completely free of aspirational thinking. In many ways, it's better to think of them as more mature shonen comics without the censorship, and which are willing to go to more extremes to shock and titillate their audiences.

Just remember that when writing seinen manga, the audience wants characters who are forging their own way in the world and doing what the audience wishes they could do, but can't. Seinen stories are more often power fantasies, and their characters change the world around them, often by destroying the old order and remaking it in their image. They are disruptors who cause change just by existing, and this brings them many enemies who benefit from the old way of things and don't want it to change. This creates a natural greyness to seinen stories, because both sides are often doing what they do for the right reasons, and the readers know that neither side is completely wrong.

THE AUDIENCE FOR SHOUJO MANGA

Shoujo manga are manga for girls 8-14 years of age, and includes titles like *Boys Over Flowers, Sailor Moon, Card Captor Sakura, Fushigi Yuugi, Vampire Knight, Ouran High*

School Host Club, *Glass Mask*, and *Skip Beat.* The audience for shoujo comics is both very much like the one for shonen comics while at the same time being very different.

In terms of similarities, the shoujo audience follows many of the same rules as the shonen one does- they're a combination of 8-to-14-year old middle grade students who are figuring out how they're going to be part of society and 12-18-year-olds who are trying to become their own person. The younger ones want funny and interesting stories about characters who fit in, and the older ones want dramatic and exciting stories about characters who create their own way in the world. They also want lead characters who are 12-16 years of age whose experiences they can relate to.

However, these manga are different from shonen stories in a few important ways. First, a lot depends on whether the audience is "real" shoujo readers (8-14) or *josei* (girls 15-25), just like it is with younger and older boys. Unlike shonen comics, girl's manga readers tend to not have as much crossover. Younger and older teen boys are more similar in their tastes than younger and older teen girls. So, while boys of many ages read *Shonen JUMP*, girls manga for younger girls will have a very different audience than girl's manga for older teens, with the younger girls liking more adventurous stories and the older girls preferring more drama and romance. It all depends on what stage of life they're at.

Also, because shoujo comics are for girls, and written and drawn largely by women, they are also very different from shonen comics in a variety of important ways. Women see and experience the world differently than men, and the stories they read and write reflect these differences. The most important of these being that while all manga are about expressing emotion through art, shoujo comics practically overwhelm their audience with it. Everything in a shoujo comic is about feeling the experience the characters are going through, and not just feeling it but being immersed in it.

Some of this comes back to the manga principle of exaggeration, where you take the things you want to focus on and heighten them- and since emotion is the thing the readers of shoujo comics want, that's what the story is there to give them. Young shoujo readers are learning to understand and direct new and challenging emotions, and shoujo manga are there to let them experience and play with their emotions in a safe and controlled way. By living vicariously through the characters in a shoujo manga, the readers are able to try different emotions and feelings on for size and at their own healthy pace.

You can see this emphasis on emotion if you look at the art in shoujo manga, which places emphasis on medium shots, close-ups, and extreme-close ups of characters. Everything is designed to reflect how the characters feel moment by moment, and these are the most intimate ways of framing characters. In fact, they place so much emphasis on characters, that shoujo manga literally have pages with no backgrounds, or have backgrounds made of shapes, symbols and patterns that are designed to convey feelings instead of place. Instead, large images of faces and other parts of characters dominate the page and highlight how each character feels and reacts to the events.

This gives some shoujo comics a dreamlike quality, where the characters exist outside of time or place, and the only thing that's important is how they feel in the moment. The artist lingers on each expression, and each emotion, working their way through the complex sets of feelings the characters have as they spin around each other and towards whatever destiny awaits them. Romantic shoujo comics are known for this style, which sees only characters, and the backgrounds are merely sets for their romantic dramas to play out on.

However, even the more grounded shoujo comics, like *Anonymous Noise* by Ryoko Fukuyama, still place an emphasis on how the characters feel and react over story events and setting details. They are thick with sympathetic characters and situations, and the audience is drawn in to the inner emotional life of the lead characters who are trying to navigate difficult and important life choices. The goal is to wring as much emotion out of the audience as possible, and play the audience's emotions like a master musician plays their instrument of choice from start to finish.

Of course, shoujo manga aren't only dissimilar from shonen manga in their heavy focus on feelings, they're also different in their core philosophy. If we take *Shonen JUMP*'s motto of "Friendship. Effort. Victory." as the central idea behind shonen manga type stories, then the motto for shoujo manga writers would be something like "Relationships. Aspirations. Fulfillment." Or, summarized, "through navigating relationships and working towards aspirations, you can find fulfillment."

Let's break it down further.

Relationships

Despite the stereotype, not all shoujo comics are about romance, nor do they all even contain romance. Yes, it's true that the majority of shoujo comics have some romantic element in them someplace, but that doesn't mean it's always the focus. There are popular shoujo manga about adventuring, solving mysteries, horror stories, superheroes, fantasy, science fiction, and almost any genre you can name- because girls like reading about all of these things too.

However, what almost all popular shoujo stories will have in common is that they place a strong emphasis on interpersonal relationships. This can be romantic relationships, but it can also be friendships, family relationships, or even the relationships between people and pets. This also includes relationships between individuals, or relationships between groups, and any kind of group dynamics is fair game for exploration in a shoujo comic.

Shoujo readers are hungry to understand interpersonal interactions, and they want to see how different people deal with difficult social situations. The main readers (and writers) of these comics are Japanese, which means they come from a group-oriented society where personal connections are everything, and then on top of that female Japanese society is even more complex. Thus, shoujo comics are there to help their readers navigate the hard realities of life for young women entering a new and often confusing world.

Aspirations

Like shonen comics, shoujo manga are about doers. They are stories about characters who have dreams and goals and work to make those dreams and goals into reality. These might be simple goals like making friends, or more complex goals like becoming an empress or CEO, but shoujo lead characters are always trying to accomplish something that's difficult for them.

The goal here is to encourage girls to be assertive and to fight for what they want. Japanese society is highly competitive, and modern Japanese women are still fighting for both social equality and a place in the work world. With many forces working to hold them back, shoujo comics are there to inspire girls and let them know that they can achieve great things in life if they don't give up and work to the best of their abilities.

Fulfillment

And finally, shoujo manga have a clear promise that comes with them- through understanding others and giving it your best, you too will achieve personal happiness. Shoujo heroines get the things they want in the end, and the stories assure the readers that they too can be happy if they don't give up and fight for what they want.

Karma runs strong in shoujo manga, and the characters who take the wrong path end up paying for their misdeeds in the end, while virtue is rewarded with the golden prize, whatever that may be. That doesn't mean all shoujo manga have happy endings (many have bittersweet endings), but they do have endings that reassure the reader that the whole thing was worth it somehow, and that their world is a better place for their efforts.

Thus, shoujo manga tell their readers that the path to personal happiness is through working with others to be their best selves and find their place in the world. It's a strong, simple and clear message that resonates with girls, who are often plagued by doubts and worries in their early teens, and it encourages them to give it their all.

TOP 10 THINGS SHOUJO MANGA AUDIENCES EXPECT

Shoujo audiences have their own sets of expectations, and naturally a good writer thinks about these things when they're planning a shoujo story. Again, the best way to know how to handle these things is to read what your audience reads, and do your best to understand both what you want to write and how to get that across to your readers.

So, here's the things your shoujo readers are going to be looking for...

1)   Intense Emotion

It was covered above, but bears repeating- shoujo comics drip with emotion. They grab their readers by the hearts and pull them into the scene, milking every bit of emotion they can out of the big moments of the story. The characters don't just have small ups and down, they have catastrophic emotional swings as they're dealt situation after situation of gut-wrenching decisions and consequences.

2)   Difficult Choices

Shoujo stories are safe places for girls to explore dangerous situations. Through the heroes, they can enter into dangerous places, try risky things, and face choices that they might never have to face in real life. Shoujo lead characters never have easy lives because they're about doing things the hard way, and seeing what can happen when you have to give it your all to make it out. They need to be brave, tough, and resourceful to find their solutions, and in the process teach the audience what it takes to make their dreams into reality. Never let your shoujo characters do things the easy way, and your audience will thank you for it.

3)   Tragedy

Nothing brings out emotion like a little tragedy, and characters in shoujo stories have tragic lives galore. Loved ones die like there's a war going on, betrayal is the name of the game, and everything important in a shoujo main character's life is precarious. If they have a mentor figure, that character is almost certain to die before the story is over, and if their family is rich at the start of the story, their dad will be in jail for embezzling and they'll be dirt poor by the end. Even in less heart-wrenching stories, the main character is going to start with a difficult life and then it's going to get a lot worse before it gets better.

4)   Hope

While things are never going to go as planned, the main character will have a flame of hope inside them that won't die, or something else that won't let them give up no matter how hard things get. And, there will be times of hope, even in the darkest of stories, when a happy moment with friends, or a cherished time with a loved one shows that life can be better, and it will be, if they keep trying. Older readers can handle darker and less hopeful stories, but young shoujo readers need a clear sense of hope in their stories and the feeling that everything will work out in the end.

5) Humor

With such strong negative emotions floating around the characters, there needs to be balance, and that comes in the form of humor. Shoujo stories, especially those for younger girls, use humor to keep the tone of the story even and offset the harsher parts of the character's lives. Everything from happy little surprises to full-on comedy serve to bring smiles to the faces of the reader and make them feel safe and warm inside this story. Much of the humor is visual, like funny expressions and reaction shots, but funny and unexpected situations keep the audience smiling while making the characters more appealing and relatable.

6) Hyper-reality

Again, going back to the principle of exaggeration, characters in shoujo manga don't exist in the real world, but a hyper-real world where things are greater than they are in real life. Characters speak like the audience wishes they could speak, dress like the audience wishes they could dress, and act in ways the audience wishes they could act. Clothes look nicer and more fashionable than they would on real people, food looks so great it makes the audience's mouth water, and places pop with feeling and emotion. A coffee shop in a shoujo story is the perfect cozy coffee shop with the smartest dressed servers that you'd like to visit every day. A remote house is the most intimidating and scary place that you can imagine, with dark corners and eyes looking at you from everywhere. It's all used to generate strong feelings in the audience, and make the usual, unusual.

7) Beautiful People

Readers of shoujo stories want to immerse themselves in the lives of the characters and put themselves in the shoes of the lead character. That means the lead character can't be ugly, because the reader always likes to imagine themselves as attractive. Of course, they shouldn't be too attractive, or they again become unrelatable- so shoujo heroines are always "cute," but rarely beautiful. Similarly, the love interests in the story should all be attractive to the reader, since they're a big selling point to the story as well.

8) Fashion

Shoujo stories aren't just about beautiful people, they're about beautiful *stylish* people. What the characters wear and how they wear it is extremely important to shoujo audiences who are trying to find their own fashion styles. Shoujo heroines dress in unique and interesting ways that make them stand out and look good, and they give the audience suggestions about what to wear. The supporting cast will show

45

off their fashion sense too, and a lot of cues about character and personality will be suggested through fashion and style choices.

9) Sexuality

Shoujo stories for young girls will usually avoid sex and stick to fairly chaste romantic ideals, just like their shonen counterparts. Hand holding, kissing, and other romantic gestures are as far as your typical shoujo title will go as far as sexual content. They also don't usually have much in the way of fanservice nudity, with most shoujo love interests being skinny and simply drawn men who look better with their fashionable clothes on. However, unlike shonen stories, as soon as shoujo comics are targeted towards older teen girls, the characters usually start having sex- a lot. The act itself is usually implied, not shown, but they don't shrink back from making it clear that the characters are sexual creatures that want and enjoy sex as part of their relationships. (Plus, sexual activity leads to more complicated emotions to explore.)

10) Friendship

One of the ways that shoujo characters survive their ordeals is through the power of friendship. It's their connections to others that give them strength and are shown to bring meaning to their lives. Every shoujo hero needs at least one friend who can help her get in and out of trouble. Friends are always there for shoujo heroes, and for younger girls the stories are usually more about friendship than they are about romance. As the audience gets older, friends get even more important, but as advisors and confidantes who help the main character navigate their way through the confusing events that the stories throw them into.

THE AUDIENCE FOR JOSEI MANGA

Josei (lit. "young women") like a very different style of manga than their younger sisters. This includes titles like *Chihayafuru*, *Gokusen*, *Nodame Cantabile*, *Princess Jellyfish*, *Paradise Kiss*, *Usagi Drop*, *Karneval*, and others.

While shoujo manga tend to be light and adventurous stories that are often pure flights of fantasy, josei titles tend to be much more grounded and down to earth. The 15-25 year old audience for josei stories are there for the drama, the relatability, and the intense emotion, and they want stories set in the real world and about realistic people.

Josei magazines are heavily focused on romance stories, and not the casual, coy romances of shoujo, but the deep, passionate and heady complexity of more mature relationships. They are filled with sex, ambition, adultery, infidelity, lust, awkward situations, and romantic tension- all of this experienced by young characters who are dealing with difficult emotions and situations for the first time. Also, unlike shoujo stories, josei stories are often filled with consequences- what characters do to others and themselves matters, and affects lives. Pregnancy, suicide, financial ruin, and other life-changing events can happen in josei stories as a result of what characters do and say.

That isn't to say that josei manga are all hard drama, and in fact like seinen stories josei stories are still intended for a young audience who want hopeful and positive messages in their fiction. Despite all their trials, josei heroes still usually get the guy in the end, and everything works out for the most part. Nobody wants to be depressed by what they read, so while josei stories might wallow in darkness at times, they always leave a light on for the reader to find their way out.

Lastly, josei heroines tend to have real ambitions in their lives. Unlike shoujo heroes, who sometimes just want to be the love interest's wife, josei stories are often about young women trying to carve their own little place in the world. They are looking for ways to move up and make their ambitions real, and are strong or finding the strength they need to reach for their dreams. Sometimes the focus of the story may even be their goals, and the romance may just be secondary to that, but like shonen heroes they aren't sitting still and waiting for things to come to them.

Other Manga Audiences

As mentioned at the start, it isn't just the young who read manga. There are manga for every demographic, for example:

- *Kodomo* Manga – for young children, under eight years of age
- *Seijin* (Adult) Manga– comics for adult men, mostly about gambling, detective, and salaryman stories
- *Redisu* (Ladies) Comics – comics for middle aged women, mostly romance
- *Gin* (Silver) and *Jin* (Golden) Manga – for retirees (Gin) and seniors (Jin).
- *Ero* (Erotic) Manga – pornographic manga
- *Gekiga* (Dramatic Pictures) – alternative manga that often explore non-mainstream, literary, or experimental topics.
- Hobby Manga – manga focused on a single hobby, like golf, fishing, horse-racing, pachinko, model kit building, etc.
- Educational and Informational Manga – manga textbooks, nonfiction, and guides
- *Yonkoma* (four-koma)– comic strips, usually humor and slice of life.

Each of these audiences has their own tastes, requirements, and styles, and their desires can only be understood by thinking about those people and their tastes, as well as reading what they read to get a feel for what they like.

The main thing to remember is that understanding the audience of a manga, like understanding the audience for any writing, is the key to successfully reaching them. Research, thought, and discussion will help you to find the golden way to reach your goals, and put you ahead of your competition who aren't willing to put the work in.

And, of course, there's this book, which will be your guide to many aspects of understanding manga.

Hajimemashou! (Let's begin!)

Language Note:

Some clever readers might notice that this book uses "shonen" and "shoujo" to describe the two major manga reader demographics, when in fact the first syllable at the start of both should be the same word-"shou" (which means "young"). Or, in other words, it should be "shounen" just like it's "shoujo" when those words are written in English.

However, in common use, few people use "shounen" and instead choose the more common "shonen," just as fewer people seem to use "shojo" and instead render it "shoujo." This book has chosen to go with the more common versions of those two words to keep things simple and because both are six letters, which gives them a more balanced look next to each other

UNDERSTANDING STORIES

Six million years ago, a man told a story.

"I walked into a cave," said the man to others around a campfire. "Then a giant bear attacked me!"

"What did you do?" Asked one of the other men, staring at his friend.

"I grabbed some sand and threw it in the bear's face! Then I ran as fast as I could!" Said the storyteller.

The other tribespeople around the fire laughed and went on drinking and eating.

Two days later, one of tribespeople who heard that story went into a cave and encountered an angry bear (probably because it had sand in its eye). He tried to run, but the bear was faster, and it ate him.

One week later, one of the other tribespeople people who heard that storyteller encountered that same bear (who had learned how tasty these two-legged piggies were). The bear charged him, looking for another feast, but then the man remembered the story and grabbed a handful of dirt to throw in the bear's eyes.

Thanks to that, he managed to escape the bear, and not get eaten. Then, he and his fellow tribespeople got together and did something about the dangerous bear. At the end of the hunt, the tribe ate well, and the storyteller got a new bearskin cap. The second man who escaped the bear would also go on to have many children, grandchildren and great-grandchildren.

In fact, everyone you know today is related to that man, or people like him- people who listened to the stories of others, and learned from them. By listening to stories, they learned how to plant crops at the right time, how to cure sickness, and how to care for a crying baby. They learned the skills and knowledge they needed to survive, have children, and keep the human race going even through the darkest times in history.

The people who didn't listen to stories, who didn't learn, didn't survive.

The ones who did grew and prospered.

Today, we are the children of listeners and storytellers, and our brains are built to absorb stories like a sponge- suck them in and get all the survival information they can. In fact, as soon as your brain hears a story, it perks up and pays attention, in case there's something good in there it can use to increase your chances of living to old age.

Stories are essential parts of human life like food and air, and without them people don't know what to do with themselves.

But, here's a question for you- what are stories?

If you had to answer this right now, could you give a clear answer? Do you know where stories start and stories end? Do you know what the parts of a story are? Do you know how to build one? For something so important and precious in people's lives, most people don't know a lot about them.

Let's fix that.

WHAT STORIES ARE

"Someone does something and gets a result."

That's it.

At their very heart, stories are about causality – why things happen or happened. Not so complicated, is it?

There are three basic parts to a story- a subject, an action, and a result. The subject is the person or thing who does something (or has something done to them), the action is what they do, and the result is what happens because of the action.

(Subject) + (Action) = (Result).

If you have all three of these things, and they fit together logically, you have a story. A simple telling of something that happened and the outcome of that thing happening. This is the basic information your brain needs to learn from a story, and as long as those three things are there, an audience will consider it a story.

Read the following sentences and decide whether each is a story or not:

1. Bill studied for a test and got a great mark.
2. Susan walked her dog.
3. Tanya led her soldiers into the field and defeated the invaders.
4. Mingyuan ran a race, biked three kilometres, and then climbed a mountain.
5. Kori biked across three states to raise money and her flower wilted.
6. Greg and Grace dated for six weeks and then got married in Las Vegas.
7. The puppy was bitten by a dog and had to get rabies shots.
8. Tumbled down the hill and got muddy.
9. On the grassy green, over the hill, in the castle, is the fairy princess.
10. Yvonne drank three milkshakes and then got hit by a car.

Keep in mind that you can only work with the information in the sentence. There might be more information that could turn something into a story which isn't, but if it's not there, you can't call it a story now.

Got it? Let's see how you did!

1. Story.
2. Not a story- no result from Susan's actions.
3. Story.
4. Not a story – two unconnected events, more information would be needed to connect them.
5. Not a story – no result, just actions.
6. Story.
7. Story – Subject is receiver of the action.
8. Not a story – no subject.
9. Not a story – no action, no result. (Is and have are stative verbs, not action verbs.)
10. Not a story – the result isn't connected with the main action.

So, as you can see, just having a character doing something isn't enough, the story needs to connect that character's actions with the result.

First Rule: Stories must have a subject, an action, and a result that's connected to that action to be a complete story.

ADDING DETAILS

Of course, just knowing these three simple things isn't enough for your brain.

The more information your brain has, the more it can learn and increase your chances of survival.

So, at the very least, your brain wants to know the following:

- **Where** does the story happen?
- **When** does the story take place?
- **Who** is involved in the story?
- **Why** do they do what they do?
- **What** happens? What goes wrong (or right)?
- **How** does it all turn out?

This basic information (also called the 5WH) can transform a simple story into a much more detailed one. For example, compare the following:

Bill studied for his test and got a good mark.

as opposed to

Bill (who) wanted to get a good score on his history test to impress his mom (why), so he recopied out his notes at home (what, where), had a group study session with his friends after class (what, who, when), and asked the teacher some extra questions (what). As a result, he got a perfect score on the test. (How it turned out.)

The first one lacks information needed for people who are in Bill's position. The second one, however, lays out an example that any student could use to do well on a test and get good marks. By adding the extra details, the basic story is transformed into something much more useful and interesting for the audience.

Some of you might be asking- "But what details do I include and what do I leave out?"

The answer is, you just need to include the things which help the audience understand the point of the story, or that make the story more interesting. If something doesn't contribute to the audience's enjoyment of the story, or help make the results of the story clearer, then leave it out!

Saying "Bill wore a blue tie to the study session with his friends" doesn't add anything to the above story, so we could leave it out. Unless, of course, we're using that blue tie to show something about Bill's personality, or it connects into the story in some way, in which case including it would be fine. Things which make the story better are always welcome, but things which don't add to the story should always be avoided.

If you're still not sure, ask yourself this- if I don't include this thing in the story, will it change anything?

If the answer is no, then you don't need it, so you can delete it.

The other way to know what to include and what not to include is to think about the Spine of Action...

Second Rule: Stories need details to be useful, answer most of the 5WH in any story.

THE SPINE OF ACTION

No, this isn't Aquaman's sidekick – the Spine of Action is the main thing that the lead character in the story is doing. Longer stories often have lots of characters doing lots of things, but the story itself is held together by one central action, and this is called the Spine of Action.

The Spine of Action...

1.   Tells us where the head of the story is- the subject/start.
2.   Connects the parts of the story together – the actions.
3.   Shows us where the bottom of the story is- the result/ending.

Let's look at the example of studious Bill to see this at work.

•   Bill studied for his history test and passed with a perfect score.

In this story, the key words here are "studied for his history test," which represents the Spine of Action for this story. This means that everything in the story must be linked to Bill, and his studying for that history test, from the things he does to the details of how he does them.

So, the actions of the more detailed version...

1.   Bill wanted to get a good score on his history test
2.   So, he recopied out his notes at home,
3.   Had a group study session with his friends after class,
4.   And asked the teacher some extra questions.
5.   As a result, he got a perfect score on the test.

All make sense, because they're connected to that central goal/point of studying for the history test and getting a good score. However, if you were to add some other actions...

1.   Bill wanted to get a good score on his history test
2.   So, he re-copied out his notes at home
3.   Took a nap
4.   Sang Karaoke
5.   Had a group study session with his friends after class
6.   Asked the teacher some extra questions.
7.   Invited his classmate on a date
8.   As a result, he got a perfect score on the test.

You have a messy and unclear story where the audience can see some things fit, but now has to wonder how the other things are connected. (Short answer- they're not.) Naps, karaoke and dating are great for Bill, but unless they affect the story in some way, they don't belong in this story, and should be left out.

However, the Spine of Action doesn't just tell you what to leave out, it also tells you what to include. Since you know where the story starts and ends, you now have a clear map that shows your beginning and your destination, so all you need to do is plot your route between those two points.

Every major action has a bunch of little actions or steps that go with it- things that you have to do to accomplish that goal. And, once you know what your story's Spine of Action is, you just need to sit down and think about the way your character is going to try and accomplish that goal.

How the character does it will be mostly decided by the character and story, so the bad news is there's no single magic formula for doing this. On the other hand, the good news is that there's no single way to do it! Whatever way you have your character do it is the right way for that character, or wrong way if it doesn't work out.

For example, let's say the main character is Lisa, and Lisa wants to get her driver's license.

The first thing you'd need to do is sit down and think about what steps someone goes through to get their driver's license. Typically, you need to go take a written test to get your learner's permit, then you need to practice driving for a while, and finally you can take the test. So, breaking it down you can see what looks like one action "Getting her driver's license" is actually three actions.

1. Write written test.
2. Practice driving.
3. Take driving test.

Now you know what the three major parts of Lisa's story are, and if you add a beginning and ending, you get...

1. Lisa decides to get her license so she can drive to the beach
2. She writes the written test to get her learner's permit.
3. She practices driving.
4. She takes the driving test.
5. She passes the test and drives to the beach.

Here, you have a complete story about Lisa getting her license, and you know what the major steps of the story are going to be. Of course, you don't have to include all the steps of a process in a story, just the ones which are most interesting and which reflect your story's point, and you can leave some steps out or spend more time with some steps than others.

For example, if you want to tell a story which focuses on how Lisa is afraid of driving at first, then most of the story's focus will be spent on the driving practice part, and the final test will be where you show that she's overcome her fear. You won't spend a lot of time on the written test because that's not related to her fear of being behind the wheel.

Remember the golden rule of storytelling- While details are important, only include important details. The brains of your audience only want to know what they need to know to understand why the character's main action succeeded or failed at the end, they don't want to know what your character posted on Instagram (unless it's connected to the story).

Third Rule: Know what your story's Spine of Action is- it will tell you what fits and what doesn't fit, and decide where it starts and ends.

Fourth Rule: Only include details which are relevant to the story and which make it more interesting to the audience.

THE THREE-ACT STRUCTURE

You now know that a story has three parts – the subject, the action, and the result.

Writers and writing teachers have a special name for this incredible trio- they call them the "three-act structure," and it's considered the most basic way to organize stories. The only catch is that the first part "subject" is usually called "setup" or "introduction" in the three-act structure because it covers a lot more than just who is involved.

But, besides that, the three-act structure is still based on the three must-have parts of a story, and is still about a character doing something and getting a result. It doesn't matter if the story is a single sentence or a hundred-thousand-page novel, there will still be a three-act structure linked together by a Spine of Action there someplace because that's what's needed for the audience to consider it a story.

Knowing the three-act structure is also important because it lets you break down your story into smaller pieces that you can more easily control. Just like cutting your food into smaller parts lets you eat it easier, breaking stories down into their three major parts lets you start to see how the whole thing comes together.

Let's look at the three-act structure in more detail to understand exactly what each part does.

Act 1: Setup (aka the Situation, Introduction, or Beginning)

Length: usually between the first 10% to 35% of the story, averaging 25%.

Questions Answered: Who is involved? Where are they? When does this take place? What motivates them? Why are they doing what they're doing?

Details:

The first phase of any story unit exists to tell the audience everything they're going to need to know to understand the rest of the story. This doesn't just include characters, time, place, and other matters of context, but also includes the motivations and problems that the characters face. The story begins here with a character and a goal or need, and this will be the central idea that carries the story from here to the end.

Notes:

- Act One should always introduce some problem the main character has to deal with, even if it's just that they're thirsty. Whether it's a single sentence or a whole series, the character should be given a motivator like a need or goal which guides them and makes them get off their sofa, put down their phone, and take action.
- Act One doesn't have to be the "real" first part of the story, it's just the point where you drop your audience into the story. The story itself often started long before the main characters or audience get involved, and the first part is about playing catch-up while the action is already in progress. However, this is still the first part of the story you're telling because it's still performing a setup function. In cases like this, the first act might only be as long as 10% of the story because the author wants to get the characters and audience up to speed as soon as possible and get on with the action.
- Nothing should happen in the story which isn't laid out in some way during the first act. It might not be directly shown, but everything that happens should be a natural outgrowth of controlling ideas and story elements which

are presented to the audience in the first part. If there's a storm in the Third Act/Result phase, clouds should be gathering in the First Act/Setup phase.

- Opponents sometimes aren't shown directly in the first Act of a longer story, but their presence is hinted at in some way or suggested by the situation.
- Story guru Michael Hague often remarks that "all story problems can ultimately be traced back to the first act." He's right, so think through your Setup phase carefully, and look here when you have problems writing later parts of the story.

Act 2: Action (aka the Development, Conflict, Event, or Confrontation)

Length: extremely flexible, but usually the middle 40%-80% of the story, averaging 50%.

Questions Answered: What happens? How does the main character try to solve the problem? What gets in their way? How do they overcome challenges?

Details:

The middle phase of any story is where most of the story's action is going to take place. The main character of the story tries to accomplish some goal, and may or may not make progress towards achieving that goal. They may succeed, fail, meet resistance, or discover new information which complicates the situation and changes or modifies their goal. There are many possibilities, which is why this phase is so flexible in length. The main requirements for the Act Two/Action phase are that it's interesting to the audience and that everything that happens is built around what was introduced in the Act One/Setup phase.

Notes:

- Typically, most stories are conflict based, which means that they're about a character in conflict with themselves, another person, society, or the world around them. In these stories, the Action phase is where the character comes into conflict with a someone or something that prevents them from accomplishing their goals. Whether they succeed or fail is left for the Result phase to decide.
- The Act Two/Action phase often ends with some kind of surprising twist or dramatic turn that changes the situation (often for the worse) and increases the level of drama going into the Result phase.
- Sometimes you will see people talk about a four-act structure- this is just the three-act structure with Act 2 broken down into two halves to make it easier to organize. Similarly, if you see five, seven, or nine-act structures, they're still just the three acts broken down into smaller bite-sized chunks.

Act 3: Result (aka the Resolution, Denouement, Climax, or Ending)

<u>Length:</u> usually the final 10%-30% of the story, averaging 25%.

<u>Questions Answered</u>: How does it all turn out? Does the main character succeed or fail? How do they accomplish (or fail to accomplish) their goals? What happens to them after the story is done? What are the consequences of the actions they took in the story?

<u>Details:</u>

The end Result phase of any story is there to bring everything to a satisfying close. It usually contains the climax, where the main character finally overcomes the last great obstacle between them and their goals, and the ending, where you see the results of everything the main character did come together.

<u>Notes:</u>

- Audiences want satisfying endings more than surprise endings, and a satisfying ending is one which is logical and earned by the main character. It is the result of the actions taken in the story, the choices they made, and feels "right" to the audience based on everything which has taken place.
- If possible, endings should also surprise the audience in some way for the best dramatic effect, but surprise is less important than satisfaction. The audience knows all along the main character will generally succeed and wants it to happen (at least at the end of the story), but they also want to know how the character does it and see it happen in an interesting way.
- There should be no major loose ends (unless the story is part of a larger one), and everything introduced in the Act One/Setup phase should be resolved in the Act Three/Result phase unless you're planning a sequel.

You might have noticed that this explanation of the three-act structure is a bit simple and vague, and that's on purpose. For you see, everything written above can work with a story which is a sentence, a paragraph, a whole play, a movie, a novel, or whatever you want to use it to write. It is a simple, universal pattern that humans use to organize stories based on our own way of seeing the world.

Fifth Rule: All stories follow the three-act structure (setup-action-result) to some degree.

THE PLOT

So far, we've talked about how stories are organized, but what about what happens inside the story?

That's where plot comes in.

The Spine of Action of a story tells the writer and audience the story's direction, and possibly the ending, but it doesn't tell the writer **how** the character gets there. The plot of a story is the path the storyteller (and lead character) chooses to take to go from the story's start to the story's finish. It is what makes this story different (or similar) to others, and decides how the events in the story play out.

To give a comparison, if you pull up the Maps app on your phone and ask it to find a way for you to get to the next town or city, it will show you several different routes you could take to get there. One or more for each type of transportation, and one or more for each of the available roads or transportation systems.

All of these involve you going from where you are now to where you want to go in the end, but by changing the way you get there, or the path you take, it will be a different journey. If you take the bus, you might have a noisy journey and meet lots of interesting people. If you drive, it might be a quieter and more relaxing trip filled with music and thought. If you ride a bicycle, it might be a nail-biting slog through hazardous weather.

All of these were you going from A to B, but by changing how you did it, you changed the journey.

The plot of your story is the way you plan to have your characters get to where they're going. It might be a route that many have taken before, or it might be a completely new path. It might be a straight line, or it might be a winding and twisting route filled with lots of backtracking and sudden surprises. In any case, it's how your characters get to where they need to go.

Knowing your story's plot is important for several reasons. First, because it will reflect the themes and ideas of your story, you need a plot that fits your goals. For example, if your theme is about working hard and being rewarded, then a rags-to-riches plot, where a poor person works hard and becomes rich, is probably the way to go. Or maybe you want to talk about how true love conquers all? Then the standard romance plot will do the job nicely, as it has for tens of thousands of other writers. Or maybe you want to put the human spirit on display and show how strong people can be when they try? Then a survival plot about a group of people trying to make it through a disaster might be your ticket to getting your ideas across.

If you want to know more about these common plots, you can find books like Blake Snyder's *Save the Cat!* (which includes his 10 Story Genres), *The Seven Basic Plots* (by Christopher Booker), and Ronald B. Tobias' *20 Master Plots: And How to Build Them*. Any of which can teach you about the way the most common plots play out. Also, later in this book you can find a collection of common manga and anime plots you can use.

Second, you need to know the plot of your story because it will help you avoid making your story exactly the same as all the other people who also use the same plot. The audience knows these plots as well as the storyteller does, and while they like them, they also like to see them done in different ways with an added twist to them. So, if you know which plot you're following, and the way it's often done, you can play with the audience's expectations to give them something they don't expect or see coming.

If the typical fantasy story would have a knight rescue a princess from a dragon, then you can have a princess rescue a knight, or the princess rescue a dragon, or a dragon rescuing a knight from a princess. It's all the same rescue plot, but by playing with the different combinations of the story, you can get different results and maybe explore new ways to take the rescue story.

And third, you need to know your story's plot so you can keep it on track and not waste time on side-trips or other directions that might annoy audiences. Your audience is smart, and the moment they feel that the story is losing direction, or getting confused, or starting to get boring, you're going to lose them and they're going to start doing something else. A storyteller must always have their audience's attention, something that's even harder to keep in today's age when there are literally endless distractions to pull them away from your story. So, to avoid losing your audience keeping the plot tightly together and moving is essential.

Know what your plot is, and where it's supposed to go, and you won't have to suffer from writer's block, wasted time writing, wasted time brainstorming, and wasted effort in general. You'll get from where the story starts to where you need to go on time, and in the most interesting way possible- which is what all good storytellers want to do.

Sixth Rule: Know your story's plot to stay on track and avoid wasting time.

THE FOUR ESSENTIAL STORIES

While there are an infinite number of possible stories, the vast majority of them fall into one of four categories. These four "essential" stories are the most basic forms of the stories that humans tell, and by understanding and using them you can quickly put your story into a simple framework that lets you know where your story starts, goes, and finishes. Not only that, knowing these four essential stories lets you weave together more complex stories than just a character doing something and getting a result, and turn it into a story which is layered and satisfying for readers.

So, what are these four essential stories?

They are stories about Milieu, Inquiry, Character, and Events, which you might notice can be remembered using the very handy mnemonic of MICE. This is why you'll often see them referred to as the "MICE Quotient" online as different writing teachers discuss and explain them. The "quotient" part refers to their use in helping new writers understand how to use them to add layers and plot threads to stories, but before you learn about that, you have to understand what each of them is.

Milieu stories are about setting change, Inquiry stories are about gathering knowledge, Character stories are about character change, and Event stories are about characters trying to restore balance and order to their lives. Together, all four are the fundamental patterns that we use when shaping stories, and by understanding them you will move towards your mastery of storytelling as a craft.

Let's look at each in turn.

Milieu

In a milieu story, a character enters a setting and then either changes that setting or is changed by that setting. Usually, setting refers to a place, but it can also cover things that are part of a setting like plants, animals, peoples, cultures, technology, or anything else. The story starts when the character arrives at the setting, and it ends when either the character leaves or decides to stay in that setting. Often these types of stories are told as a way of exploring a setting with the main character as a window to that setting for the audience.

The Three Acts of a Milieu Story

Act 1 (Setup): The lead character's environment changes to a new one. Usually, the character goes to a new place, or something is added to a familiar place which changes it into something new to the main character.

Act 2 (Action): The main character adapts themselves to the new environment and faces situations where the character, environment, or both change in some way.

Act 3 (Result): The lead character reaches a point where they can no longer change the world, or it can no longer change them. They must then make a decision whether to stay and be part of the setting or leave based on their own needs or situation.

Sample Milieu Stories:
- A wandering ronin comes into a small farming town where he offers to help with the harvest in trade for a place to stay for the winter until the local lord recruits soldiers the following spring. Through working alongside the

farmers, he finds a new purpose in life, and as the winter drags on, he slowly becomes part of the community and finds love with the farmer's daughter. When spring comes, men from the local lord come into town recruiting soldiers for the lord's army, but he decides to keep his new life as part of the community and stays to become a farmer. (The soldier entered the milieu, was transformed by it, and chose to stay as part of the community.)

- A student comes to work one day to discover they now have a new teacher. The teacher has a strange an eccentric style of teaching where everything involves acting and creativity. The very practical student doesn't like this change, but their classmates do, and slowly the practical student comes to appreciate the new classroom environment as they see how the others respond to it. In the end, the practical student is given a chance to transfer to a new school, but decides to stay and explore new sides of themselves. (The student's milieu was transformed, they adapted to it, and chose to stay part of it.)

- A young office worker is hit by a truck and killed, waking up in a world that resembles a fantasy role-playing game. The world they have entered into is chaotic and filled with demons and monsters. They don't know why they are there or how to get home and must turn themselves into an adventurer to survive. Through adventuring and making allies, they discover that they were summoned to replace the guardian of a magical tree which is the source of magic energy in the setting. They choose to become the new guardian and take their place with the tree, restoring the dying tree to life and banishing the corrupting influence. (The office worker entered the milieu, saw it was in chaos, adapted to it, and stayed in the new land they became a part of.)

Notes:

- Change to a character through exploring a milieu can be as simple as learning or understanding something that wasn't understood before. It doesn't have to be serious and significant character change, but it should feel consequential to the reader.
- Milieu stories can be internal or external. In an internal milieu story the character's perceptions of the world around them changes and they must adjust to experiencing the world in a new way ("Well, I can see ghosts now. This is new."). On the other hand, in an external milieu story, the character's environment changes and they must deal with this new setting ("Where am I? How did I get here?").
- See the chapter on Exploratory Manga for more details on one type of Milieu story.

Examples of Milieu manga and anime: *One Piece, Bakuman, Overlord, Kurosagi, Lone Wolf and Cub, Pokémon, One-Punch Man, Fruits Basket, Ouran Koukou Host Club, Hikaru no Go, Assassination Classroom, That Time I Got Reincarnated as a Slime, So I'm a Spider, So What?, Ascendance of a Bookworm, The Devil is a Part-Timer, Konosuba, Boys Over Flowers,* etc.

Inquiry

In a story about inquiry, a character is faced with a question that must be answered and tries to find the answer to that question. The main character may be a detective trying to solve a mystery, or a scientist trying to cure a disease. They might be an athlete who needs to find out if they still have what it takes, or they might be a chef trying to find the perfect soufflé recipe. However it goes, they start the story by being presented with a problem, and at the end of the story the problem will either be solved or they will be forced to give up trying to solve it. Everything that happens in between is linked to their efforts to solve that central problem that drives the story.

The Three Acts of an Inquiry Story

Act 1 (Setup): The main character has a question that for whatever reason (job, curiosity, survival, etc.) must be solved.

Act 2 (Action): Often facing setbacks and challenges along the way, the main character follows the steps they need to answer the question. Everything that happens in the story is somehow linked to the solving of the question or the understanding of the answer to the question.

Act 3 (Result): The main character answers the question or gives up trying to solve it.

Sample Inquiry Stories:
- A man is found dead and a police detective is put on the case. The detective learns that the man was a low-level city clerk who lived along and had no family, so he interviews the clerk's co-workers and discovers that the clerk had noticed missing money in a bank account and reported it to his boss. Using that information, the detective soon arrests the clerk's boss for murdering the clerk to try and cover up his theft of the money. (The detective was given a puzzle of who killed the clerk and why, worked through the possibilities, and solved the problem.)
- A mysterious disease is turning people into zombies and a team of researchers race to find a cure for it. While collecting samples, they learn that a village exists where nobody was turned into a zombie despite exposure and race there to find the reason why. Eventually they learn

that the zombie virus is cured by an element in the town's well water and they use that knowledge to cure the zombies and turn them back into humans. (Scientists are faced with a zombie plague, they try to learn how this happened and how to stop it, and eventually find the answer in a small town's well water.)

- A young office worker is hit by a truck and killed, waking up in a world that resembles a fantasy role-playing game. They learn that the tree of life which powers the world's magic is dying and nobody can stop it, so they go on a quest to find a solution and save the magic because it's the only thing that can send them home. In the end, they learn the tree was poisoned by demons and find a way to break the spell so the guardian of the restored tree can send them home. (The young office worker was given the problem of how to save the magical tree of life, searched for a solution, and eventually found it so they were able to return home.)

Notes:

- If the story is a Detective story, usually the problem to be solved is one of three types: why something happened, how something happened, or who was responsible for what happened. (Or some combination of the three.)
- Most stories have Inquiry story threads inside them somewhere, since there are always dramatic questions to be introduced and answered, but a real "mystery" story is only about the question and the hunt for the solution.
- Horror stories are very often Inquiry stories, where the main characters are the victims trying to solve the mystery behind the "monster" before they all die. Usually the "monster" is the result of a "sin" which has left the world unbalanced and the main character(s) need to learn that sin and set it right in order to stop the killings.
- Inquiry stories can be internal or external. An internal Inquiry story means the character is trying to answer a question that has come from within themselves ("Why do I feel this way?") whereas an external inquiry story is about them trying to answer a question from outside themselves ("Why is my brother acting this way?").

Examples of Inquiry manga and anime: *Detective Conan, Dr. Stone, The Promised Neverland, Uzumaki, Ghost Hunt, Liar Game, Steins Gate, Monkey Peak, etc.*

Character

In a story about Character, a character struggles with personal change. In this type of story, some inner part of a character changes from what it was before to something different. This change can be as small as deciding they now like vanilla ice cream to completely becoming a totally new person. The key is that they are somehow different than they were before at the end of the story. This change can be good or bad, and may even go between positive and negative before it reaches some final position.

The Three Acts of a Character Story

Act 1 (Setup): An event happens which begins a character's transformation as a person.

Act 2 (Action): The character faces one or more situations that cause them to confront parts of themselves which prevent them from reaching their goals or becoming their best self.

Act 3 (Result): The character has finally transformed into a different version of themselves.

Sample Character Stories:
- A troubled student is forced to start a new high school when they get kicked out of their old one for fighting all the time. At the new school, they meet a student council president who they clash with right away and the two hate each other. Through a series of events, the two are forced into being together in different situations and slowly come to understand each other. The troubled student slowly comes to realize they need the student council president in their life and must face their own insecurities that make them reject other people. They open up to the president, who returns their affections, and the two start a new relationship together. (The troubled student meets a person who forces them to confront their inner demons if they want to live a better life and changes into a new person so they can be together.)
- A poor young student is hired to become the driver for a rich man. Working as a driver, the student carefully observes how the rich man acts and operates and realizes they have habits which are holding them back in their life. Soon, the student has changed their ways and started an online business and begun to make money they use to pay off their family debts. Eventually, their online business becomes so big they're able to sell it to the rich man they drove for, and become a rich businessperson themselves who invests in smaller businesses to help others. (The student wants to be rich but doesn't know how, so they study and learn from the more successful businessman, and then change themselves to be more like their model to succeed.)
- A young office worker is hit by a truck and killed, waking up in a world that resembles a fantasy role-playing game. The office worker was a shy introvert who never stood up for themselves and just tried to get through

each day with as little human interaction as possible. However, they find a baby dragon which needs their help and so to help keep the dragon alive they must learn how to interact with the local people. Over a series of adventures with the growing dragon, they become a confident leader who helps the local people overcome a tyrannical lord. In the end, they become the new lord and mentor a new generation of dragon riders. (The shy office worker must find the confidence they need to protect their new dragon partner and ends up becoming a great leader through standing up to the local "boss".)

Notes:

- In these stories the main character usually starts unhappy with some part of themselves or their life and then a catalyst appears which offers them a chance to change.
- The most common version of this story (when used as the main storyline) is one where the main character knows they need to change in some way but refuses to change and instead does everything they can to avoid changing. Then, when they hit rock bottom at the end of Act 2 (Action), they are forced to change in order to fix the problems their poor choices have created.
- Character change stories usually have a main character and a "guide" who is the one who forces them to face their need to change or who acts as a reason they need to change (or both). This guide doesn't even need to be a person, just someone or something that acts like a speck of dust in the character's emotional eye that they can't get rid of unless they change.
- Romance stories are mostly Character stories where the main character must change themselves or their love interest (or both) to achieve happiness.
- Character stories can also be internal and external. In an internal character story the motivation for change comes from within the character ("I'm unhappy. How do I not be unhappy?") and in an external character story the motivation for change comes from outside the character ("My boss says unless I learn to be a better salesperson, I'm fired.").

Examples of Character manga and anime: *Naruto, Magu-chan: God of Destruction, Skip Beat, Blue Flag, Anonymous Noise,* etc.

Event

In an Event story, external things happen that throw the character's life out of balance and the main character spends the rest of the story dealing with the repercussions of those events. This event can be as simple as discovering they're out of food and need to shop, or as complex as trying to survive an alien invasion. The event could be the unexpected result of something the character did or something totally unexpected that was outside the character's control. Either way, the character now has to deal with the consequences of that event and find a way to adapt and overcome the problem.

The Three Acts of an Event Story

<u>Act 1 (Setup)</u>: Something happens to the character which can't be ignored without consequences.

<u>Act 2 (Action)</u>: The character reacts to what happened and tries to find a way to deal with the situation.

<u>Act 3 (Result)</u>: The character solves the problem created by the event or finds a new balance in the changed situation.

Sample Event Stories:

- A dying martial artist gives the youngest of his three students the secret techniques that made his martial arts invincible. The two older students attack and try to kill the youngest student who barely manages to escape alive. The youngest student wanders the land while mastering the secret techniques and meeting friends along the way who help him understand the meaning behind martial arts. When the youngest is forced to face the elder students in a tournament, he shows them he has taken the secret techniques to a new level and defeats them. He founds a new school to teach his refined techniques to the next generation.

- A nerdy high school student's father re-marries and now they're living with the captain of the school volleyball team. The volleyball star keeps getting into weird situations and the nerdy student keeps being forced to rescue them because of their new family ties. Eventually, the volleyball star and the nerdy student come to an understanding, and accept they're now family. (The nerdy student is forced into a new family situation, must deal with the events that come with that new family situation, and they find a way to live peacefully in this new situation.)

- A young office worker is hit by a truck and killed, waking up in a world that resembles a fantasy role-playing game. They make friends, discover they have magical powers, and build an alliance of kingdoms based on freedom and justice. With their new allies, they defeat a great demon lord and then settle down with their beautiful love interest in a peaceful and happy land.

Notes:

- Event stories are the "catch-all" story category when the story's focus isn't about setting change or character change.
- Even stories can be internal or external. In an internal Event story, the event which causes them to act comes from inside the main character ("I'm hungry, time to find food.") whereas in an external Event story the driving force for acting comes from outside ("Godzilla is attacking the city!").

Examples of Event manga and anime: *Demon Slayer: Kimetsu no Yaiba, Naruto: Shippuden, Jojo's Bizarre Adventure, Kaiju No.8, Attack on Titan, Dragonball, BLEACH, Glass Mask, NANA, Fist of the North Star, Tokyo Ghoul, Berserk, Slam Dunk, Death Note, Hunter X Hunter, My Hero Academia, Sakamoto Days, Chainsaw Man, etc.*

Now, some of you might have noticed that technically, all four are "event" stories in the sense that they all tend to start with some occurrence (usually called the "inciting incident" by writers) which sets of the chain of events that follow. However, the difference is where each type of story goes after that initial event launches the story into action. In Milieu stories, the inciting incident changes the main character's environment and makes them adjust to a new situation. In Inquiry stories, the inciting incident presents the character with a question, and that question needs to be answered in some form by the end of the story. In Character stories, the inciting incident triggers a path to character change which the main character will accept or reject in the end. Finally, in actual Event stories, the inciting incident will lead to other events, which will lead to other events, and finally result in a new status quo.

Also, these are meant to be very broad categories, and many stories could in theory fit into multiple categories. However, the trick to finding which type of story is really being told is to look at the Spine of Action for a particular story and what is really happening in the story as a whole. If the story is about conflicting with the world, it's a Milieu story. If the story is about seeking knowledge, it's an Inquiry story. If the story is about personal transformation, it's a Character story. And finally, if the story is about reacting to what's thrown at the main character, it's an Event story.

Since most manga are continuing serials, they usually try to avoid stories built around character change since they don't want the lead character to change much except over long periods of time. Thus, they avoid Character stories when possible and usually stick with Event stories where the main character is thrust into a difficult situation and spends the rest of the series dealing with the ramifications of those initial events. Sometimes, they also tell Milieu stories where the main character enters a strange new world or life situation and the real stars are the people and setting around the main character so the main character doesn't need to change much. And rarely, they tell Inquiry stories where the main character's overall goal is to solve some greater problem through solving a bunch of smaller mysteries.

Using the Four Essential Stories in Your Writing

The first thing to understand is that these essential stories are not plots that tell you what happens inside a story, they're frameworks to help you understand the very rough shape of the story. A good comparison might be the way we think of buildings – instead of Milieu, Inquiry, Character and Event we have Houses, Apartment Buildings, Factories and Stores. Calling something a Milieu story is like calling something a House, it tells us the purpose of the building and the rough shape it will take, but it doesn't tell us the details. It's the same with these essential stories, which tell us the very rough shape a story will take but doesn't tell us any details about it.

To continue the house metaphor – the builder (author) decides they want to make a house (Milieu story) and then they decide whether they want to use pre-planned designs that have worked for other builders (story plots) or make up their own design. Then they will put up the framework (write a story outline) and begin planning out the details of how it will all come together. When they have all their materials (ideas and characters) in place, they will start building (writing) the house and putting it all together.

So, the usual order when using these essential stories is as follows:

Essential Story > Story Structure (Three Act/KSTK) > Story Plot > Details

You figure out your essential story, and that gives you the story structure, which helps you decide what kind of plot you're going to tell, and then you start to figure out all the plot details.

For example, what if you want to tell a story about a young boy trying to get his younger sister to a shelter in a city that's just had a major earthquake? Well then, that's clearly an Event story, so you automatically know that Act One will start before, after, or during the (Event) Earthquake. Act Two will be them trying to get across the disaster zone and the challenges they face. And Act Three will have them arrive at a safe place of some kind.

Now you just have to figure out if you want to use a plot from some other source, or make up your own to help you fill in the details. This story could become a tragedy where the boy is dying and trying to get his sister to safety before he dies. It could be an action story where the boy and girl are being hunted by a group of robbers because they witnessed something they shouldn't have seen. It could be a comedy where the boy turns the trip into a fun adventure to keep the scared girl calm.

Those are all different plots, and while the MICE story they're built on helps determine where the story will start and end, it doesn't tell the writer the details of what happens in between, just helps keep everything organized and on track.

In fact, another good use of the essential stories is to use them to help you figure out what your main story is going to be. You can do this by taking your story idea and trying it out with different MICE stories to see which one is the most appealing to you to write.

For example, let's use the story idea above about the boy and girl trying to reach safety after a major earthquake.

Milieu Story: The story could be about them adapting to the changed world and figuring out how to survive in the post-earthquake environment. Or maybe they will be viewpoint characters and it'll be a story about how the different people they meet deal with a disaster situation where society's rules are out the window.

Inquiry Story: The story could be about them trying to find out why their mother isn't answering her phone, and so they go on a quest across the city to find their mother and learn if she's alive or dead.

Character Story: The story could be about the boy having to take responsibility for the first time in his life and learn to use his head instead of fooling around. Or maybe he's always been jealous of his younger sister and all the attention she gets, but now he comes to realize how precious she is in his life as they journey together.

Event Story: As above, the children could become witnesses to a crime of opportunity being committed which is using the earthquake for cover and become the targets of the criminals trying to eliminate any witnesses.

Each of these could easily become a separate and very different story, and by laying them out like this the writer can see the different story possibilities these characters have and decide which one is the best overall story they want to tell. You can only use one of the four as your main story framework, so choose the one which produces the most exciting and interesting ideas.

Of course, that doesn't mean the other ideas will go to waste. They can become storylines that still get used insider the bigger story the writer wants to tell...

Why is it also called "the MICE Quotient?"

As mentioned previously, you will usually see these referred to as the MICE Quotient and not as "the four essential stories" in other sources.

Writer Orson Scott-Card, originator of the MICE Quotient, pointed out that long stories are often made of a whole bunch of shorter, smaller stories, and each plot thread or storyline inside a bigger story is also one of these four essential stories. In fact, it's rare to have a story that's longer than a few pages that doesn't have more than one of these essential stories running inside it at the same time. So, a certain percentage (or "quotient") of a story is actually made-up other smaller storylines that the writer must keep track of and make sure to pay them off in the end.

Let's look at a generic *Isekai* story where a person is transported to a fantasy world. In this case, the Character story about the shy introvert who finds a baby dragon after they arrive in a new world.

The main overall story is a Character story where the hero learns to be brave and fight for what they believe in, however, there will be a number of other storylines running inside that overall story. Here are just a few of the possible other stories layered inside the main one at the start of the story.

- A Milieu story about the main character learning to survive in the forest where they wake up at the start.
- An Event story about the character finding a baby dragon and freeing it from a trap set by hunters without being attacked by the scared and angry young dragon.
- A Character story where the baby dragon learns to trust the main character.
- An Inquiry story where the main character needs to figure out what baby dragons eat.
- An Event story where the hero has to venture out to find something for himself and the dragon to eat.
- A Milieu story about the main character trying to interact with the townsfolk from the nearby village and figure out how to trade with them.

Each of these can be their own small chapter of the story, or they can be intermixed with each other and happening across many chapters and scenes at the same time. Everything the character does is either a reaction to something (Event), someone struggling with personal change (Character), them getting used to the setting (Milieu), or them trying to find the answer to a question (Inquiry). And these can be long stories that run throughout the whole greater story, or something so small and short it's over in a few sentences.

For most writers, trying to keep track of all the different MICE stories inside a novel or long work would be too much and require a lot of book-keeping. However, you don't need to keep track of all of them, just the important ones that make up the major threads of your story. Such as the different Character plotlines for the main character and any supporting characters, Inquiry stories for the mysteries that pop up during the story, and the major Event stories that come from what happens in the overall story to the main characters and others.

If you want to know more about the MICE Quotient, look up Mary Robinette Kowal's website, as she's one of its strongest proponents and has videos and examples there about how she uses it and others can as well.

Seventh Rule: Know which of the four Essential stories you're telling as your main story, and what the major MICE storylines inside your main story are.

SPECIAL EFFECTS

"Wait!" You might be saying if you've read other books on writing. "What about plot points, and the rising action, and the climax? Don't I need to know those too?"

The answer is that those are tricks that various writers and writing teachers have come up with to add to the basic three-act structure to make the story easier to organize. In fact, you'll find many different people giving advice about storytelling, and each will have their own way they tell others to organize their stories. However, these are all just their own formulas, or the formulas they learned from others for making stories; they're just extras that they think make it easier to write stories and entertain audiences.

The Japanese too, have come up with their own tricks for writing manga and organizing the stories, which you'll find in the chapter called The Rhythm of Manga, and in the later chapters on genres, meta-genres, and plots. Don't let yourself get too confused by all this, and stick to the simple basics of understanding the three-act structure and the rules that go with it and you'll be fine.

IN SUMMARY

Thus, we have the basic rules of storytelling.

First Rule: Stories must have a subject, an action, and a result that's connected to that action to be a complete story.
Second Rule: Stories need details to be useful, answer most of the 5WH in any story.
Third Rule: Know what your story's Spine of Action is- it will tell you what fits and what doesn't fit, and decide where it starts and ends.

Fourth Rule: Only include details which are relevant to the story and which make it more interesting to the audience.

Fifth Rule: All stories follow the three-act structure (setup-action-result) to some degree.

Sixth Rule: Know your story's plot to stay on track and avoid wasting time.

Seventh Rule: Know which of the four Essential stories you're telling as your main story, and what the major primal storylines inside your main story are.

With these, you now understand what stories are, how to organize them, how to decide what to include and what not to include, and how to avoid wasting time writing them and telling them. This gives you a solid foundation when it comes to making your stories, and is a good start.

But the truth is, this doesn't teach you how to tell interesting stories, just stories.

To tell interesting stories that grab and hold your audience's attention, read on...

ENGAGING YOUR AUDIENCE

Telling stories isn't just about the shape of stories – if it was, then stories could be written like mathematical formulas: 1 + 1 = *War and Peace* – it's also about getting the audience's attention and then keeping it. Doing that well isn't easy, and it takes a lot of time, skill, and craft to master it, but there are five basic principles that make storytelling engaging in some way, and if you can use them well, then you're already on your way to telling better stories.

In short, these five principles are sympathy, exaggeration, surprise, suspense and change.

And, by using these five simple principles in different ways, in different amounts, and in different combinations, you can achieve an incredible number of effects. You can hold audiences spellbound, make them weep, make them jump with joy, and even make them tremble with fear. You can play with their emotions, tickle their brains, jangle their nerves and make their hearts explode out of their chests. And, you can make them think, consider new ideas, ponder new points of view, and understand what they could never understand before.

In a nutshell, these five principles are at the core of what brings stories to life and make them engaging pieces of art that shape feelings, lives, and thoughts. They are the root of what makes stories into stories, and by mastering them, you master the craft of storytelling itself.

However, before you dive in, just remember one thing- mastering these principles will take time. Just try to use them in simple ways at first, and then slowly experiment with them as you develop and expand your craft. Each of them is like a powerful spice that can ruin a story if overused, but transform the ordinary into the extraordinary when used carefully. Don't be afraid to use them, but don't think just dumping them in will make something good. That's where experience and technique come in, and what separates a new writer from a professional.

Got it? Then let's begin!

THE THREE KEY PRINCIPLES

A lot of storytelling, from making stories to presenting them, is based around the three key principles of sympathy, exaggeration, and surprise. Together, these three principles will help to guide you in both creating stories and presenting them, as opposed to suspense (which is about building drama), and change (which is connected with planning stories). All five principles are important, but the big three are the most important of all.

SYMPATHY

The first, and most basic, principle of writing an engaging story is using sympathy to connect the characters, events, and situations with the lives of the audience. The word sympathy itself comes from the Greek words "syn" (together) and "pathos" (feelings or emotions)- or in other words, sympathy is anything that lets people feel an emotional connection with the world around them. This can be an emotional connection to individuals, groups, ideas, places, situations, objects, and even events that cause a person to have some feelings when they encounter or think about those things.

Scientists think sympathy evolved to strengthen the bonds between people in communities, and encourage people to work together and help each other out. If you feel an emotional connection to your neighbor, or their situation (say, they're hungry, and you've been hungry too, so you know how that feels), then you are much more likely to help them. This creates stronger social bonds between people, and improves their mutual chances of survival.

And, this reaction applies not just to people you know, but to people you hear about as well. So, when you hear that a grandmother doesn't have enough money to pay her heating bills, a shopkeeper keeps cheating his customers, or a child overcomes cancer, you feel sad, angry, or happy even though you don't know these people personally. You know people like them, or have had similar experiences, and that's enough for you to feel some emotional sympathy towards them.

Stories, of course, are built on using this effect. You present the audience with a main character who has positive relatable traits, or is doing positive things that the audience can relate to, and suddenly you have a character who the audience feels a connection to and wants to support. They want to see this character succeed, they

75

want others who oppose this character to fail, and they get concerned if bad things happen to this character. The character becomes a part of their "community" and that bonding social evolutionary trait mentioned earlier makes them feel like that character is someone they're connected with.

No wonder some people feel that fictional characters are as real to them as the people they see every day in their own lives!

So, how can you start to use this in your own writing?

Actually, it's very simple. When you first introduce a character you want the audience to connect with, do one or more of the following things:

- Show them living under sympathetic **circumstances**.
- Show them doing sympathetic **actions**.
- Show them having sympathetic **connections** to the world around them.

Each of these things by themselves will naturally make the audience want to like them, and start the bonding process between the audience and the characters. Presenting more than one of these things, and layering them onto a character, will continue to strengthen those bonds and continue to make them and the audience even more connected.

Thus, if you have a character who is a homeless teenager living on the streets (circumstances), but who is kind to other people (connections) and feeds stray animals (actions), you will have a character who the audience is going to think favorably about. Similarly, if a character has just won the lottery (circumstances), takes their family and friends on a round the world vacation (actions), and spends the whole trip sorting out the complicated relationships they have with their family members (circumstances) then the audience is also likely to feel a connection with them.

The next time you watch a movie or read a story, pay attention during the introduction phase of the story and you'll see that a good film or story spends time at the beginning quickly presenting a series of circumstances, actions, and connections around the main character that the audience can relate to. The point here is to make you bond with the main character, and you can do this in your own stories too.

But, what if you want to make audiences dislike characters?

Well, then you do the opposite!

- Show them living under un-sympathetic **circumstances**.
- Show them doing un-sympathetic **actions**.
- Show them having un-sympathetic **connections** to the world around them.

Having the character do things the audience can't relate to will instantly distance the audience from those characters and make them reject bonding with them. They'll feel the character is "other"- not part of their community – and because of that will have neutral or even hostile feelings towards them. This will make the audience okay if bad things happen to this character, and possibly they'll even cheer it on.

To see this in action- next time you watch a story or movie, pay attention to the first time a "bad" character is introduced, and you'll see that they'll almost always do or say something to make the audience dislike them right away. If the bad character will die in that scene, then the first words they say or actions they do will be something terrible. Usually they'll be shown bullying innocents or saying something bad about women, which tags them immediately as a bad guy who must be punished in the minds of the audience.

However, sympathy isn't just about characters- it can also be about how the audience relates to the story and its situations as a whole. Places, actions, sensations, and even events can generate sympathy in the audience and make them feel more connected and invested in the story itself. For example, if the audience has had an experience like the one the character is going through, that will generate sympathy between the character and audience. Being stuck in traffic, having to write exams, going on a bad date, or missing a loved one are all experiences that most people have had, and thus when those things happen in a story it will make the audience subconsciously relate more deeply to what's happening.

Of course, the other side is true as well. If the audience can't relate to something in a story because they haven't experienced it, they will feel little or no connection to it. This is why some stories resonate strongly with certain people while leaving others flat- those people who can't connect with the story's elements won't get anything from it and thus won't enjoy it. If a story is about the experience of being a middle-aged woman, then it becomes hard for men or younger women to relate, since they don't have any connection to the things a middle-aged woman is going through in her life. And, this is also why certain stories are very different experiences depending on the context and situation of the reader. If you read the same book in your teens, thirties, and fifties, it can often be a completely different experience because your connections to the book, your sympathies, are different.

Thus, you can see that sympathy is an important principle in storytelling because it brings the audience and the story together and makes it possible for stories to become emotional journeys.

In the following chapter on *The Power of Emotion*, you'll see how to use sympathy to generate emotions in your audience and bring out different feelings in your audience to dramatic effect.

SURPRISE

Everything you just read isn't true. It's all lies.

You didn't expect to read that, did you?

And now, your brain is paying extra attention to find out if that's correct or not. (It's not.)

As neuroscience writer Jonah Leher says, "nothing focuses the mind like surprise." And, it should, because surprise is there to keep you alive. It's a primal reaction that our ancestors developed to deal with the unexpected and unusual.

Something strange happens? You freeze. Your brain wakes up and gathers as much information as possible. You make a decision. That's a survival trait we've developed as a species to avoid getting eaten by lions and bears. It's an unconscious and automatic process that happens in seconds whenever we encounter something we didn't expect.

And it doesn't just happen in real life, but also when we're consuming stories. Our brains don't know the difference between what's real and what's fiction, and take everything coming in as though it's real. So, when a character you're bonded with opens a door and there's a lion there, your brain reacts just like it would if you'd opened the door and found a big kitty waiting for you. It jumps into overdrive, tries to figure out how this happened, if this is a threat, and how to deal with it- then starts making decisions.

Surprise makes us sit up and take notice, whether it's something that's happening to us personally, or characters in stories, and it's a trait that skilled entertainers exploit to keep their audiences interested, involved, and emotionally engaged.

How?

Unexpected things (to the audience) happen, and characters must deal with them. This can be small things, like unforeseen reactions, or more complex things, like a planet blowing up, but in order to keep an audience interested a storyteller must give them a steady stream of unexpected events and situations. Preferably ones which make sense based on the other elements of the story.

This is something storytellers have learned to use to their advantage, and a good storyteller is always looking for ways to gently surprise their audience to keep them actively involved in the story.

These are just a few of the ways that storytellers surprise their audiences and keep them involved with what's going on. And, it isn't just what happens, but what doesn't happen can also surprise the audience. When the audience expects something to happen (because of the storyteller leading them, or their own assumptions) and it doesn't happen- the audience is again thrown off guard and forced to pay attention to what's happening. Anything that interrupts the patterns and rhythms that you have created in the minds of the audience will act as a surprise and get a reaction. The more unexpected it is, the bigger the reaction.

Good storytelling, then, is about controlling and creating patterns and rhythms in the minds of the audience and then playing with those patterns. The most basic way to do this is to subvert the audience's expectations- you let them think they know where the story is going, and then things happen which aren't what the audience would normally expect, but which still make sense.

However, that's only one way to do it. A good storyteller is giving the audience a stream of small surprises in different ways that keep them stimulated and interested, and slowly building up to even bigger surprises. Think about it- if you constantly hit the audience with one major shock after another, they're going to get tired and fatigued, and the surprises will have less and less effect on them because they'll become numb to the constant shifts. Therefore, a good storyteller needs to both alternate between the surprising and expected, and they need to also change up the types of surprises they're giving the audience.

This can include...
- Introducing a new character, problem, or situation
- Moving the story in an unexpected direction
- Having characters say something unexpected
- Startling decisions from characters
- Stopping a scene or chapter at a critical moment
- Changing points of view
- Jumping between events
- Taking a break to explain something the audience needs to understand
- Giving them incomplete pieces of a puzzle
- Sharing a story or anecdote related to what's going on

A surprising character revelation could be followed by an unexpected shift in points of view to give the audience time to digest what they just learned, which could be followed by a new problem being introduced, which could be followed by a startling decision by a character, which could be followed by a jump to other character's points of view, which could be followed by a new revelation brought about by the previous one. Each of these shifts acts as larger or smaller surprise to the audience and keeps them thinking about where the story is going and what's going to happen next. And, by keeping them wondering and off-balance, the writer keeps them engaged and actively focused on the story.

However, surprise is not only about keeping audiences engaged, but also about stimulating their emotions. Surprise actually amplifies the emotions associated with the surprise, making the audience feel them more strongly. How much more strongly? According to LeeAnn Renninger, in her book *Surprise: Embrace the Unpredictable and Engineer the Unexpected*, "Research shows that surprise intensifies our emotions by about 400 percent, which explains why we love positive surprises and hate negative surprises."

When something unexpectedly good happens, we go through the roof. When something unexpectedly bad happens, we take it as a serious emotional blow. And remember, this doesn't just apply to us, it applies to the experiences of characters we're bonded with (thanks to sympathy) as well. We experience their emotional highs and lows as our own, and their emotional surprises as our own as well.

So, when the big moment hits, adding some elements of surprise to it will make the audience's feelings more intense and all the sweeter.

And finally, surprise isn't just involved in telling a story, but even in the way you plan it. Characters, situations, and settings in a story should have some surprises connected with them to make them more intriguing and interesting for the audience. A character or situation with a good surprise twist connected to them can sell a story or keep an audience hooked as they're driven by curiosity to find out how that surprising twist turns out.

The coming chapters on Making Manga go more into detail about how to use surprise to your advantage when you're planning your stories.

EXAGGERATION

Remember that weird kid in your class? The one who would talk in funny voices, and act in over-the-top ways that made the rest of the class laugh and your teacher sigh? Most of you probably questioned how that kid was wired, and used words like "weird" and "dumb" to describe them.

Well, it turns out that kid was way ahead of the curve.

They'd already mastered a very important formula that everyone who wants to hold the attention of an audience needs to tattoo onto their brain.

Exaggeration = Attention.

Think of exaggeration as being like a magnifying glass that puts people's attention onto something and makes them aware of it. By making something greater (or lesser) than it normally is in real life, thanks to its connection to surprise, it causes people's brains to sit up and take notice. Exaggerated things catch people's interest and imagination, making the audience want to know more about what it is that they're looking at.

Great speakers have known this for centuries, and have used the power of exaggeration to sway audiences and change the world. They don't talk about what is, but what could be, and by exaggerating things in the minds of their audiences, they make the audience dream of the possibilities of tomorrow if only they acted with strength and conviction.

Great actors too, know the power of exaggeration. The best actors have the ability to exaggerate their reactions and emotions in a way that the audience responds to – but that is in no way realistic. That's the difference between an actor and real people in everyday life- an actor can exaggerate certain parts of their speech, body language, and actions to make their emotions crystal clear to audiences. Real life emotions are hard to understand clearly, but these exaggerated emotions are ones the audience responds to and sympathizes with, bringing them into the actor's world of performance.

And great writers also know the importance and power of exaggeration. The best writers have the ability to pick the right things to exaggerate to bring out the reactions they want from their audiences. They exaggerate details, actions, events, places, words, and other things in their stories that captivate and interest the audience- holding their attention and keeping them focused on what the writer wants them to focus on. It's through exaggeration that writers express theme by picking certain elements of the story to concentrate on, and keeping those elements front and center while the rest of the story plays out around them. It's through exaggeration that writers take their audiences on emotional roller coasters through the story and its events. And, it's also through exaggeration that writers find the best and most interesting parts of reality to craft into engaging stories.

So, as you can see, exaggeration is very powerful and important, and mastering it is one of the keys to being a successful performer of any kind.

And, for you, the exaggeration starts from the very moment you pick the premise of the story.

Your story will be built on some piece of reality that you've chosen to exaggerate, and by doing so stimulate the imaginations of the audience.

"A man takes a dog for a walk," isn't interesting.

"A man takes his dog on a thousand-mile hike through the mountains," brings nothing but ideas to both you and potential readers.

"A boy and a girl fall in love," doesn't fly off the shelves.

"A boy billionaire falls in love with a female archeologist," has serious potential on the romance stacks.

And, if you look at a list of successful books or movies, one of the first things you'll notice is that they have a clear, exaggerated premise behind each and every one of them. People don't want things which are normal- normal is boring. People want to escape from their boring, normal lives into fiction, and they pick the stories they consume based on whether it stimulates their interest and imagination.

So, like a good public speaker, when you decide what story you're going to tell, your first job is going to be finding the most interesting and exaggerated take on that situation to sell both yourself and your audience about the possibilities of that idea.

Then, once you have that settled, it's time to use the power of exaggeration throughout your story to keep everyone's attention as the story plays out.

- Locations should be the most interesting places you can think of
- Characters should have larger than life traits that make them compelling
- Situations should be ones that don't happen everyday
- Emotions should be pushed to the limit
- Actions should be the most interesting ones the characters can take
- Reactions should be the most interesting and unexpected
- Dialogue should be what people wish they could talk like if only they were wittier
- Details should vividly describe the story world
- Ideas should be taken to their extremes to find their limits and potentials
- Themes should be written in the sky in big letters

These things, and more, are ways that writers can capture the imaginations of audiences and keep them immersed in the story. By thinking about ways to make the story larger than life, the potential of the story is unlocked, and that potential will make audiences interested.

However, there are also two other important guidelines that writers should remember about exaggeration.

First, while normally exaggeration refers to things being bigger, it can also refer to things being smaller. Just as a character having five seconds to defuse a bomb is more interesting than them having an hour to do it, making things smaller can also act to emphasize them in many different ways. Don't get stuck on the idea of making everything larger, and instead think of how making things more extreme can make them more interesting. The most interesting ideas are found on the fringes- the strange, the rare, the unusual, the unlikely. That's where exaggeration can take you, and produce some of the most original characters and stories.

And second, if everything is exaggerated, then nothing is. Exaggeration only brings its powers of clarity and focus if it's used in limited and controlled ways. Too little will produce a bland story nobody wants to read, and too much will create an over-the-top mess. You need to only exaggerate the right things in the right ways to get the best results.

But what to emphasize and what to leave alone, then?

That's a matter of judgement that only works on a case-by-case basis, but two good tips are to study how the creators you love use exaggeration in their works, and then to go slow when you start using exaggeration yourself. Knowing how others do it will show you what writers in your genre emphasize and what audiences like, because it does vary by genre. Young Adult stories tend to pump up the emotion to extreme levels, for example, while stories for older readers will tone down the emotion and play up the unusual situations. Similarly, you should experiment to find what feels right for you by slowly trying different approaches, and finding what it is that makes your readers react the best to your work.

In any case, remember that exaggeration is what brings readers and writers to the heart of the story, makings things story-worthy, and keeps them there by stimulating their emotions and imaginations. It is a powerful tool that is hard to master, but whose use separates the amateurs from the professionals.

SUSPENSE

One upon a time, there was a powerful Thai king who was tired of the extravagant food he ate each day and made a declaration- "Whoever gives me the most delicious taste in the world will be showered with riches!"

Naturally, this brought an endless parade of people to his palace, each one of them claiming to offer him the most delicious food in the world. He tried them all, and while he liked many dishes, there were none that he felt could be called "the most delicious."

Then as he was getting tired of it all, one morning an old woman appeared and said to the king- "I can give you the most delicious taste in the world, but you must agree to follow my commands for three days."

The king laughed and said that for him to taste the most delicious taste in the world, following her commands for three days was nothing. What did she want him to get? What did she want him to give? What was he to do?

The old woman shook her head. "If you want the most delicious taste in the world, you may not eat anything today. You can drink water, but no food. Do you agree?"

"I do," said the king.

"Then I will come again tomorrow," said the old woman.

And so, the king didn't eat anything for a whole day, merely sipping on water to quiet his growling stomach.

The next morning, the woman again appeared. "Did you eat anything since we last met?" She asked.

"No!" Said the king, ready for his meal.

"Good," replied the old woman. "If you want to taste a taste beyond compare, then you must continue your fast for another day. I will return tomorrow."

The king, who was very hungry, wanted to argue, but his desire to taste the greatest taste in the world made him hold his tongue. He merely watched as the old woman left, and grumpily went about his day, trying to ignore his twisting stomach and yelling at his servants.

The next morning, the woman appeared again, and again she asked. "Did you eat since we last met?"

"No!" Barked the hungry and unhappy king. "I have not had even a seed to eat! Where is this food you promised me?"

The old woman smiled and said, "You shall have it for dinner tonight, my king. All you need to do is wait a little longer. Do not eat until you see me again and your wish will be granted, I promise you."

The king cursed and considered that this old woman was making a fool of him, but decided that a few more hours was worth the price for the greatest taste in the world. If she did not give him what she promised, he mused, he would take a terrible revenge on her.

"Be at your dinner table tonight before sundown, and I will bring you your meal." Said the old woman who again left the palace.

The king, who was feeling so weak he could barely walk, was waiting at his table just before sundown as the old woman instructed. And, as she promised, the old woman appeared with a cloth-covered tray, walking across the grand ballroom to where the king sat.

"Your great majesty," said the old woman placing the tray before him. "I present to you, the greatest taste in the world."

But, when the cloth was removed, all the king saw was a steaming bowl of plain white rice. No side dishes. No toppings. Nothing but a simple, unadorned bowl of rice.

At first, the king was angry, and a thousand punishments flashed in his head for this woman who had tricked him and made him starve for three days! However, he decided that could come later, he was too hungry to think any more and he grabbed the bowl of rice and gobbled it down.

When he finished, he stopped and stared at the bowl.

Then, he ordered that the woman be given the gold and riches he'd promised her.

Because to a starving man, that plain, simple rice was the most delicious taste in the world.

So, what does this old parable have to do with suspense?

As you have probably guessed- everything.

Holding an audience in suspense not only keeps their attention, but also makes them emotionally engaged and invested with what's happening in a story. Like the Thai king, the audience finds themselves wanting to know the answer to a question, and the more they wait to get it, the more important to them the answer to that question becomes. (And the sweeter the result.)

Again, there is science behind this. According to Anthropologist Dr. Helen Fisher, when humans are given some information and then left with a mystery, it triggers a flow of dopamine that gives them a natural high and hooks them to want to know more. The human brain wants to understand more about the world to increase the owner's chances of survival, so when people are given a puzzle, they're driven to find out the answers. Marketers call this the "curiosity gap."

In a large part, this is why people love stories so much.

Audiences are presented a sympathetic character with a problem (a puzzle, like what the most delicious food in the world would be) and then they're naturally driven by instinct to find out the answer to that problem. In fiction, the puzzles which pop up in stories are called "dramatic questions"- questions which stimulate the interest of the reader and make them want to know more. Then, storytellers use that trait to keep audiences hooked by not giving them answers right away and making them wait for the answer to the puzzle. The answer to the story's biggest question is the end of the story, and in between the audience is treated to other smaller pieces of the greater puzzle, surprises, and interesting situations that help keep their attention focused until the end of the story.

Thus, to create suspense a storyteller should...
- Give them a dramatic question they must read on to find the answer to.
- Give them a surprise that creates a dramatic question and make them wait.
- Give them pieces of the puzzle, but not the whole thing until the end.
- Give them a pattern, and then let them expect something to happen that follows that pattern.
- Give the audience information the characters don't have (dramatic irony), and then let the characters walk into the situation the audience thinks (or knows) isn't going to go the way the characters expect.

Of course, to get the most out of suspense, the storyteller needs to combine it with surprise to achieve maximum effect and make the audience feel their attention was rewarded. Whenever a dramatic question is created, the storyteller needs to answer it in the most interesting and entertaining way possible. This is usually done by following the old showman's wisdom which says that when the audience wants something- don't give it to them. Then, give it to them in a time or way they don't see coming.

By using this technique, it creates maximum emotions and reactions in the audience, since like a starving man, they've built up their hunger and just want the answer. And, when they get it in a way which is not only satisfying, but extra satisfying, they love it even more.

However, suspense is a tricky thing to work with, and writers should be careful with it. If the writer goes on too long without giving an answer, the audience will lose interest. Similarly, if storytellers don't pay off their smaller dramatic questions and puzzles well to earn the trust of their audience, the audience will lose faith in the storyteller and find something else to do. The audience needs to feel their attention and suspension will be rewarded, and a writer must never abuse their faith by not living up to their side of the bargain.

To master suspense, follow the masters- analyze the stories you love and see how they're using the principles of suspense to keep you hooked and unable to put their work down. See how they play with you until the very end, keeping you moving forward with small rewards until the final payoff at the end. See where their scenes and chapters end, and how they slowly reveal the truth behind the story's mysteries and dramatic questions. Until, like the Thai king, the audience eats that final delicious bite of the thing they've been craving the whole time.

CHANGE

The final element that storytellers need to know to engage their audiences is change.

As was discussed in a previous chapter, stories are about characters trying to do something. And, that thing they're trying to do, whether it's an active thing like baking a cake or a reactive thing like surviving a forest fire, needs to have some kind of result. The audience wants to see how the character's actions came together to produce the end results of the story, and how the character's situation was changed as a result of what they did.

As usual, this is human brains trying to find out more survival information by learning what combinations of actions and situations will produce what results. The hope here is that by learning what leads to what, the audience member in question will be able to use that information to get or avoid the same kinds of results that happened to someone else.

Accordingly, this means that audiences naturally love stories where something changes- where things at the start of the story are different than things at the end of the story. They feel satisfied when they can look back at a story and see how everything came together to produce a result at the end.

What kind of result?

That depends on the story, the audience, and storyteller.

However, there are generally speaking two kinds of change in stories- character change and setting change.

Character change happens when a character starts in one way, and then finishes differently than they were when they started. Maybe their perspective changed, maybe they changed physically, maybe they changed as a person, maybe their social situation changed, or their financial situation. Regardless, the foundation of this type of story is that the character is the one changing, usually because of their experiences during the story and the world around them. This change may be caused by things they do, or things done to them. Often, it's the result of meeting other characters and those interactions are what changes the character.

Setting change, on the other hand, is where the character at the center of the story alters the world around them in some way. The character themselves may or may not change, but the setting does as a result of the character's actions or inactions. Maybe the character builds a well, or helps start a revolution, or creates a plague, or solves a crime- in some way the character's existence and actions have changed the world around them. Sometimes that change can even be restoring order- like in crime fiction where a murder has occurred at the start and the criminal must be brought to justice to restore balance to the world – but the character is the bringer of change to the setting.

In most stories, you will find some combination of both types of change, but stories which are perfectly balanced in both character and setting change aren't very common. Largely, stories will lean heavily one way or the other, with the focus being about how the character changes, or the focus being about how the world changes, but not both. For example, crime fiction, superhero fiction, adventure fiction, and most fantasy and sci-fi tend to be about setting change where the main character changes only a little or not at all. (They are usually stand-ins for the author and audience, so they don't change much.) On the other hand, dramas and romances are all about character change, and how interacting with other people causes the characters to become someone new and a better version of themselves.

Regardless of what type of story a storyteller wants to tell, this all means that they must decide two important things at the start of the story- 1) is this story about character change or setting change, and 2) what changes will happen by the end.

First, knowing whether the story is about character change or setting change is important because it can change the entire way the story is presented. The change in the story needs to reflect the themes of the story, and so the emphasis on what the change is, how it happens, and how it turns out, needs to be known so the theme and change can be connected with each other. For example, if the story is about how working together lets people do great things, then the characters at the start of the story are probably going to be distrustful loners who come to see how they need others to accomplish their goals. Or, if the story is more setting based, it will be about how a great project needs to be done, and that project is accomplished by many people who all contribute their own part to its success.

As you can see, the focus and emphasis shifts depending on whether the change in the story is linked more with the characters or setting, and needs to reflect the story's themes. A character-based story is usually about how the characters are changed by the setting and the situations produced by that setting, and a setting-based story is about how the setting is changed by the characters working to change it in some way. Each has a different approach, and each has its own focus.

Some writers naturally lean towards character change stories, while others naturally fit with setting change stories. Which you best work with will depend on your own tastes and style of writing, and you should experiment to see what works best for you. As a general guideline, younger writers and male writers tend to gravitate towards setting change stories, while more mature writers and female writers tend to gravitate towards character change stories. Which is right for you is something only you can decide.

BRINGING THEM TOGETHER

Together, the three key principles -sympathy, exaggeration and surprise- shape both story creation and storytelling. At the same time, suspense keeps audiences engaged and focused where the storyteller wants them, keeping their interest on the story itself. And, it all leads to the end, where the audience can see how the characters or setting have changed as a result of the story's events.

As you may have noticed, these elements are all interconnected, and don't just work on their own. Surprise and exaggeration are linked, and so are surprise and suspense. Sympathy is linked to change, because the audience wants sympathetic characters to escape their poor situations and go forward to better lives. And exaggeration and sympathy work together to create clearly defined characters who are more ideals than they are real people, but still connect to the audience on a deep level.

Using all of these principles together when planning a story (whether it's visual elements or text) makes stories into something that captivates audiences from the start and makes them want to come back for more.

They also help to shape an audience's feelings and emotions as they experience the story, so read on to learn more...

MAKING THE AUDIENCE FEEL

Good stories are felt, not understood. Just as a musician plays an instrument, a storyteller plays the emotions of their audience. They lead their audience through a series of ups and downs, using the principles of engagement to keep their audience focused and moving along an emotional journey through the story.

To be a good storyteller means to be good at controlling and directing the emotions of your audience, preferably without the audience realizing they're being manipulated. A good story feels natural, unforced, and as though it were something which is really happening in the hearts and minds of the people experiencing it.

Of course, the audience knows that they're going to have their emotions controlled by the storyteller- that's why they're there. But they don't want it to be obvious because that breaks the immersion of the story experience. They want to be so swept up in enjoying the story that they fall into the arms of the storyteller like the aforementioned instrument and allow their emotions to be played and massaged into bliss.

So then, how do you control what your audience feels?

In the previous chapter, you learned about the key principles of storytelling, and the first of those basic principles was sympathy. Sympathy is what bonds an audience to a character, and creates a connection that lets the audience feel what the character feels. It links them together, and makes the audience emotionally invested in this character just like they are in the people they know in their own real lives. The character's ups and downs are the audience's ups and downs, their accomplishments are the audience's accomplishments, and their hopes and dreams become the dreams of the spectators.

But, once the storyteller has created that bond, what do they do with it?

How to shape the emotions of the audience depends on the emotion you want to generate. Each has their own characteristics, and tricks to bring them out. The following is a collection of the more common emotions and how you can get your audience to feel them. It is by no means a complete list, or the only ways to bring out these emotions, but is meant to help you get started in developing your own ability to bring your stories to life through emotion.

SADNESS

It might surprise you to learn that the easiest emotion to make audiences feel is sadness. And, in fact, a type of sadness, pity, is the most commonly used emotion at the start of most stories. Sadness creates sympathy, and so it's customary to start most stories with the main character in a poor state of affairs because that almost automatically makes the audience connect with them. Everyone has been in bad situations, they know how it feels, and they don't like it, so they want the character to feel better so that they too feel better.

Sadness can be created in many ways, but the simplest is to make the character pitiable. Maybe they were born into a poor family? Maybe they got cheated on? Maybe they're sick? Maybe they just lost their job? Maybe they have no friends? Whatever it is, luck has put them in a bad position that they're struggling with and can't easily get out of. Poor fortune makes the audience's hearts go out to a character, and the more they're struggling, the more the audience feels for them.

Of course, other things will trigger sadness in the audience. Putting the character in sympathetic situations of loss can bring out strong emotions. Generations of children cried for hours after Bambi's mother was killed, and few remember anything about the film after that moment because they were so overwhelmed by the main character's tragic loss. Similarly, characters going through heartbreaking situations in their attempts to find love or happiness will connect with audiences and mix their own memories of sad times with the ones the character is experiencing.

However, the one thing to be careful of is to avoid there being a clear character to blame for the sadness. Sadness comes when the cause is the setting and world around the character- fate, destiny, bad luck, poor planning and poor timing generate sadness. If there is a villain- someone doing immoral things on purpose to the character- that generates an entirely different feeling in the hearts of the audience...

ANGER

Making the audience mad is also fairly simple- show them injustice and their tempers will quickly begin to rise. Everyone experiences times in their life when they've been treated unfairly. Even the calmest person can remember the hard times of childhood and teenaged years, when others were cruel to them. Or has dealt with difficult co-workers, bosses, or customers that have forced them to swallow their pride and just grin and bear it. Thus, as soon as the audience's surrogate, the main character who they're bonded with by sympathy, is treated unfairly by others, those memories will come rushing back like hot lava waiting to explode.

Anger and sadness are similar, except while sadness is generated when the bad things are due to impersonal forces like bad luck, anger is generated when there is a clear and very personal cause of the character's bad situation. Anger needs a villain-someone to blame, and preferably someone who the audience doesn't like to begin with. It needs a character who is causing these bad things to happen to the main character out of their own selfishness, greed, malice, or other sinful reasons.

A likeable character missing their chance to confess their love because the traffic was bad will make the audience feel sad. A likeable character missing their chance to confess their love because their business rival slashed their tires will make them feel angry. A likeable character missing their chance to confess their love because their business rival framed their love for murder will make them feel furious.

The bigger the injustice, the angrier the audience will become, and the more they will come to hate the villain and the person who is inflicting the injustice. Not only that, the more the audience likes the characters suffering, the angrier they will become as well. This is where exaggeration comes in- the worse the things that the villain does to their favorite characters, the angrier the audience will become. So, if you want your audience to really hate a villain, then look for ways to have them do really nasty things to the characters they love.

Besides injustice, another trigger for anger is the abuse of power. This one often hits closer to home (generating sympathy) for most adults, who have to deal with situations in their lives where they feel powerless and out of control. Having a character in the story abusing their power will remind the audience of their own experiences, and sympathetic anger will naturally flow. Look for chances to show villains abusing power, and you'll find ways to build audience anger quickly.

Finally, anger can be layered. A series of small injustices or abuses can sometimes be even more effective than a single larger abuse. Watching a bonded character suffer again and again makes the audience feel both sadness and anger, until a last straw happens and both the main character and audience's anger explodes into rage. Just remember to not let it go on too long, or the audience will start to lose their anger and just feel tired and helpless instead.

JOY

You might think that making the audience feel happy would be simple- all you need to do is have good things happen to the characters they like and they'll be happy too. However, happiness isn't as simple to generate in audiences as it is to feel in real life. In real life, any good thing happening to you – from finding money, to seeing a beautiful sunset, to getting a good night's sleep – can make you feel happy fairly easily. (At least, in the short term.)

But, if you think about it, you'll realize that those things happening to a character in a story, even one you like, won't actually make you feel much of anything at all. So what if the lead character gets a good night's sleep? So what if they see a beautiful sunset? So what if they find money? It was them (not you) that experienced those good things, so it doesn't really affect your emotions much at all.

Even if you're tightly bonded with a character, their victories aren't really yours.

Except when they are.

The key to making audiences feel happiness is when they feel like they got something from the story. Storytellers do this by literally giving them something that they want, and these things can be broken down into five categories that you can remember using the mnemonic SPICE.

Skills – If the audience feels like they've learned how to do something through the story, they'll feel happy about the experience. This is usually done through learning a skill at the same time as a character does, but sometimes through the storyteller directly talking to the audience and explaining how something is done. Not just learning how to do a skill, but seeing it used, and learning the ins and outs of that skill will stimulate an audience that's interested in it, and make them feel happy and satisfied.

Perspective – If a story offers a new way of seeing the world, or conversely, confirms or supports the way the audience already sees the world, then they will likely consider it interesting. In your life, you only really know your own point of view, and stories let you see the world as others see it- that's one of the wonderful parts about experiencing a story. On the flipside, you naturally want your own views of the world to be the correct ones, and stories that back up and support those views will resonate with an audience that wants those views to be true. Being told you were right makes everyone feel warm and happy, even if it's by a character learning that a certain way to see the world is the right way. So, giving new worldviews and confirming existing ones can make audiences happy.

Information – If a story offers the audience knowledge about a subject that they're not familiar with, they will feel happy. This is different from Skills in that it isn't teaching the audience how to do something, but giving them information about a topic or topics. This can be history, culture, fashion, philosophy, sports, nature, geophysics, religion, and everything in between. If the audience is interested in this topic, or made to be interested in it by the presentation of the story, then they'll enjoy hearing about it. Audiences remember the plots and conflicts of great fiction, but those books were often also filled with information about the world as well, which subtly helped to make them the classics they are.

Creativity – When you give audiences a new experience through the story- they'll feel happy. This can be any aspect of the story from how it makes them feel, to the way it's told (character, plot, setting, style, structure, etc.) to the content (skills, perspective, information) that is new to the audience. Give them something they don't know, they haven't seen done, or they haven't seen done this way, and you'll have a happy audience on your hands. (But never sacrifice quality for novelty- novelty might carry a short story, but it will rarely carry an entire book by itself.)

Emotion – Making the audience feel emotions actually makes them happy as well. Whether it's watching a character accomplish something hard so that they too feel a sense of accomplishment, or escaping a monster alongside another character, or falling in love with a character. These emotional experiences that a story gives its audience can make an audience feel pleased. Even better is when they've gone through a rollercoaster of different emotions, shifting from one to another until it reaches a final satisfying peak. All good stories should make the audience feel something, and certain kinds of stories are even built around producing specific kinds of emotion. (Horror, Romance, Erotica, Comedy, Tragedy, etc.) If you can elicit emotions from your audience, and it's emotions they want to feel, then they'll smile and enjoy the emotional ride.

These five approaches will make your audience happy because they will feel they got something from the story. Of course, a big part of accomplishing this is knowing your audience and what will appeal to them. If your audience isn't interested in fixing cars, then unless you're really skilled at making it interesting, teaching them how to fix cars in a story is more likely to bore them than make them feel happy and interested. Thus, choose carefully and think deeply about the best ways to make your audience happy.

Also, never forget that yes, good things happening to good characters will make an audience happy because it makes them feel like good things will happen to the audience members in their lives. However, for characters those good things must be earned for it to make the audience share in their happiness. The characters getting things they don't deserve will make the audience feel the storyteller is cheating them.

So, a pitiable character getting a lucky break is something that will make the audience happy because that character deserves good fortune in the minds of the audience. But a character just randomly winning the lottery probably won't make them feel happy if they don't feel the character deserves it, or earned it in some way.

ANXIETY/FEAR

Getting the audience to feel anxiety, or it's bigger and stronger brother fear, is all about tapping into the bond between audience and characters. As was mentioned before, human brains don't know the difference between what happens to fictional characters and what happens to you or the people around you. Human brains react to fictional threats like they do real ones, especially if the threat is to someone who the audience closely identifies with.

Therefore, all you need to do to make an audience feel anxiety is to put the goals of the characters they closely connect with in jeopardy. Or, to make them feel fear, put the characters in actual danger of losing their lives or worse. Just so long as the audience is tightly connected to the characters and their goals, the audience's own natural feelings of unease will flare up.

Of course, sometimes just watching things happen to other, innocent people is also enough to trigger feelings of anxiety and fear. Master of suspense Alfred Hitchcock once famously described the difference between surprise and suspense as the difference between two men sitting at a table with a bomb underneath. If the audience could only see two men chatting and then a hidden bomb suddenly exploded, that would produce a brief surprise but not much else. On the other hand, if the audience could see the bomb but the men couldn't, and the audience had to sit there and watch the clock tick down to the explosion, then that would create suspense. In this example, the audience feels anxiety and maybe even fear because they're watching two people who could be like them be threatened.

This example of Dramatic Irony works and generates anxiety in the audience because everyone has a primal fear of death, and even watching it happen to two complete strangers is enough to trigger the fight or flight response. But if the audience is closely familiar with the characters, that anxiety will be even greater. Imagine the power of watching two of your loved ones sit at a table with a hidden bomb and being forced to watch it tick down to their deaths while not being able to do anything about it. Many people would be unable to watch because it would be so intense.

Naturally, tapping into other primal fears will also make audiences feel anxiety. Fear of the unknown is a big one, since people instinctively try to avoid situations where there could potentially be danger. So, presenting an audience with an unfamiliar situation where danger is hinted at will cause the audience's own imaginations to fill the unknown with things that could be far worse than what the storyteller actually has in mind. This can produce anxiety, fear, or even horror depending on how intense it gets and the consequences involved.

In fact, the key is making the audience feel that there will be serious and maybe permanent consequences to what the character is doing. The bigger the stakes and the worse the potential consequences, the more nervous the audience will become. Death – physical, spiritual, social, financial, or any other form – is automatically the greatest consequence most people can think of, and sympathetic characters facing it will cause their audience to get anxious as they watch the characters put themselves more and more into dangerous waters.

OTHER EMOTIONS

The four emotions above, combined with surprise, cover the most common emotions that storytellers work to create in their audiences. Using different shades of these emotions and combining them in different ways can give the audience an emotional experience they'll enjoy out of a story. Very often stories start by making their audiences sad at the main character's circumstances, then anxious as the main character is thrown into troublesome situations. After that, they'll feel angry at the villains who are standing in the way of the main character and their goals, and finally joy when the main character succeeds at the end of the story. In between, they'll feel other emotions, like curiosity, contentment, excitement, disgust and a few other common emotions.

Let's look briefly at some other common emotions that audiences feel while enjoying stories.

Awe – Generally, getting the audience to feel awed requires showing them something spectacular they haven't seen before. This feeling usually comes from extreme novelty- where the storyteller gives the audience something they aren't expecting in such an amazing way that they can't help but be impressed. This can be the way in which the storyteller presents the story or its parts, or it can be something that happens within the story which leaves the audience awestruck. Examples could include brilliant ideas, deft showmanship in art or description, a complex turn of events the audience didn't see coming, or a situation that leaves the lead character and audience unable to believe their senses.

Contempt – If characters are shown doing immoral things, then the audience will naturally feel contempt towards those characters. Usually when characters are shown giving into negative traits completely (cowardice, greed, lust, laziness, ruthlessness, ignorance, etc.) the audience feels contempt towards those characters. Contempt is about judging them, and their actions as being low or inferior to others.

Contentment – This feeling comes when everything is going fine, and the characters are doing well. If the audience feels there is no danger to the characters they love, and everyone is safe, then they will feel contentment. To achieve this, show characters enjoying themselves, relaxing, and showing they feel they are safe. Avoid any looming sense of danger.

Curiosity – This is created when the audience is presented with a puzzle or problem that needs to be solved. Humans are curious animals, they want to know about the world around them, and so when presented with a question or mystery, especially one where the available clues look interesting, they want to know more.

Disgust – This is the result of triggering the audience's innate disgust reflexes. If the audience is given repulsive imagery, or there are situations in a story which the audience finds sickening, then they will feel disgusted. Generating disgust is all about knowing what the audience will find revolting, and this will change depending on the audience, their experiences, and their imaginations. That said, there are always a few standbys that work most of the time- insects, filth, bodily fluids, and especially things connected to disease will trigger disgust in most people.

Excitement – In a way, excitement is like reverse suspense- the audience (and maybe the characters) know that something good is going to happen and they can't wait for it to happen. Excitement is based on expectation, and can be created by introducing new things to the story which will benefit the main character and make the story more interesting.

Love – Love is a lot like disgust – each member of the audience has their own preferences and desired traits that make them strongly attracted to someone or something, and by triggering those innate reflexes the audience can come to love a character. In stories, this usually means that the characters have the basic qualities most people find desirable - attractive appearance, good personality, good background, intelligence, wealth, etc. – and then also have their own special qualities that make them especially pleasing to a particular group of people. Love can mean sexual attraction, or it can be the love of a fan or admirer. Usually, if a storyteller wants an audience to fall in love with a character, they present that character as the storyteller's own ideal lover, and then that either works for the audience or it doesn't. The trick is the more detailed the storyteller makes the character, the fewer people will actually fall in love with them (more things for some audience members to like are more things for others to dislike), and it's all about finding the right amount of key details that let the audience fill in the blanks with their own desires.

Lust – Making the audience feel lust can be done in three ways. The first is to offer sexual contact to the main character- since the main character is linked with the audience if the main character is being offered sex the audience will also feel like they are being offered sex. The second way to make the audience feel lust is to give them sexually stimulating imagery. And, the third way is to include sexual situations that stimulate the audience's imaginations or memories. All these ways can be combined, and are used extensively in erotica.

Relief- Relief is like contentment, but the result of danger having passed. The characters were in danger, but now they've overcome it, and things are returning to normal. It's the result of having gone through hard times and come out okay.

THE RHYTHM OF MANGA STORIES

One of the key differences between manga and the stories that get told in English is the way they organize their stories. Manga storytelling has its own unique rhythm that evolved differently than the rhythm used by storytellers in Europe and the west. This way of structuring and presenting stories gives manga its own flavor and works well with the serialized format that most manga use. It is still based in the three-act structure (which is universal to human storytelling), but has a twist to it (literally) that it isn't based on conflict and instead based on what's more entertaining for the audience.

HOW JAPANESE STORYTELLING IS DIFFERENT

The Greek philosopher and playwright Aristotle once wrote (in 335 BCE) that all stories could be based on four essential conflicts:

- Man versus Man
- Man versus Self
- Man versus Nature
- Man versus Society

These are the central dramatic conflicts that dominate western drama (people would add more later) and are the simplest ways to look at the core of western stories. This is a natural framework based on the Euro-centric outlook which sees the relationship that people have with themselves and their world as an adversarial one. People struggle against the world to survive. They struggle against each other for resources like food. They struggle against the selfish and animalistic sides of themselves to be civilized.

This is the western worldview, and it permeates everything in western culture, including our approach to storytelling.

On the other hand, the Japanese worldview is a co-operative one. Culturally, they don't see the world as an adversarial place like westerners do, but instead see the world as a co-operative system where different parts have a role to play and everything interacts. This is true from their religion (animistic Shinto) to their view of how society works.

With their group-centric culture, the Japanese see man's place in the world as being part of a greater system. People are not individuals- they're members of society, members of families, citizens of the state, part of the natural cycle/world, the servants of the gods, etc.

Thus, to the Japanese, stories aren't about conflict.

They're about interaction.

To a Japanese storyteller, it's...

- Man meets Man
- Man meets Self
- Man meets Nature
- Man meets Society

The central point of drama in a Japanese story is the interesting interaction between two or more things, or more specifically, what interesting thing happens when two things come together? Instead of two things fighting each other, it's two things negotiating their place in the world with each other and understanding how they can (or can't) co-exist with each other.

American story- Man conquers outer space.
Japanese story – Man finds his place in outer space.

Most Japanese stories in any media are extensions of this philosophy, and ultimately the characters are people who are engaged in an existential game of give and take with each other. It isn't about confrontation, but compromise, and their ability to do so (or not do so) in the world they live in.

A good manga example of this can seen in what western fans of the manga/anime *Naruto* often complain about something called "talk-no-jutsu," which is a term referring to the fact that the main character in *Naruto* usually defeats his opponents by talking to them. He might fight them in huge duels using ninja superpowers, but at the same time he's arguing with them, and in the end of the fight his opponents often give up or withdraw because he basically talked them out of their reason to fight him.

Western *Naruto* fans laugh at this and many find it annoying and silly when this happens in *Naruto* and many other manga. The term "talk-no-jutsu" itself making fun of the fact that most ninja-magic superpowered techniques in Naruto's world are called "something-no-jutsu." Naruto basically has the magic ninja superpower of talking his opponents to death from their point of view.

However, from a Japanese perspective what Naruto is doing is perfectly reasonable.

To Japanese audiences, everything in the story is about the interaction between Naruto and his opponent, and is all ultimately a negotiation of their positions and places in the world. They first argue their positions, and then unleash their attacks against each other through the form of cool ninja superpowers, but then ultimately that doesn't work and they have to find a way to co-exist. Or, in the case of the truly evil, that they can't co-exist and the hero is forced to kill them to bring balance to the world.

American story – Man conquers a mountain and climbs to the top.

Japanese story – Man learns how to work with the mountain's terrain and nature and reaches the top.

Yes, there is conflict, but the underlying story philosophy is about negotiation, and the only way the battle can end is by figuring out a solution to their conflicts. This reflects Japanese society, where large numbers of people live in close proximity to people they may or may not like, but who they need to find a way to live and work with regardless. At the same time, humans in Japan have always had to learn to work with nature, especially because in any conflict nature generally wins, so the focus is on co-existence and not on conquest.

The Japanese story structure you will learn in the following section, the Ki-Sho-Ten-Ketsu (KSTK) is built to naturally focus on this, with its conflict-optional approach to storytelling, but the truth is that this philosophy isn't linked to any single story structure. In fact, Hollywood already uses this storytelling philosophy from time to time even though they don't use the KSTK story structure, and many of the best American situation comedies like *Big Bang Theory* have used it as their base. Although even then, they tend to focus on the conflict aspects of character interactions rather than the softer situations that rise up due to natural differences.

As you write your stories and think about manga, just try to remember that story interest and drama comes from interaction, and that might be due to the conflict, or it might just be due to different ways of living. In either case, the heart of Japanese dramatic philosophy is watching them try to find balance, and the challenges, humor, and surprises that come with dealing with those unbalanced situations.

THE KI-SHO-TEN-KETSU

During China's Tang Dynasty, there was a popular poet named Meng Haoran (孟浩然), who developed a flare for writing four-stanza poems. These poems were built on a simple structure where the poet first introduced an idea, then expanded on it, presented a twist, and then finally resolved the poem in an interesting way. His approach would go on to influence many (including Li Bai (李白), one of China's most famous historical poets), but it was especially influential on the Japanese poets of the day.

This style of poetry would eventually come to be called *Ki-Sho-Ten-Ketsu* in Japanese, with each word coming from a Chinese Kanji character used to represent a different phase of the poem.

- Ki- Introduction
- Sho- Development
- Ten – Twist (Activity)
- Ketsu – Resolution

As this way of writing poems remained popular for a long time, it wasn't long before storytellers too began to make use of this form, realizing that it provided a simple but entertaining way to organize their stories and present them. This is little surprising, since its form is basically a three-act structure that divides the central action into two phases to create four acts instead of the standard western three. With the "action" being divided into a "development" phase were the writer builds up the drama and suspense, and an "activity" phase where the climax happens along with other exciting events created by the "development" phase.

Used this way, it's easiest to compare it to an archer shooting an arrow.
- Ki (Introduction)- The archer stands and faces the target.

- Sho (Development) – The archer inserts an arrow and draws back on the bow, taking aim.
- Ten (Activity) – The arrow is loosed and strikes the target.
- Ketsu (Resolution) – The archer lowers the bow and checks his score.

This version is essentially a four-act structure, where emphasis is placed on setting up the action which occurs in the second half of the story and which has a short introduction and short ending to keep the focus on the events in the middle.

The key here is that the story starts small with the introduction, and then begins building at a steady pace, alternating between positive and negative events to create excitement and suspense before finally building to a climax where everything comes together in a big glorious moment. After that, it's just about showing the results of the whole thing and finishing the story off in an emotionally satisfying way (or not, if you're writing serials).

This is the KSTK story pattern, and while it's simple in idea, it's more complex in its execution, at least if you don't grow up with this type of story.

THE PHILOSOPHY OF THE KI-SHO-TEN-KETSU

One of the hardest things to understand about the KSTK for non-Japanese is that it's built around a fundamentally different approach to storytelling than traditional European and American storytelling is. Western storytelling is based on rising drama, with the events and interactions that happen being the focus of the story. Characters have conflicting goals, and because of those conflicts drama is created- this is the core of a typical Three-Act story the way western storytellers understand it. Sometimes we call this "conflict-based storytelling," because everything is built around the idea of one side versus another, even if the opposing force is a character's own mind, illness, technology, nature or society.

The KSTK is based on another very different storytelling philosophy- rising interest. In a KSTK story the goal is to keep the audience interested, and the story is a vehicle for giving them an entertaining experience. Conflict-based interactions, like two characters or sides opposed to each other to create rising drama, can be the focus of a KSTK story, but it doesn't **have** to be. In this approach to storytelling, conflict is just another tool that the storyteller uses to entertain the audience, but there are many other tools they can also use instead like surprise, mystery, imagery, sounds, or anything else which will delight and please the audience.

So, for example, a typical three-act American story might involve a mother wolf trying to bring food back to its cubs and the challenges it faces as it tries to reach them with the food. This is a conflict-based story, and the rising drama would be created by the harder and harder obstacles it faces on its journey, or other challenges the wolf experiences.

Alternatively, a KSTK approach to the same story (wolf trying to bring home food) might focus on the things the mother wolf sees and experiences on the journey back, and how this makes her appreciate the cycle of life. Seeing a fox chase a rabbit, mother birds protect their nest, and fish swimming up a waterfall could be interesting sights that make the wolf (and audience) reflect on the drive to survive and procreate. She could be trying to make a decision, perhaps about whether to reject a lame cub, and seeing these things helps her to reach a decision, giving the story form. Or maybe she is just being thoughtful and reflecting on her place in the world.

Thus, there are only two guidelines to a story made with this philosophy:
1)   The audience's emotional engagement should increase as the story plays out.
2)   Stories built using it are based on build and release approach.

The first is created through a combination of positive and negative feelings which generate excitement and suspense. You present the audience with unexpected, interesting, or stimulating things that draw them in to the story and make them want to find out what happens next. This about giving the audience a growing stream of new or interesting things to keep them engaged. The main rule here being that there needs to be sense that what's coming next will be better than what came before, or at least has to the potential to be better. It all comes together in a climax that is the most spectacular point in the story/performance, and then things are allowed a brief cool-down.

The other hallmark of KSTK stories is that they're based on a build and release pattern- something is introduced, then developed through the promise of its potential or dramatic questions, and then finally released. Then the next cycle starts, and it promises to be even bigger than the last one- in a constant series of bigger builds and bigger hits. For example, a character might be trying to haggle over a pair of shoes, so they make their first offer, which gets refused, so they think and come up with another better offer, and that fails too, and finally they give in an offer everything they've got- and they get accepted. Each of these was a cycle of build (coming up with a new offer) and release (trying it and failing/succeeding), with the audience being engaged by the question of whether they'll succeed or other dramatic questions.

But, this build and release pattern can also be based around expectations of emotion created by imagery or events. You could show a box being placed on a table, then that box with the flaps open from the side, and then that box from an upper angle with the inside shrouded in darkness, and then characters reacting to what they see in the box, and then finally the reveal that there's a rabbit inside the box. This too is the KSTK build pattern in effect- the audience is given an image that creates a question, then the possibility of the answer to that question is teased out to increase suspense and curiosity, and finally the truth is revealed, creating emotional release.

Used this way, the KSTK form is based on curiosity, suspense, and anticipation-making the audience wonder about what will happen next or hope for something, while keeping them in suspense about when/if it will happen, and then finally giving them what they want. However, this is where the principle of surprise comes in-because you don't give them what they want in the way they were expecting it. You give it to them in an unexpected way- whether that's giving them something slightly different than what they were expecting, giving it to them at a time they weren't expecting it, or overdelivering/underdelivering and giving them more or less than what they were expecting.

You make the audience want something, and then you let anticipation build before you give them what they want in an unexpected way- this is the heart of the build and release approach that KSTK is put together around. It's a showmanship approach to storytelling and based on the principles that magicians, storytellers, and other entertainers around the world have been using since the dawn of mankind.

Together, these twin concepts of rising emotional engagement and the build and release pattern are the heart of the KSTK form, and can be used in stories and performances of any kind. And, the stories don't even have to follow the KSTK story structure below to make use of them, just so long as they follow the philosophy of rising interest which guides the KSTK form.

USING THE KI-SHO-TEN-KETSU WAY TO WRITE MANGA

It didn't take long before Japanese writers realized that there were ways to adapt the KSTK form to narrative storytelling, and over the years they have developed many different approaches to using it. This isn't really surprising, since after all the KSTK pattern is at its heart still following the setup>action>result pattern that all stories are built on, they're just dividing "action" into a "development" phase and an "activity" phase to heighten the drama.

Manga creators too developed their own approach to using the KSTK form to tell stories, and eventually worked out different story structures that optimized the strengths of the KSTK form when telling their stories. Different types of manga, from *4-koma* gag strips, to action-driven *shonen* manga, to romantic *shoujo* comics, to horror comics all developed their own ways to use the KSTK form to maximum effect when telling stories that appealed to their audiences.

Over the years, the writers and editors of manga and anime have developed a few "standard" patterns which you'll see used again and again in Japanese storytelling. The charts below show what this pattern roughly looks like when mapped out around the feelings of excitement and suspense that keep their readers engaged.

KSTK – POSITIVE TEN CHART – "THE TWO VALLEYS"

In this first pattern, the story is alternating between cycles of positive developments that make the audience feel excited, and negative developments that make them feel suspense about what will happen to the characters. The wavy line represents whether the audience is feeling overall excited about what's happening, or overall worried or uncertain about what's taking place, while the "Calm Line" represents the point where the reader is feeling neither suspense or excitement.

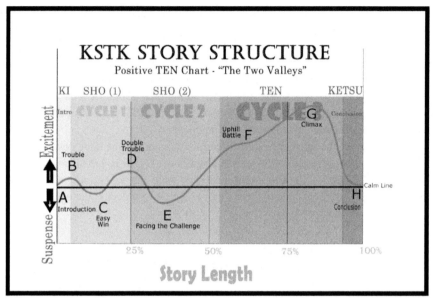

Laid out like this, it's easier to see where the focus of the story is at any given point. This type of story starts out interesting, then makes the audience worry a bit, calms their fears, and then hits them again with a much bigger load of worry. After that, the story is about progressively more interesting things happening until a climax is reached, and then everything is allowed to gently settle down. The early worries heighten the feelings of excitement as the escalating events play out, and the audience is left with an emotionally satisfying ride.

Let's look at each phase of this particular Ki-Sho-Ten-Ketsu pattern to understand what's happening there.

KI – Introduction (5%)

In the Introduction phase, the audience is quickly brought up to speed as the basic information they need to understand the story- Who's involved? Where are they? When is it? What are they trying to do? Why are they trying to do it? Why should the audience care? Almost all of these questions should be answered as quickly and plainly as possible using the art, dialogue, or text of the story. Even though the audience might know who these characters are, and what they want, it's good to refresh their knowledge and makes things clear exactly what their goals and motivations are at this exact place and time.

Some writers take their time in answering these questions, while other writers combine the Introduction (KI) phase with the first development (SHO) phase by introducing the character already in trouble and trying to deal with a situation. However you choose to do it (and there are many possible combinations), remember your audience won't be happy until they have a clear main character with a clear goal for understandable reasons. So, make sure you give it to them.

SHO – Development (20%+30%)

The development phase is where the characters begin working towards reaching their goals, but find that there's something in their way. If the characters could just walk straight to their goal the story would be over, and interesting stories come from overcoming adversity, so the writer begins putting some challenges in their way. By watching the character deal with challenges, we learn about the character and how someone deals with the kinds of situations they find themselves in.

You might notice there are two development (SHO) phases on the chart. This is a pattern which has developed over time in manga storytelling, and has come about because each of them has a slightly different job.

The first development phase, SHO (1), is there to set things up for the rest of the story. It is really an extension of the Introduction phase, and it's there to let us know more about the main character by seeing them in action. By watching them do what is usually a small task, we learn who they are and what they can do. Sometimes this small task is the thunder before the storm, and other times the character's reactions to this small challenge are what causes the events of the rest of the story. Regardless, by the end of the first SHO phase the audience should know everything they need to know to understand the rest of the story.

Which leads to the second development phase, SHO (2), which is there to exclusively set up the main challenge that the lead character of this story is going to need to face to win in the TEN phase. In this stage of the story, you give the audience a reason to believe the character is going to fail, and show them why in great detail. This should be no simple task, because the challenge presented here is going to be one which is going to take the rest of the story to sort out. The bigger the challenge, the longer it will take and harder it will be, but the opposites are also true. Pick your challenges carefully.

After the challenge is properly set up, the main character is shown beginning to work their way out of it. After their initial success in the first development phase, they're feeling confident and positive, and pretty sure they can beat this if they try- so they roll up their sleeves and get to it.

TEN – Activity (35%)

The activity phase is where all the magic happens. The preparations are complete, and now the real show is about to begin. In this phase, the main character must come face to face with the challenge or challenges which stand in their way and find ways to overcome them in a series of ever more exciting and interesting events.

If everything was set up properly during the first two phases, what happens here should be obvious to you and your audience. But, that's where the principle of "surprise" comes in, and why this phase is also called the "twist" phase in the KSTK traditional form. Because you're going to give the audience what they expect here, but you're not going to give it to them in the way they expect it. You need to come up with interesting situations, events, art, and other things which are going to give the audience an entertaining show. Just make sure that it all makes sense, and is reasonable based on what was set up in the introduction and development phases, and the audience will love it.

The activity phase is also where manga writers will play around with the pattern the most, trying different ways to surprise and delight their audiences. Sometimes this phase is actually a bunch of small ups and downs as the characters face a series of challenges, while other times it's a roller-coaster ride between heaven and hell with giant twists and turns. The two most common versions of this are the "Positive TEN" (see the above chart), and the "Negative TEN" (see the chart below) patterns. Each of which plays out quite differently than the other, and is worth taking the time to look at.

The above "Positive TEN" chart, also called "The Two Valleys" because it only has two dips into real suspense, is based around progressively more positive events and feelings happening. Sometimes, the main character is winning, then winning, then winning some more, until they finally reach their goal in a glorious fashion. They may experience some small stumbles along the way, and there will be moments of doubt for them and the audience, but each smaller challenge will be solved in some way. Other times, this phase may mostly be them preparing for one shot at the big challenge, readying themselves for a big moment so they can seize it when the time comes. As long as everything is moving in a positive direction overall, then it's all going the right way.

On the other hand, the chart below, the "Negative TEN" chart called "The Three Valleys," takes a different approach and goes deeply into the realm of suspense to shake the reader up and keep them on the edge of their seat. Instead of everything going in a good direction, just when victory is in sight everything goes wrong and the character is cast down into a personal hell. This is the pit of fire which forces the character to dig deep into their personal resources and find something, anything, which can get them out. Hidden strengths are revealed, trump cards are played, and the character either wins or loses everything. If they do find the way out, it's a glorious burst of emotion and relief for the audience who were trapped in deep suspense with them, and it can lead to an amazing finish.

How you write it is up to you, but one tip is to try figuring out your climax first, and then planning out how to get there in interesting ways with your characters and situations. On the other hand, some writers prefer to figure things out as their characters do, and go out the journey together. There is no wrong way to do it, only what works and what doesn't.

KETSU – Conclusion (10%)

Everything that happened in the story is going to have an effect- so what was it? The conclusion phase is there to answer all the remaining questions in the story, explain any twists, and show how the characters continue their lives (or not) afterwards. It's also there to set up any further stories, plant seeds for future plot developments, and remind the audience why they like these characters and want to see more of them. It's all about presenting the "new normal" for these characters, and leaving the audience satisfied.

One trick that manga creators often do during the middle of story arcs is move some or all of the conclusion to the start of the next episode, leaving the audience hanging. This is a simple way of making them come back if they want to know how it all really turned out. The next episode will have a combined introduction and conclusion, setting up the current situation for the audience and characters which the story will then move forward from.

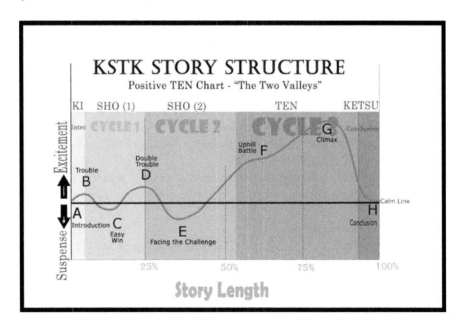

Key Events of the Positive TEN Chart

Looking at the chart above, you'll notice there are certain events marked to indicate key moments in the story progress. These are there to help you understand the chart better and gives you a structure to think about when planning your own stories.

Let's look at each...

A. **Introduction**: This is (usually) the first scene, where the audience is quickly introduced to the characters, setting, and situations of the story. The key here is to let them know about the motivations and goals of the protagonist so that they understand what they're trying to do and why.

B. **Trouble**: An obstacle to achieving their goal appears, and the main character/supporting cast runs into their first challenge. They now have to work to overcome it and figure out a solution- fast.

C. **Easy Win**: Through fortune or by working at it, the character/supporting cast seems to solve the Trouble that has come their way and manages to get things under control.

D. **Double Trouble**: Something even worse happens! The character/supporting cast is faced with an even bigger challenge, the "real" one which will require everything they've got to overcome.

E. **Facing the Challenge**: The character/supporting cast digs in and tries their hardest to make their goals happen, taking things seriously and using their talents and abilities to solve the problem.

F. **Uphill Battle**: The character/supporting cast faces a series of challenges as they try to reach their goals. Complications, twists, misunderstandings, and mistakes plague them as they advance toward their target, but thanks to the help of others and their own inner strength they don't give up.

G. **The Climax**: This is the big exciting finish, and it should be the logical result of everything that came before while still offering some surprising and interesting twists. Usually this involves a display of the character's special strength that makes them unique.

H. **Conclusion**: Everything gets wrapped up in the final scene(s), hopefully in a way which makes your reader want to read more about these characters.

Example: **The Comic Artist**

A. **Introduction**: A talented comic book artist living in the big city has just gotten their first big break- a contract to draw a new comic for a major company.

B. **Trouble**: Their editor calls and asks if the story can be done a week earlier due to printing needs. The artist knows it will be hard, but they want to impress, so they say okay.

C. **Easy Win**: The artist puts away their video games, sets a rigid schedule, and begins drawing like a machine to get the work done. It goes pretty well.

D. **Double Trouble**: A week before deadline, the artist's mother gets in a car accident and is sent to the hospital in a coma. The artist must fly home and be there to help, but this is going to kill their schedule.

E. **Facing the Challenge**: The artist takes their drawing tablet with them home, and tries to keep up with the schedule while dealing with doctors, insurance, and other interruptions.

F. **Uphill Battle**: Staying at their mother's bedside, the artist works hard to keep drawing while watching over their mother. Things get in the way, but the artist makes friends with a nurse who has artistic talent and loves comics, and the nurse even brings a tablet in and starts to help with some of the background work in their spare time.

G. **The Climax**: As the deadline looms, the artist is still terribly behind, but thanks to the nurse a few more hospital staff join in during the final crunch to try and help the artist out. Working together, it goes down to the wire, and then they let out a cheer as they cross the finish line together. The artist's mother is woken by the cheer to find her room filled with hospital staff laughing and crying.

H. **Conclusion**: The artist's editor is happy, their mother will be okay, and they now have a growing relationship with a cute nurse. Then they get the hospital bill, and realize they're going to need to raise more money fast...

KSTK – NEGATIVE TEN CHART – "THE THREE VALLEYS"

The other very common pattern is the chart below, the "Negative TEN" pattern which is all about suspense and drama. For the most part, it's the same as the Positive TEN chart, but you'll notice that the "Uphill Battle" is now "Disaster" and "Glimmer of Hope" to reflect the dramatic downward turn that the story takes when it reaches this point.

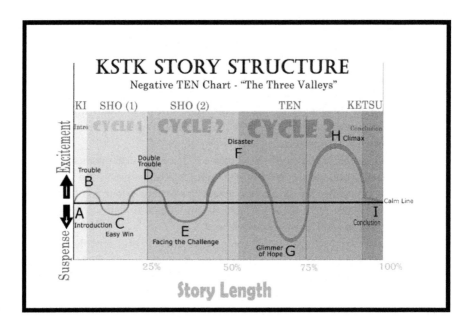

Most of the key events are the same, but here's the whole list with the changed parts underlined:

A. **Introduction**: This is (usually) the first scene, where the audience is quickly introduced to the characters, setting, and situations of the story. The key here is to let them know about the motivations and goals of the protagonist so that they understand what they're trying to do and why.

B. **Trouble**: An obstacle to achieving their goal appears, and the main character/supporting cast runs into their first challenge. They now have to work to overcome it and figure out a solution- fast.

C. **Easy Win**: Through fortune or by working at it, the character/supporting cast seems to solve the Trouble that has come their way and manages to get things under control.

D. **Double Trouble**: Something even worse happens! The character/supporting cast is faced with an even bigger challenge, the "real" one which will require everything they've got to overcome it.

E. **Facing the Challenge**: The character/supporting cast digs in and tries their hardest to make their goals happen, taking things seriously and using their talents and abilities to solve the problem.

F. **Disaster**: They seem to have managed to beat the Double Trouble they found themselves in, and say those fateful words to themselves: "Y'no? I think I got this." Murphy's Law kicks in, and one last great obstacle appears to throw everything in doubt. Just when things couldn't get any worse- they do. This is here to add extra suspense going into the climax of the story and make the audience question whether the goal will be realized or not.

G. **Glimmer of Hope**: When everything looks hopeless, the main character/supporting cast digs into their supply of skill and luck and finds a way to bring it all back around. What happens here should be something that only this main character/supporting cast can do, and represent their "special strength" that gives them an edge over others and lets them cross the finish line unto victory. (Note: Avoid Deus ex Machina, no matter how tempting they are!)

H. **The Climax**: This is the big exciting finish, and it should be the logical result of everything that came before while still offering some surprising and interesting twists. Usually this involves a display of the character's special strength that makes them unique.

I. **Conclusion**: Everything gets wrapped up in the final scene(s), hopefully in a way which makes your reader want to read more about these characters.

Example: *The Dragon Slayers* (Fantasy Action)

A. **Introduction**: A group of brave knights are passing through a peaceful mountain valley village in a fantasy setting.

B. **Trouble**: A dragon appears, attacking the local farms.

C. **Easy Win**: The knights rush to fend off the dragon, and succeed in killing it.

D. **Double Trouble**: The dragon turns out to be a baby dragon, and the much larger mother dragon is drawn to the village by the baby's dying cries.

E. **Facing the Challenge**: The knights try to fend off the mother dragon, and through sacrifice one of them manages to hurt it enough that it retreats.

F. **Disaster**: The wounded dragon sets the valley forest around the town on fire, and is now waiting atop a nearby mountain for everyone to burn to death- ready to attack anyone who tries to leave.

G. **Glimmer of Hope**: Just when things are looking bad, the leader comes up with a plan to save the village and sets the knights and craftsmen to work making a makeshift ballista. Meanwhile, the knights have the townsfolk prepare wagons and horses for a caravan to get people out of town.

H. **The Climax**: The dragon sees the caravan of covered wagons trying to escape and swoops down and destroys the caravan with a fire attack from the air. When it comes in to check to make sure it got everyone, the lead knight attacks it from the nearby forest with a ballista bolt- putting it through the dragon's chest and killing it. (Having planned an ambush point in advance.)

I. **Conclusion**: The knights have lost some of their members, but they have saved the villagers and gotten them away from the village before it burned down. When the fire is burnt out, they'll be able to sell the dragon parts to get enough money to rebuild the village. The remaining knights continue on their quest, heading to their next adventure.

Example: *Coffee Lovers* (Romantic Comedy)

A. **Introduction**: A nerdy girl gets a job at a coffee shop where a handsome boy she likes studies each day in hopes of getting to know him.

B. **Trouble**: The first time the girl serves him coffee, she's so nervous she spills it all over him, and he rushes to the bathroom.

C. **Easy Win**: The boy still comes back out and makes a joke about what happened, not seeming to care.

D. **Double Trouble**: He discovers his exam notes for his final exams were ruined by the coffee, and gets stressed out, he yells at her when she apologizes and storms out.

E. **Facing the Challenge**: The girl notices the ruined exam notes he left behind and decides she's going to try to save them for him. She takes them home with her and after some research tries burying them in rice in hopes of drying them out enough to read.

F. **Disaster**: She chose the wrong kind of rice and used sticky rice to bury the notes. The powder from the rice stuck to the pages and made them a goopy un-readable mess. Then, as she's looking at them, the boy shows up at her front door, having been told she took the notes home and come looking for them. He says he found a way to recover them, and is angry when he discovers them ruined.

G. **Glimmer of Hope**: It turns out the subject the boy was studying hardest was math, a subject that the girl is an ace in. She offers to tutor him to pay him back, and he reluctantly agrees.

H. **The Climax**: The pair work together to prepare the boy for the math exam, and in the process spend a lot of time together and get to know each other. In the end, he takes the exam and aces it thanks to her help.

I. **Conclusion**: The boy asks the girl to go out with him to celebrate, making her dream come true, but then another stylish-looking girl calls out to the boy and rushes over, hugging him. Where has he been, she demands! And the nerdy girl wonders -Who is this girl? What's their relationship? Read the next chapter to find out!

As you can see in the various different examples, these patterns give you the flow of the story, but doesn't tell you exactly what happens. They're a series of escalating events, but what those events are, and how they escalate will depend on the story being told. The only constant is that the audience is treated to a series of growing complications to the main character's attempts to solve some goal, and we watch how the main character (or characters) react to the events playing out.

These patterns are the most common KSTK patterns you'll find in manga and anime, and represent how a typical story unfolds. A character with a goal appears, faces two or three cycles of mounting obstacles on their way to achieving that goal, and finally comes out on top in a way which is unique and special to them. In the case of the Negative TEN pattern, they usually limped through the first two challenges because they weren't using their full potential (their "special strength"), but it's when they finally unleashed their true best that they're able to overcome the opposition and win. (Teaching the audience to believe in themselves or whatever the theme of the story is.)

Which Pattern to Use?

You might wonder which of these patterns you should be using in your stories, and the actual answer is- both. Different situations and types of stories lean towards one pattern or the other, but a good writer is using a mix of the two and playing with them to keep the story fresh.

Positive TEN stories can work with any story type, but tend to fit better with the tone of lighter, optimistic, and romantic stories. Comedies, dramas, adventure stories, action stories, romantic stories and sexy stories all lean heavily on the Positive TEN pattern because they're about excitement and fun, not so much about suspense and heavy drama.

Negative TEN stories, however, are a natural fit with thrillers, mysteries, gritty noir stories, horror stories, and even hardcore action and heavy drama. When the stakes are life and death, the Negative TEN pattern will deliver a thrill ride that the audience won't easily forget. However, you can still use versions of the Negative TEN pattern in stories with low stakes if you want there to be more tension.

Actually, for beginners, the Negative TEN pattern is often easier to use, especially if you come from reading Battle Manga and want to write your own high-action stories. It makes it clear what goes where, and you just have to worry about having interesting characters and filling in the blanks. The Positive TEN pattern, however, is a little vaguer and requires more thought- which is why it's better for more experienced writers.

But, in the end, whichever form you use is up to you, and you should try looking at your favorite manga and anime to see which they're using, and where they're using it. Also, experiment with it, and once you get the hang of it, you'll find it naturally lets you bring the best out of your stories and uses the principles of audience engagement to maximum effect. Once you start to see the patterns, you'll be well on your way to finding your own KSTK way!

THE THREE CYCLES

Another handy way of looking at the KSTK form is seeing it as Three Cycles of the situation going from good to bad and then back again. Each of the Three Cycles serves a slightly different role, and has their own unique characteristics, so it's worth taking some times to look at each.

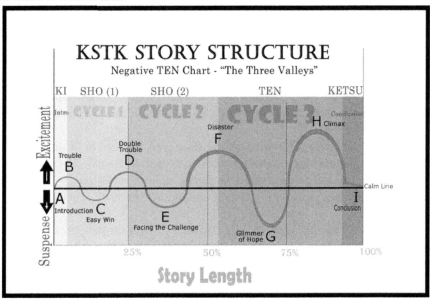

Cycle One: Introduction + Sho (1) "In this corner..."

Purpose: Introduce character abilities and give them a moment to shine, set up coming challenges, introduce plot points and character flaws.

The first cycle is there to give the audience a small taste of the problem which will be facing the character(s) in this story. The point of this cycle is to show that there is trouble coming, and through their actions show who your main character is and what they can do. Sometimes this cycle introduces the main problem in a small way, or is the small event which sets off a series of larger events which are yet to come. Typically, the first cycle is fairly easily solved, which is deceptive because it makes the audience and characters think that later problems will also be easily solved.

The first cycle is also there to set up the story by giving the audience more information about the situation and telling them anything they need to know to understand what's to come. Nothing should be introduced into the story which isn't in some way foreshadowed or set up during the introduction and first cycle phases. If there's information the audience needs to know, they need to be told it here; if there's a trick that will be played later, it needs to be set up here; and if there's an action which will bear fruit later on, set it up here as well.

Don't underestimate the importance of the introduction/first cycle, your story will often succeed or fail based on how you set things up at this stage.

Variations on this cycle:

- In many manga, the first cycle and the Introduction phase are combined to both introduce the characters and start the action as quickly as possible. Often the story will start with action, pause to introduce the characters, and then finish off the rest of the first cycle.
- This cycle doesn't always have to end in victory for the main character, sometimes they lose and the cycle is a set-up for them being in an even worse position.

Cycle Two: Sho (2) "And, in that corner..."

Purpose: Introduce main problem of the story, build drama and suspense before the main conflict, set up reasons for character change (if any).

The second cycle is the real problem that will challenge the character(s) for the rest of this story. This should be presented in a way which makes it clear just how big a problem this is- preferably by how the character(s) react to it. This is where the real suspense in the story is going to come from, so the writer shouldn't be afraid to make the situation extremely bad and then work to build up the tension. However, there should still be room for hope, and not everything should go wrong (yet).

In serials, this phase is sometimes used to delay conflict, by switching to another character or event and focusing on that before coming back to the main conflict in the third cycle. The principle of Sho is building suspense by making the audience wait for what they want, so writers have come up with many ways to use the Sho phase to build suspense while avoiding the main conflict.

Don't be afraid to have the main character(s) hurt or make sacrifices to get out of this phase, it will only build the drama when the audience sees just how vulnerable they are in the face of this opposition.

Variations:

- Sometimes this cycle is used to introduce opponents, giving some of their backstory which makes it clear just how dangerous they are, especially to the main character(s). In that case, the suspense is coming from the audience seeing just how overwhelming the opposition is and the phase will end with them about to face the main character in conflict.

- A common trick in Battle Manga is to jump to supporting characters' perspectives during this phase, and have them talk-up the opponent and explain to each other (and the audience) why this opponent is such a difficult one for the main character. They may also explain rules or other things the audience needs to know to better understand the fight or what's coming.

- In lighter stories, this phase is often just about the main character trying to solve some problem and then discovering just how big a problem it really is. The suspense comes from the character and audience realizing just how much trouble they're in.

Cycle Three: Ten "Ready?!? GO!!!!!"

Purpose: To show the characters at their best and worst in a big dramatic finish.

The third cycle is where the main character is faced with the main problem/opponent of the story and must find a way to overcome it to move on. This problem can be internal or external, but there will almost always be something physical which represents the problem and which the character must overcome in order to reach their goal at the end of the story.

The trickiest part when using the Negative Ten pattern are the Disaster and Glimmer of Hope waves, which will determine a lot about whether your story succeeds or fails. On the chart, the Disaster wave is shown as being a deep pit that the character falls into and must find a way to get themselves out of, however not all writers use it that way. If the story is a romantic comedy, then the great pit might be more of a large dramatic pothole that make them face metaphorical death and almost fail rather than being a life-threatening development. Generally, the higher the stakes, the deeper the pit will be, but also the lower the stakes of the story the shallower the pit will be.

Sometimes, it's just a small bump to add drama instead of an actual crisis moment, and that's fine too.

Conversely, the Glimmer of Hope wave is where the character must find a way to climb out of the trouble they've gotten into in a way which reflects the themes of the story and is dramatic and exciting for the audience. The Glimmer of Hope should always feel like a natural, organic extension of everything which has come before it, and be reasonable and logical based on the characters and situations involved. At the same time, there should be an element of surprise to it when possible, a little twist which the audience doesn't see coming but which makes the whole thing extra satisfying.

In many manga stories, the Glimmer of Hope phase usually involves the main character breaking through some kind of personal limit that they've been trying to overcome through the story. This might be a physical limit they've been training to break, but more often it's an emotional or psychological limitation that they need to overcome to prove themselves and unleash their potential. For example, this might be them accepting that they can't do it alone, or that they need to have confidence in themselves, or maybe that they can overcome their fear. Whatever it is, it's a problem that was set up back at the beginning of the story, and in the fires of hardship they're changing as a person.

The key here is that the Glimmer of Hope is where the lesson of the story is taught, usually something that reflects the theme of the story. It may or may not involve character change, but needs to be the result of what was set up before to feel satisfying.

Variations:

- A common trick if there isn't character change is to have the character do something small in Cycle One that now bears fruit when the Glimmer of Hope comes around. For example, the character helps an old man with groceries, and now the orange that old man gave him becomes the key to winning. (Thus, giving the message that helping others bears fruit.)
- Sometimes, especially if this episode falls in the Sho phases of a story arc, the third cycle won't have a Glimmer of Hope phase, and will in fact be all Disaster, ending on a bad note for the hero.

Examples of Three Cycle Plots

These are some of the many possible ways you can use the three-cycle pattern to plan out the plot of a story, using some common situations. Each of these is only one way among many to do it.

The Hero Cycle

- C1: A heroic character is introduced and faces a small challenge which lets them show off what they can do. This challenge leads to them facing a larger threat.
- C2: The hero faces off against the real threat, and learns that it's much tougher than they initially thought. By putting their skills to the test, they manage to hold their own against this dangerous opponent and make things even.
- C3: The opponent reveals that they've been holding back and unleashes their full force against the hero, driving them into a corner. At their darkest hour, the hero manages to find a solution to their problems and rally against their opponent, defeating them.

The Comedy Cycle

- C1: There's a misunderstanding between two characters, but maybe they can work it out.
- C2: Nope! Thanks to a twist, things get twice as bad, and there's going to be real consequences. But there is still a chance...
- C3: The chance for understanding falls apart and the only solution is now the hero coming clean (if it was caused by their own unwillingness to do what needed to be done) or a display of their special strength. The misunderstanding is cleared up and their relationship is healed, usually becoming stronger for the experience.

The Murder Cycle

- C1: Someone has been killed and a detective uses their skills to find their first clues that lead them to a suspect.
- C2: The detective finds the mystery is even harder to solve when their first suspect is also killed by the murderer, or the first suspect has a solid alibi. They're left back at square one.
- C3: The detective finds a new direction that leads them into a confrontation where they face several suspects and explain how the crime was done. Then they point out the murderer, who confesses under the weight of evidence.
- Note: The "Glimmer of Hope" in the Murder Cycle is when the detective has an "ah-ha!" moment that lets them piece the whole thing together and solve the crime.

The Romance Cycle:

- C1: The lead is romantically interested in another character but their first attempt at getting closer with the other person fails.
- C2: The lead gets another try at getting closer with the other character, often due to circumstances, but this attempt not only fails but makes the love interest seem to dislike them.
- C3: The lead gives it their all and confesses their feelings to their love interest, usually as part of an apology, and finds that the love interest doesn't hate them at all. The two of them find a way to start a new relationship with each other, one that's going in a positive direction.

USING THE KSTK PATTERN FOR DIFFERENT STORY LEVELS

You might think that the above story structure is just for episodes (chapters of a manga), or maybe for telling short stories, but the truth is that it will work for all levels of story- from scenes to overall stories spanning across multiple story arcs. Let's look at how it functions at each level.

Scenes

A typical scene is basically a mini-story that happens at a single place and time, and is part of a larger story. But it is a story, and follows the rules of stories- setup>action>result, or in the case of a KSTK story, setup>development>activity>resolution. A character is introduced who has a goal, they try to accomplish that goal and then either fail, succeed, or partly fail/succeed. Whether it's a character trying to find a book in a library, do brain surgery, navigate a space warp, or just decide what to have for lunch, there is always a character, a central thing they're trying to do, and some kind of result.

In the KSTK style, the character may experience several setbacks as they try to accomplish that goal even in a single scene. These won't usually be major problems, but they will be challenges that the character has to navigate as they try to solve their problem, and it often still comes in threes. For example, here is one using the Negative TEN pattern:

- Introduction: Bob is throwing his wife a surprise birthday party and walks into the kitchen of their house with the specially made cake.
- Sho (1): Suddenly his wife Sue comes home early and heads for the kitchen. Thinking fast, Bob stuffs the cake in the microwave oven so she doesn't see it.
- Sho (2): Bob greets his wife and asks how her day was. She has a migraine headache and left work early. Now she just wants to get some herbal tea to help. With mounting horror, Bob sees her prepare a cup of water and head for the microwave to heat it. He quickly tells her that the microwave is broken and it was sparking earlier, so she had better use the stove to heat the water. She nods and puts the kettle on.
- Ten: As the kettle heats, Sue goes to check out the microwave, thinking there might be something inside causing the sparks. Bob rushes to stop her and tells her that their daughter's school left a message on the machine, and hasn't checked it yet. Sue refocuses on checking the answering machine in the other room and leaves, letting Bob switch out the cake to another safer location in the pantry.
- Conclusion: When Sue comes back and says there was no message, Bob apologizes and says he must have misheard a telemarketer or something. Then relaxes as Sue checks the microwave and gets her tea, that is until she discovers they're out of honey, and goes to get some from the pantry...

As you can see, this is all one scene, but we go through an entire three cycle KSTK story pattern of escalating events as the character(s) try to accomplish their goals.

Cycles

A cycle is a special term referring to a single wave of the KSTK pattern. It starts with a problem being introduced, follows that problem down through the uncertainty and suspense it creates, and then back up as the character tries to recover and solve the problem. Basically, it runs from the time the character makes an attempt to solve a problem until they "finish" their attempt at solving it, through a full cycle of suspense and excitement.

The important thing to understand is that cycles can have cycles within them. Just as a single scene reflects the KSTK form, a series of scenes can happen inside a cycle, and the set of them represents another KSTK cycle. Like was mentioned in the chapter on Understanding Story, it's KSTK cycles all the way up and down.

Episodes/Chapters

The standard KSTK pattern is designed for episodes/chapters of a manga, and works very well with them. The most common versions used in episodes are either ones which end by introducing another problem to be faced, or which end somewhere around the climax, and then the introduction of the next episode resolves the unanswered questions of the climax and begins a new KSTK pattern which ends early again. This way the reader is always forced to check out the next episode to find out how the whole thing resolves. The cycle only ends when the story arc is actually finished.

Also, because episodes are so short, single episodes of a manga usually stick to the rule of just being about a single character trying to accomplish a single goal, and the obstacles they meet. Sometimes it's about two or three characters, but there will generally be a lead character who is the focus of the episode, and possibly an opponent or some other kind of opposition. However, this episode lead character doesn't always have to be the main character of the overall story, and can be members of their supporting cast, opponents, or other new characters who are connected to the main story.

However, that doesn't mean the audience can't also be shown connected pieces of other stories, flash-backs, flash-forwards, or side events which are happening to other characters as well. These are usually short interludes set up to create drama, introduce new characters or elements, or sometimes to heighten suspense.

Story Arcs

Manga are serial by nature, so they don't usually have stories so much as story arcs- a single story which runs across many episodes. Together these episodes form the parts of the story arc. There are minor story arcs (story arcs which are just made up of one story) and major story arcs (story arcs that have other story arcs within them), but no matter how you slice it up they all still use the KSTK form. Each story arc consists of three (or more) KSTK cycles broken down into smaller episodes/chapters that represent the pieces of the story.

Since your typical manga collected *Tankobon* volume holds eight episodes of a manga, the usual target for story arcs is often eight episodes per arc. However, this is due to publishing preferences, and if the manga is being produced/released for online distribution then it really doesn't matter how short or long a story arc is. Stories like *One Piece* have major story arcs that run a dozen or more collected volumes, although even there, the creator, Eiichiro Oda, tends to break them down into smaller minor arcs to keep the story manageable.

Something to keep in mind as you look at the KSTK Cycle chart is that the KSTK cycles tend to roughly double in length with each new cycle, and as the story is getting more intense and involved. So, if Cycle 1 is one episode, then Cycle 2 is two episodes, and Cycle 3 is likely three or four episodes. Even putting the Introduction and Conclusion phases into the first and last episodes, that's a story 6-7 episodes in length. Separate the Introduction and Conclusion, or add some stand-alone episodes, and you end up with an eight episode story arc pretty easily.

Overall Story

The final level that the KSTK pattern plays out on is the Overall Story, in other words- the whole thing as a single story. On this level, the main units are Story Arcs, and the KSTK pattern plays out divided into story arcs which get more and more intense as the story goes on, usually getting longer and more detailed with each new story arc cycle.

While it's rare that a manga creator has the whole overall story planned out in detail, it's a good idea that they have a rough idea of how the whole thing will come together at the end. This rough plan might be modified or changed as the story goes on, but it should be there to ensure that the story really does have a clear direction. Also, this will help the creator avoid the "endless clone villains" syndrome where each time the hero defeats an opponent, another one who is basically the same but slightly more powerful pops up to stand in their way.

Audiences quickly tire of reading the same story arc over and over again with only cosmetic changes, and the story will lose popularity and die. So, instead it's better to have a clear set of objectives right from the start, and work to make each opponent and story arc different from the others while still reflecting the themes of the story. With just a little planning, the story will work as a whole, no matter how long you intend it to be, and can become more exciting and thrilling as it runs.

So, pick a ballpark length for your story and start planning it out using that rough length and the KSTK cycle chart. An "easy" way to do it is as four arcs- an introduction arc (consisting of the "pilot" story which introduces the characters and situations), the Cycle 1 arc (where the hero faces their first real opposition), the Cycle 2 arc (where the hero enters into the big leagues), and the Cycle 3/Conclusion arc (where the hero uses everything they've learned to defeat their strongest opponent). For more details, see the different meta-genres and their overall story patterns.

Keep in mind, the Overall Story cycles can have story arcs inside their story arcs, which can be divided up however you like.

B-Stories

Many types of stories, especially film and television, have more than one storyline running at the same time. These are often referred to as the "A-story" and "B-story," with the B-story being a smaller second storyline (or storylines) running alongside the main one. B-stories can involve support characters, opponents, or even the main character having some other small thing they're doing alongside working on the main story problem, and usually at some point will connect with the main A-story.

Generally speaking, there isn't room for a full B-story in an 18 to 20-page manga episode, and so most manga episodes don't have a full B-story running inside them. Instead, B-stories are added to manga in several different ways.

Sometimes, episodes will have pieces of a greater story arc's B-story inside them, which are used to increase the excitement or suspense by cutting away from the main story to other events. For example, the character might be winning this battle, but we can see their friends are in danger elsewhere. Or maybe the character is preparing a special meal for their love interest, but at the same time their rival is making a move at work. These might not be things that affect the current episode, but will affect things in a later episode or the story arc as a whole.

Other times, manga creators avoid intercutting with other events in a story arc, and instead simply alternate whole episodes between different characters and their points of view. So, while character A might be trying to defeat the main villain, his buddies character B and character C are facing off against the villain's lieutenants with each of their fights getting whole episodes to show how they turned out.

The important thing is that B-stories are stories, and so they too have a character trying to perform some action and achieve some goal, usually with a typical KSTK story pattern to their own efforts. Also, when possible, the story should be relevant to the main story and connect to it in some way. This doesn't mean that the B-story can't have a separate resolution than the main story, but just that it should interact with it in some way. For example, the B-story of a detective looking for a missing girl might allow them to be in the right place at the right time to both solve the missing girl's case and help the main character avoid becoming another victim.

Like the main story, the B-story is there to explain why the story ends the way it did to the satisfaction and interest of the audience.

THE THREE KEY PRINCIPLES AND WRITING MANGA

The three shaping principles of exaggeration, surprise and sympathy also form a major element of the way manga creators plot their stories. Their goal when planning stories is to get the maximum amount of emotion out of the reader, and they do this by putting the main character in a series of unusual situations which go in unexpected directions while still being relatable in some way.

Usually, a manga main character already has a story seed that goes along with them that gives an idea of the overall direction and focus of the story. As we covered in the Manga Characters chapter, at the start of the planning process a creator should try to come up with an exaggerated character who is in a surprising situation (but is still sympathetic) and use that as the starting point for your story. However, how that story plays out is where plot comes in.

As a creator, you should always be looking for ways to have your characters be put into extreme situations, because those naturally generate drama and opportunities for surprise and sympathy. People can experience real life outside their door anytime, but it's only in fiction that they can experience thrilling or unusual situations that let their imaginations wander. This is why having a larger than life situation can be a major element of making a thrilling story.

Like with characters, creators should try to come up with "plot seeds" that can be used to bring these stories to life. These plot seeds are a way of trying new ideas, and finding ones which jump out at you and have real dramatic potential.

The formula for making these seeds is pretty simple, and should be familiar to you by now:

(Character and Exaggerated situation from real life), **but** *(interesting twist that the audience wouldn't expect)*. **Also,** *(sympathetic aspect that connects with real life problems)*.

So, for example:

- A man takes his dog on a thousand-kilometer trek through the mountains, but the man has cancer and sees this as a final journey. Also, he's trying to find a reason to fight for life and undergo chemotherapy.
- A martial artist must defeat a hundred foes to finish his training, but he must do it blindfolded. Also, his master is dying, and this might be his only chance to try the challenge.
- A girl must learn to play the piano at a professional level in three months, but she doesn't know how to play it in the beginning. She needs to do this to

<u>take her twin's place in a concert because her famous twin has had a nervous breakdown.</u>

Naturally, these are a bit generic, and would be more interesting if they were tied to a specific character seed, but it gives you the idea. These would then be fleshed out more, and matched with a KSTK manga story pattern to try to turn them into fuller and more realized stories.

When using the KSTK pattern, you should also be looking for ways to incorporate the Three Key Principles into your writing at all levels during story planning. Even if you are writing stories about students in a high school, or people at a job, looking for ways to exaggerate situations, add surprising twists, and connect with your reader's heart strings can add a lot of zest.

One way to work with these is to pick one of the four elements of conflict (emotional connection, intensity, level of stakes, and level of challenge) and then exaggerate one or more of them.

Emotional connection is already built into the Japanese approach as sympathy, but the other three elements are definitely going to be something you can play with. By taking a normal situation like taking notes in class, and making it more intense than normal (there's going to be an important test based on these notes at the end of class), you can turn an everyday school situation into something greater than life. Similarly, if that test at the end of class will determine someone's whole academic future, then the stakes are much higher than normal. Or maybe they need to take those notes, but the teacher is going too fast for them to keep up, making it extra challenging.

Emotion, intensity, stakes, and challenge can all be used to turn an ordinary situation into an extraordinary one just by raising the bar on one or more of them, and make the story more thrilling and interesting to read. Just remember not to make them too ridiculously high, unless that fits with the story you're telling.

Also, be on the lookout for interesting spins on normal activities which can make your situations into something that will catch and hold the attention of readers and add surprise. So, for example, while taking notes could be made more interesting through added conflict, it could also be made more interesting by having the students do it blindfolded, having the class taught by an alien, or setting the class in an unusual place like atop a mountain or in a prison. It will all depend on the nature of your story and setting, but there are always different twists on any activity which can come into play if you think hard enough about it.

Lastly, never forget to add sympathy to the situations and plots you come up with. Sometimes this will flow naturally, especially if you have a character that audiences really connect with, so anything they do becomes sympathetic. However, sometimes you will need to add a little extra sympathy, usually through making sure there will be emotional consequences for the character if the character fails. In the "taking notes" example, this could be a character's family future riding on how they do in the test that follows, the character's goal or dream being in jeopardy if they don't take good notes. Also, the character's condition can influence the audience, so if the character must take a class while sick (an experience many have had), that will make the audience feel sympathetic towards them as well.

Once you have gotten practice at incorporating the Three Principles into your writing, it will become second nature to you, but when you're just starting out make a point of brainstorming lists of ways to generate exaggerated and sympathetic situations when you begin planning a story. On a sheet of paper write down as many plot ideas as you can for your character's story, and then look at ways to incorporate the Three Key Principles into them to make them stronger, clearer, and better at reaching your audience.

HOW TO PLAN YOUR STORIES USING THE KSTK FORM

Once you have a plot seed, or idea of what you want your story to be, you can move ahead and start using the KSTK form to plan out your story. There are three simple ways to do this using the KSTK pattern: the Key Events Method, the Cycle Method, and using the spirit of the KSTK to do it your own way.

The Key Events Method

This way of planning the story is usually the best one for getting the most out of the KSTK form, and it's pretty straightforward and easy. Basically, you just use the key events which happen as the part of each cycle and write the story out similar to the examples of *The Comic Artist*, *The Dragon Slayers* and *Coffee Lovers* shown above. Using the different phases of Introduction, Trouble, Easy Win, Double Trouble, and so on, you know what type of things need to happen in that wave of the story so you use them to guide your own story's direction.

Just be aware that you'll find the detail increases as you go through each stage of the story. The Trouble usually has a fairly simple solution, but Double Trouble will definitely require more effort on the part of the character, and the Disaster will require a lot of cleverness on their part (and yours) to get out of. Just imagine what you'd do in their situation, and play with the ideas that come to you, looking for the most surprising and interesting ones.

The Cycle Method

Some people prefer looking at things from a bigger picture, and for them, there's the Cycle Method. In this method, you look at the story as being an Introduction, Three Cycles, and a Conclusion. Focusing on each of the three cycles of problems then solutions, you write down what happens in each cycle in general (or specific) terms instead of worrying about the details.

Generally, the Cycle Method formula looks like this:

- Introduction: The character is in a place trying to accomplish a goal because of their motivation.
- Sho(1): The character takes action, but a problem appears. So, the character solves it by taking an action which solves/does not solve the problem.
- Sho(2): But the Character encounters a larger problem, so they try to solve it by taking action, which seems to solve the problem/make things worse.
- Ten: But the character discovers there is an even bigger problem, and must take action they weren't willing/able to take before to solve it. They succeed/fail.
- Conclusion: The character is now in a new situation and has either moved closer or farther from their goals.

So, let's look at a short episode from a horror story built around this formula:

- Intro: Bob and Sue are in a haunted house and became separated.
- Sho(1): Bob is chased by a ghost and escapes into a room, then finds something surprising.
- Sho(2): Sue meets an old man who seems helpful, but then he is revealed to be a vampire. She tries to escape but he grabs and bites her. And so, Bob rushes in to find them while carrying a golden cross he found and drives the vampire away.
- Ten: Bob tries to escape with the wounded Sue, but discovers she's now under the vampire's control and she attacks him. And so, Bob is forced to fight her off, and in the end he uses his wits to lock Sue in a closet.
- Conclusion: Bob seeks out the vampire to kill him and free Sue from his grasp.

As you can see, we view the story as a series of escalating major events and use them to quickly sketch out the major ideas of what happens in the story. It's a fast way to figure out how the story will play out, and you can write down as much or little detail about each cycle as you wish, but start with simple events like the formula above. After that, you could also use The Key Events Method above to re-write the story in more detail, and then after that turn it into a full synopsis written in paragraph form. (Unless your Key Events chart is super detailed.)

The Cycle Method can also be used for fast planning out of cycles at any level of detail, from a scene, to an episode, to a story arc, to an entire overall story. Play with using it in different ways, and you'll find it a handy and versatile tool.

Let the Spirit of KSTK Guide You

The final way to plan your story is to do it however you normally do it, or like, but to try to incorporate some of the ideas behind the KSTK form into your story. As mentioned above, the KSTK form is based around escalation and creating suspense and excitement to drive your story instead of building it (only) based on conflict. While the KSTK story structure above is conflict-based, this is just one way to use the form, and you can tell stories that have little to no conflict while keeping the audience engaged through suspense and excitement.

If a character is hiking up a mountain and sees progressively more beautiful and interesting things, that's a KSTK story, but it isn't based on conflict, just seeing interesting results to the character's actions. As long as you have the audience wondering what will happen next and interested, your story is going fine, and you just need to reward their attention with things that will interest or delight them. Try playing with stories that are purely about characters, like Slice of Life stories, which barely use conflict, and yet tell amusing, entertaining, and sometimes ironic stories about life. They can be a lot of fun.

PLANNING YOUR MANGA

There are three levels or paths for creating a story for a manga

1. Episode/Single story
2. Story Arc
3. Overall Story

While they are similar, each of these three uses a different set of steps when planning it out. As a writer, you can start at any level, and use these steps (or not) as you wish, they are only a suggested guideline for how you might go about it, not the only way to do it.

It should also be mentioned that these are the steps for producing a character-driven story, and your process might be different if you wanted to write something plot-focused or setting-focused instead.

SINGLE STORY/EPISODE

1. Pick a Lead Character

Use the information found in the chapter on Creating Characters combined with your genre, meta-genre, and own ideas to create a character that lights your imagination on fire. Don't just copy an existing character and make small changes, but try to use the principles of exaggeration, surprise, and sympathy to shape a character that is unique to you and with their own story. You might hit upon one instantly, or you might have to create many character seeds until you find one which will grow and develop into a lead character that you can go on a great journey with.

Also, don't forget to ask yourself the following questions:
- What motivates this character to do what they do?
- How are they heroic? What makes them a hero?

- What is their unique strength that makes them special and will determine their true way to act?

2. Create Opponent

Create a list of possible opponents who are the natural opponents of this character and would stand in their way. Remember these people are usually dark mirror images of the lead character, and so they represent a character who has chosen the wrong path to reach the same goals as the main character. Try to match up your lead character with the opponent that is the most unexpected and surprising one on the list, and which offers the most interesting dramatic story situations. Then use the Three Key Principles to flesh that opponent out even further.

3. Create supporting cast.

Decide which characters you'll need to make this story work besides the Lead and the Opponent- each side will need someone to talk to or interact with, plus possibly other characters to motivate them or give them what they need to accomplish their goals. Think about the minimum number of characters you'll need, not the maximum. Skill as a writer comes from your ability to do a lot with a little, not a little with a lot.

4. Decide on the Essential Story You're Telling

Think about which of the four essential story types (Milieu, Inquiry, Character or Event) the real story of this episode/story is going to be. If you're not sure which one to use, then try coming up with a few ideas for how this character could be used with each of them.

5. Create plot seeds

If you don't already have a story in mind, think about the many possible stories you could tell using these characters. One way to do it might be to apply the following formula from the Rhythm of Manga chapter to generate short punchy ideas for stories.

(Character and Exaggerated situation from real life), **but** (interesting twist that the audience wouldn't expect). **Also,** (sympathetic aspect that connects with real life problems).

It might be tempting to skip the sympathetic aspect, but remember that this is where the real heart of emotion for the story is going to come from. The audience needs to feel something from your story, and sympathy is the key to making that happen.

6.   Pick a plot seed.

Which of your story seeds leaps out at you and makes you excited to tell it? Pick that one and write out a short one-paragraph synopsis of where you think it might go. If it looks good, go to the next step, but if you're struggling with it, try picking another story seed and seeing if that might work better.

7.   Think about what Common Plot pattern might fit with this story seed. (if any)

Common Plots are frameworks that stories often follow and let you focus on plugging in your ideas instead of trying to re-invent the wheel. If any of the ones in this book or elsewhere like Chris Booker's *The Seven Basic Plots*, or Ronald Tobias's *20 Master Plots*, works for you, then use them to help shape your story. Of course, Booker and Tobias have structured their plots for the Three-Act Structure used by Americans, not the Japanese method, but both can work equally well.

8.   Use the KSTK pattern to plan your story.

If you have used one of the Common Plots from this book, then your story may already be shaped by the *ki-sho-ten-ketsu* story rhythm, but if you decided to write it your own way then this is where you would use the KSTK method to think through the highs and lows of your story according to the *Rhythm of Manga* chapter. Whether you use the Key Events Method or the Cycle Method, it will give your story the flavor of manga you're trying to achieve.

9.   Script each episode out with dialog and descriptions.

Open a blank document in a word processor or free scripting software like CELTX, and then begin breaking your story down into scenes. Script each scene out with dialog and action descriptions which describe what the characters say and do as the scene plays out. Just focus on getting a fast, rough draft out first with your basic ideas, and then move on to the next scene when you're ready. Keep going until you have a whole rough first draft finished.

10. Revise

When you have a complete rough first draft, start back at the beginning and read it through. Don't worry about small details or things like typos, dialog, or grammar-worry about the big things like how the story works (or doesn't work) as a whole and how the scenes fit (or don't fit) together. You need to fix the big things first, and then work your way down to the smaller problems so you don't waste time on whole scenes that might be deleted or re-written later. Once you have your bigger problems fixed, then you can go back and start to play with the dialog and add more detail to your scene descriptions.

Important note! If you are the artist who will be drawing this manga, then you only need to give the basic descriptions and can figure out what you want to have happen in the storyboarding stage. On the other hand, if you're handing this script off to another person to draw, then you need to provide detailed descriptions for what happens because that other person isn't you and can't read your mind. Anything you leave out, they will fill in, and it might not work like you wanted it to.

11. Draw Storyboards/NAMEs

In the manga industry, a manga creator doesn't just write a script, they commonly draw a super rough draft of the comic called a "NAME" in manga industry terminology. This is basically a first draft of the manga broken down into pages and panels with dialog and notes. The characters are stick-figure level or other simple designs (this may even be drawn by the writer, not the artist) and there may not even be any backgrounds beyond lines. This is so they can show their editor the story before putting real work into it and make the changes that their editor and others suggest in a quick and efficient way.

Even if you don't have an editor, and especially if you're just starting out, sketching a NAME first before you start working on the actual comic will save a tremendous amount of time and really improve the quality of the final work. You'll be able to see how your comic comes together on a visual level, and make the adjustments you need without having to redraw whole pages or scenes. It can be hard to resist jumping right in when you have a script you're passionate about ready to go, but putting in that little bit of extra work is what separates amateurs and professionals.

12. Edit/Review

With your NAME complete, you should show it to your editor, friends, or others who you trust and get their feedback on it. Either that, or set it aside for at least a few days and then come back to it later so you can look at it with fresh eyes. (Go work on character designs or backgrounds instead, if you're an artist.) Then armed with a new perspective, edit the NAME and craft it into the best possible version of the story it can be.

13. Draw final version.

Armed with your NAME and script, draw the first real draft of your manga. Have fun!

STORY ARC OF MULTIPLE EPISODES/PARTS

1. Pick a lead character

Decide who your lead character for your story arc will be and what you want them to get from this story arc. Are they or their circumstances going to change during this story? If so, how? Or are they going to change the world around them in some way, and what change will that be? How will this story fit into their overall progression (if any), and what will they be like at the end?

2. Create Arc Opponent

Story arcs need clear opponents driving the story and the events. They are the reason the main character can't just stay at home and play games on their phone. (Unless that's part of your story!) When you make an opponent for a story arc they should be someone who is strong and interesting enough to hold the audience's attention for the whole arc while providing a challenge to the hero that they can't easily overcome. Arc opponents should be thought of like level bosses in video games- the main character can't escape the arc or finish the story without "defeating them", and they should represent a significant challenge to the main character.

3. Create Supporting Cast

Figure out who the story is going to need to work, and what roles they're going to play. Often there will be some new character(s) introduced in each arc to keep the story lively and interesting, and these characters may even be the ones going on journeys of change while the lead character is just there to be a guide and inspiration. Don't forget to think about the characters the Arc opponent will need to support them and interact with them as well- usually they'll need at least one person to talk with and express themselves to. Also, try to keep the main cast of most story arcs under 6 characters whenever possible, as any more will make it harder to write well and harder for the audience to follow.

4. Decide on the Essential Story You're Telling

Think about which of the four essential story types (Milieu, Inquiry, Character or Event) the real story of this arc is going to be. If you're not sure which one to use, then try coming up with a few ideas for how this character could be used with each of them.

5. Story Seeds

Since you have your cast, use them to think up all the different possible story situations which might happen in this story. Don't forget to consider the Three Key Principles when coming up with story ideas. Keep playing with different ideas until you get one which grabs you and makes you want to write it! You're not looking for the story you could use, but the story you **have** to use because it's such an interesting idea.

6. Think about what Common Plot Pattern might fit with this story seed.

Consider which of the Common Plots might be useful in developing and presenting the story seed you chose. Not all stories use them, but if one of them works for your story you can use it to help develop your story into something that fits your goals.

7. Use KSTK pattern to plan the overall story.

Whether you use a Common Plot or not, you'll need to create an outline for how your story is going to play out using the KSTK rhythm. Remember that this story will be broken down into multiple smaller pieces, but all of them together should match the KSTK pattern.

8. **Break the story down into episodes based on how many episodes you have to tell it in, or whatever number works best for this story.**

If you have a set number of episodes you need to break this story down into, then start to use that number to divide up your story. If you don't have a set number, then numbers like three, five, eight, twelve and sixteen are all good numbers to consider. Three and five are good for stories that aren't too long or too short and allow for fast-paced stories without much filler. Eight is the number of chapters in a typical collection, and will fill one collected volume exactly. Twelve is one and a half collections, letting you start a new story in the second volume and requiring the audience to buy the third volume to find out what happens. And finally, sixteen fills two volumes exactly, if you want to make it all fit neatly into collections of complete story arcs.

9. **Begin working on the individual episodes as above.**

OVERALL STORY OF A LONGER WORK

1. **Pick a Genre**

Decide on the genre of story you plan to tell. This may already be chosen for you by a manga or story which inspires you or a genre you're in love with. Either way, pick your genre and make sure that you understand it by doing research and consuming as many stories in that genre as you can, especially manga. You probably also want to pay attention to the sub-genre of story you've chosen, because that will have even more specific tropes and ideas that the audience will expect to see.

2. **Think about what Meta-Genre this story fits under.**

Before starting your story, you may want to take a look at the different meta-genres of manga and decide if any of them suit the story you're planning to tell. Picking a meta-genre will tell you a lot about the characters, plots, situations, and presentation of the story you're planning to tell and help you shape it similar to how the Japanese manga creators do it. You don't have to use or even think about the meta-genre, but if your story does fit under one of them, then it saves a lot of time.

3. Pick a Lead Character.

Find the most interesting character to tell this story with, using the information from the Manga Characters chapter. If you don't already have a series lead, start with…

He/she/it is the (adjective)-est (thing/role) you ever saw, but he/she/it (thing which contradicts what was just said in the reader's heads). Also, he/she/it (sympathetic trait or flaw).

4. Brainstorm Possibilities for How Your Main Character Can Grow!

Once you have your character seed, begin brainstorming and write down as many ideas as you can come up with for what that character could do in the story. This shouldn't be the actual story of the character (although you can do that if you want), but a collection of bullet point notes about where you think this character's story is going to start and the direction it's going to go in. Have fun putting all your wild ideas down here- brainstorming means nothing is too silly or wild, because you never know what will lead to ideas that will make your story shine.

5. Create a Supporting Cast.

Once you have the main character's story in mind, who are they going to need to help them along in this journey? Who are their friends, allies, mentors, rivals, enemies, and the other people who will shape them into the person they're going to be? What characters need to exist in the story to help them along the way? What characters will stand in their way and keep them challenged and struggling as they reach for the gold? Don't forget to apply the principles of exaggeration, surprise, and sympathy to each of your supporting cast as well- this way they're going to be interesting characters in their own right. (But not too interesting- you don't want them to overshadow the lead!)

6. Decide on the Essential Story You're Telling

Think about which of the four essential story types (Milieu, Inquiry, Character or Event) the real story of the overall story is going to be. If you're not sure which one to use, then try coming up with a few ideas for how this character could be used with each of them. Remember that most long-running serial shonen manga don't use

Character (change) as their essential story because it means all the arcs need to be about the character changing and growing. Instead, they have smaller Character stories inside the bigger story when it's convenient.

7. Figure Out What the Overall Story is Going to Be.

Use the story's meta-genre template to roughly plan out what the overall story is going to be in as much or little detail as you need. Focus on the beginning and the end, the middle can be left somewhat vague because you'll often change it or modify it as you go along. It's enough to know roughly what will happen or needs to happen along the way and how the main character and their supporting cast will come together.

8. Plan the Pilot/Introduction Story for This Story Using the Single-Story Plan.

Once you know how the whole thing will come together, it's time to plan your Pilot. The pilot story is basically the simplest possible introduction story you can write that sets up the characters, situations, and world of your story. It's a chance to test everything out and find the right style, voice and tone for your story before launching into a full series. You don't have to do a pilot, but it's a really good idea, even if the pilot itself is never released or used. Just remember the pilot is there to sell the characters and their story, so it's just the most interesting parts with a lot left open to mystery.

9. Use the Story Arc steps above to start planning out the story arcs which come after the pilot.

Plan out the first two- or three-story arcs of your story to give yourself a solid idea of where this story is going to go, then break them down into episodes and begin planning the episodes. Just plan each story arc in detail one at a time, then write it and produce it. Don't work too far ahead or you'll lose the flexibility to change things as you come up with new ideas and rethink things due to audience reactions.

ADVANCED MANGA TECHNIQUES

This chapter is a collection of tricks and techniques that manga writers use when planning and presenting their stories to audiences. Some of them will be useful to you, some of them won't be, it will all depend on the type of manga you're writing and your own personal style. However, even if you don't use them, knowing the thinking behind them will help you to become a better manga creator.

AVOIDING EXPOSITION

When writing manga, one of the greatest challenges can sometimes be giving the audience information they need to know without resorting to text boxes and narration which will slow the reading experience down. People who want to read large blocks of text are reading novels, and people who read things in comic form are looking for light and immersive experiences, so they don't want the writer telling them things directly when it can be avoided.

There are five techniques that manga writers use when crafting manga that not only help them to avoid exposition, but can improve the manga reading experience in other ways as well. They are infographics, fools, commentators, the manga chorus, and thought speech, and each adds its own flavor to the story where they're used.

Infographics
As manga are a visual medium, one of their greatest strengths is the ability to present needed information in visual ways, and in fact manga writers should always be trying to think their stories through visually first. People process visual information much faster than they do text information, and a good information graphic (infographic) can transform even the most complicated of ideas into something simple and easily understood with a little thought and creativity.

Just remember that any infographic must both convey the information in an easily digestible way, and also be visually appealing in a manga. Study examples of online infographics to find styles and ways of presenting the information that work best for your story and how you can use iconography to enhance the presentation. For example, most manga infographics usually reduce characters into cute little game pieces or other chibi designs to make the audience smile and the information look more appealing.

Fools

The classic role of foolish characters in stories is to add humor and relieve tension. They are often clownish figures who by their appearance, words, and actions make the audience smile or laugh and give the audience a break from the more serious drama. However, fools also have another more important role that audiences don't always pick up on- they're there to ask the "dumb" questions that make sure everyone understands what's happening in the story.

The fool is actually there to guide the audience through the more complex parts of the story, often by making the other characters explain to them the events and plans in action. And, not only that, they get the main characters to express their thoughts and ideas out into words which the audience can read and understand. This allows the writer to turn dull exposition into interesting and funny situations which flow more easily than any text box could, and the audience is entertained and learns what they need to know at the same time.

In manga, the role of the fool is most often played by the best friend of the character or an ally, who they can trust and thus will give their real thoughts and opinions to. However, in theory any character can "play the fool" in different situations because there's always someone who doesn't quite get what's going on. There doesn't have to be a set "fool", but just a character playing this role in a particular scene, and it can sometimes make audiences connect with characters more when they see they're flawed and fallible.

Just remember not to overdo it, because fools often walk the line between being amusing and annoying.

Commentators

One of the more overlooked but powerful techniques used to convey information to the audience in manga is the use of commentators- people who are commenting on the action as it happens. Usually third parties, these "other audience members" are there to lead the reader through the story in an interesting and lively way. These commentators can be allies, enemies, or neutral third parties, but they serve three important and useful purposes.

1. They act as a dialog-based way to convey information about the events unfolding to the audience (extremely useful in visual mediums like comics and film). They can inform the audience about rules, background information, and anything else the writer needs the readers to know.

2. Their reactions act as emotional cues for the audience, making the action feel more exciting and letting the audience know how they should be feeling about what's occurring. (Hopeful, worried, scared, shocked, etc. The audience will feel what the commentators tell them to feel in their reactions.)

3. They help to control pacing, as every time we cut away to the commentators it slows the action down and makes the audience wait to find out what happens next, building dramatic tension and suspense. (Or relieving dramatic tension if things get too intense, with a little comic relief!)

Not only this, but if the commentators are named characters, it also gives the writer a chance to show the audience what these characters are like. How the characters express themselves, their thoughts, and their opinions will all be made clear while they are commenting on the action before them. As a result, this technique can be used to develop characters and even set up plot points before they become part of the story.

For example, if two characters in a battle manga are dueling and the reader is getting commentary from a known villain in the audience who is showing his expert knowledge of the fighting techniques and his opinions of the fighters, it could be used to not only set up the coming duel but also increase tension. After all, the villain clearly knows the rules better than the hero does, so how will the hero defeat this expert in the coming rounds?

Like fools, commentators can come in many shapes and sizes, from announcers, to judges, to random audience members, to enemies and allies. However, most often they also come in pairs or trios, since that allows different perspectives and back and forth discussion. Very often, there will be an "expert" and a "fool" paired together as a commentator team, which brings a combination of knowledge and levity, and lets the commentary have an entertaining flow to it. (Usually with the fool getting the last word.)

The Manga Chorus

In ancient Greek plays, there was a group of people on stage called "The Chorus" whose job it was to comment on the action, express the character's thoughts, and sometimes narrate transitions. These people often wore masks, and spoke together as a faceless group representing the masses, gods, or society.

In manga, there is a similar technique used sometimes where the faceless masses of society or people show their thoughts or opinions of what's happening in the story. This is often expressed with silhouettes and voice or thought balloons which float on the page untethered to any particular characters and are representing society and the world around the characters commenting or expressing ideas about what's happening.

For example, in a high school manga if a character wore a strange outfit to school, the reader may see a shot of the character walking down the hallway while a collection of word balloons hang around them with people commenting on the character's appearance and motives for wearing that outfit.

This is the manga chorus in action, and it lets the writer express many ideas in an efficient way by giving the audience a sample of how the world around the character views them. (Or, in some cases, what the character believes the world is thinking, whether it is or not.) Also, the manga chorus can be used to provide background information in the form of "gossip" or stories being passed along, and transitions between scenes ("Did you hear Marion is meeting Bob behind the school after class?") as a way of giving the reader emotionally flavored text.

Not that the speakers need always be faceless or unshown- sometimes it's important for the audience to know what kind of speaker is saying these things and see their expressions. In these cases, the speakers will be seen, but there usually isn't any stem indicating exactly who is saying these things, and it will rarely be a named or important character. This is to show that these characters represent society or the world around the main characters, and thus are not just speaking for themselves, but others as well.

Thought Speech

The last way manga creators commonly express information to the audience is through thought speech- floating text on the page representing a character's thoughts. In non-Japanese comics, this is often done through "thought balloons", and sometimes the Japanese will use these too, but more commonly they ignore the balloon and just have the text hanging in the air around the characters.

Especially in stories with a small cast, or first-person perspective, this can be an effective way to convey information to the audience in a way that tells them about the character at the same time. Thought speech is naturally flavored by the thinker, and so it shows us not just what they think and feel, but how they think, and injects personality into what would otherwise be dry information.

Another advantage of using thought speech is that it can turn participants in the action into commentators who are also commenting on the action as it happens. In a duel between two characters, they can also be their own commentators, breaking up the action as they think about the situation and express their views on what's happening and why. They can even be their own fool, making mistakes in their thinking, or correcting themselves as they think through what's happening, or commenting on their own mistakes. (See *Kaguya-san: Love is War* for this in action.)

WRITING OP CHARACTERS

By default, heroes in stories are all exceptional.

Being a hero means having some special traits that make them someone who stands out in the story's situation, otherwise they'd be a nobody. In that time and place, the hero is the right person for the job to be the lead character, and whether this is because they have the right skills, powers, personality traits, or other qualifications, it is this extra thing which lets them shine.

Thus, all heroes in stories are powerful.

But some, are more powerful than others.

OP, which stands for Over-Powered, characters are not only good at what they do-they're too good at what they do. And, because they're a form of pure wish-fulfillment character on the part of the writer, they're usually good at almost everything important to the story. As power fantasy characters, OP characters have few weaknesses, and are usually capable of crushing their enemies like flies. They are often the best there is for their setting, gods and goddesses walking among normal mortals, and face few real challenges in their lives.

They are the writer letting out all of their dreams and wishes and painting them in glorious technicolor for all of the world to see. They are the writer having fun coming up with ways to the use the clever lines they came up with two hours after it was actually needed. They are the writer turning their weaknesses into strengths, and being applauded for it by an audience that shares those basic human needs of admiration, security, power and self-fulfillment.

And, this is great because the audience too gets to vicariously feel what it's like to be that powerful- "to crush their enemies, to have them driven before them, to hear the lamentations of their women." (At least, according to Conan the Barbarian, one of the original OP heroes.) They get to imagine what it would be like to wield that power against foes in their own personal lives, and bring righteous vengeance against that dog down the street which won't stop barking, and get the respect of the cute girl working in the coffee shop at the corner. They get to imagine themselves saying the cool and witty lines the OP character tosses off as they indiscriminately mow through their opponents like grass and know what it's like to be at the top of the social ladder, a place that's very far from where they really are. And, they get to imagine what it would be like to face no challenges in their very tough and difficult lives.

And therein lies the problem, because there is a very simple set of formulas that all writers, (especially new ones) need to memorize:

Limits = (Audience) Interest
No Limits = No Interest

This is why, as fun as people find OP heroes, they often lose interest in them pretty quickly if there is nothing the character can't do. It's the things that the character can't do that define them and make them interesting to the audience, and so without those limitations the character isn't challenged, and the story isn't interesting. A character who can do whatever they want, whenever they want, isn't one the audience can learn from, and so there is no dramatic tension or dramatic questions there to keep the audience's interest.

In other words, OP characters aren't just amazingly powerful, they're also amazingly boring.

This makes them very difficult to write well, as most writers and audiences of OP hero stories want things to focus on the OP hero, but OP heroes become dull fast, so OP hero stories usually fail. This is why, since 1933 when Superman (the ultimate OP comic book hero) was first created, there have been dozens of Superman knock-offs in comics, but you probably only know one of them (Captain Marvel/SHAZAM!). Also, writing Superman is known to be one of the toughest jobs in comics exactly because he's so powerful he's hard to come up with interesting stories for. (You can only have so many other Kryptonians show up or other alien superman clones to fight before the audience decides to take a nap instead.)

So, does this mean OP lead characters are a bad idea?

Yes and no.

It is always easier to level characters up than down, and watching characters try to overcome foes that have advantages over them is where most of the dramatic tension and energy in most stories comes from. Powerful heroes who fight those stronger than themselves to protect the weak are respected and adored for their efforts, while powerful heroes who fight those weaker than they are can easily be seen as bullies and jerks, and remind the audience more of the people in their lives they hate more than those they like. (Unless you arrange it so the audience's hate of the weaker foe is greater than their dislike of watching the strong bully the weak.)

OP characters are also hard to work with exactly because their power level makes it hard to challenge them, so the number of possible plots and situations they can be put into drops as their power levels go up. An all-knowing, all-seeing character with infinite strength can't be challenged by anyone other than another character like themselves, which quickly just turns into god-level wrestling matches as the two duke it out. Great for a few times, but it gets old fast.

This is why most stories tend to end when the character reaches OP status, because they're at their peak, have nowhere else to go, and have become harder than ever to write, so the author does the wise thing and brings down the curtain with the character in their prime. The character is then remembered as a great one who got a good ending, and the author can go on to count their cash and write something easier.

But, that doesn't mean you can't do stories with OP lead characters, and do them well. The aforementioned Superman is known around the world. *Dragonball*, with it's OP lead Goku, can almost rival Superman for global popularity, and *One-Punch Man's* Saitama (who is literally OP Man!) has used his OP-ness to rule manga and anime sales charts for a few years now.

The trick is remembering the above formula, and using a bit of slight of hand.

To begin, Limitation = Interest, so therefore the best way to handle an OP character is to limit what they can do. Limits on characters can come in many different ways, including:

- **Abilities with limits**- limited uses, recharge times, limited types of circumstances when it can be used.
- **Abilities with side effects**- everything has a downside, what is this ability's?
- **Rules of Engagement**- limits to when they can use the powers or under what circumstances
- **Codes of Conduct and Ethics**- codes against killing, codes of honor
- **Personal character flaws** – mental and physical limitations, psychological flaws
- **Situational Limits**- things like hostage situations or other limits created by circumstances
- **Secrets** – they have to hide their power for some reason, secret identities
- **Bosses or minders**- someone has to give them the okay to unleash their power

Any of these automatically restricts what a character can do, and therefore makes the character more interesting to the audience and easier to write. Things like bosses or minders mean the character can't act without permission, and so is limited by their superiors. Abilities with recharge times that can only be used infrequently are very common (Japan's "Superman" called Ultraman, can only use his powers for a few minutes each day, for example), as are codes of honor or ethics.

Another type of limitation is social limitations, like say a character who is hiding their strength because it would affect how others view them. They might not want the people in their lives to realize just how strong or different they are because it will affect their relationships with those close to them, and may destroy something precious. They could show their strength, but it would affect their lives and the lives of those around them by attracting attention. An idea that is common in Asian cultures is that success means fame, but fame also means trouble. Once you show you're strong, others will come to test you and challenge you, especially if you have a position or something they want. It can make living a peaceful or normal life impossible.

They can be the strongest woman in the world, but if everywhere they go they're mobbed by people wanting something from them, and never allowed any peace, their strength can be a curse, not a blessing.

And finally, of course, while they might be strong, that doesn't mean the people around them are. Supporting characters can become targets and victims if people know they're connected with the hero, and even if they're also strong, the stronger enemies can still get to the hero through them. The most OP characters still have emotional needs, and the connection with others is a powerful one- a connection that comes with a natural vulnerability as well.

Going back to Superman as an example, in the golden age of radio in the 1930s and 1940s there was a daily Superman radio play series that people tuned into every evening. On that extremely popular series, Superman was as powerful as we know him today, but almost never faced a single opponent who could match his strength. For two decades, he fought gangsters, spies, saboteurs, mad scientists and the occasional monster, but no supervillains as we know them today.

So, how did they make a hit show about an OP character like Superman work when there was literally nobody who could stand against him? They focused on his greatest limitation- while he could toss around tanks, was invulnerable, and could fly like a rocket, he was still only about as smart as an average man in the show. The adventures were almost always mysteries and puzzles, where Superman's power didn't matter because he didn't know who to use it against until the mystery was solved and the true villains revealed. His code of conduct kept him from just beating people up to find the truth, so he had to slowly pick the situation apart, and only then could he apply his incredible powers to bring swift justice to the evil doers.

The Superman radio show also developed his supporting cast like Lois Lane, Jimmy Olsen and Perry White, who he had to protect because they weren't immune to bullets, but were also on the case with him. Of course, this was a challenge because he had to hide the secret that their co-worker Clark Kent was really Superman from them, and it often kept him from acting against foes right in front of him. If he revealed Clark Kent was really Superman, he'd lose one of his greatest assets, and the one way he could live peacefully among humans. And finally, when the lead actor of the radio play series, Bud Collyer, was struck with a severe illness, the quick-thinking writing staff came up with a green glowing radioactive rock that made Superman too weak to move and robbed him of his powers so poor Bud could have a break. Kryptonite was such a success at generating drama, it would continue to torment the Man of Steel until this very day.

So, you see, despite being the most powerful being on the planet, Superman is also one of the most limited, and through those limitations his story really comes alive.

Nevertheless, sometimes you have characters who don't suit a lot of limitations, or who are so powerful that it's hard to reasonably come up with good limitations for them. In this case, writers can take a move from magicians everywhere and use a little slight of hand.

What slight of hand means in this case is to make the audience think they're getting one story, when they're really getting another. They think they're getting a story about the OP main character, but in reality they're getting a story about the supporting cast, side characters, or opponents. This is another time-honored trick used when dealing with powerful characters, and it's been used for so long exactly because it works so well.

These plots tend to fall into three categories- Guardian Angel, Righteous Avenger, and Bringer of Justice.

In a <u>Guardian Angel</u> story, the story is about one of the OP hero's supporting cast and them doing whatever it is they do. Then, at some point near the end, when they get into trouble, they call the OP hero in and the OP hero joins the plot to take care of the bad guys. For example, Lois Lane investigates a strange disappearance, finds out aliens are trying to poison the water supply, and when she gets caught she texts Superman for help, who shows up and cleans house. The title on the book still says Superman, but the story was really about Lois, with the hero acting as a guardian angel in case she gets in too deep. (Not that the audience will notice as long as the supporting characters being featured are interesting and the stories help to develop their characters.)

The <u>Righteous Avenger</u> story is similar, in that it's about another character instead of the OP hero, but in a Righteous Avenger story the focus is usually on an innocent side character or supporting character being tormented by a villain. The character is trying to live their life, or do some noble task, but someone cruel won't leave them alone and does bad things to them. However, once the audience has been made to hate the villain sufficiently, and it looks like the villain has won, the OP main character turns up and delivers some righteous justice on the villain, to the cheers of the audience. (Again, the audience not noticing that the OP lead was actually only there for a tiny part of the story.) See *The Righteous Avenger Plot* in Common Plots for more details.

Lastly, the <u>Bringer of Justice</u> story is where the main character is the villain, not the hero or a supporting character. This type of story is a foundation of American superhero comics, with their unchanging lead superheroes, and makes up the majority of stories for characters like Batman and Spiderman. The plot is about the villain trying to accomplish some criminal goal, usually with the hero trying to figure out what they're up to, and in the process, we learn who the villain is and why they're doing what they're doing. The villain is the real main character in the story, with the hero just there to fight them while uncovering more about the villain's story, and then bring them to justice in the end.

The key in all of these obviously being that the story focus isn't the OP main character, but that OP main character is still involved and is allowed to show off their power somewhere in the story. Using these types of plots mixed in with stories about the OP main character allows the writer to add variety to the stories without having to resort to weakening the main character or limiting them. They can be their OP best, and yet there is still a story about a character struggling with difficult decisions and situations.

Since it's hard to give specific examples of this without spoiling stories, a "theoretical" example of this in use might be an OP series where the first story arc focuses on the bored OP main character, and then the following story arcs alternate between the main character and his supporting cast, progressively spending more time with the supporting cast than the OP main character, but still having the OP lead show up and take the bad guys down in a single hit at the end of Righteous Avenger plots- often just one punch. This lets the story develop the characters and setting, while letting the main character be their OP self who has few to no weaknesses and still be there to do the cool things when needed.

Naturally, to do this well, you need a strong supporting cast and/or setting worth exploring, and one which the audience will find interesting enough to not mind spending time away from their OP hero. But, if you can pull it off, the OP hero ends up being an anchor around which a whole community of interesting characters that the audience enjoys spending time with forms. They know their OP hero will be there when needed, so they relax and just enjoy the show.

Final tips on writing OP lead characters:
- Fights with OP characters are hard to do because they just win, so unless they have limitations to make the fight interesting (or a worthy opponent), just get the fight over with as quickly as possible. There's no point in dragging out a fight between an elephant and an ant, unless the ant has some real tricks up their tiny sleeve. The elephant wins, move on to what happens next.
- There have been a number of anime/manga characters (Vash the Stampede from *Trigun*, Ryo Saeba from *City Hunter*, for example) where the OP main character acts a fool but then suddenly becomes their OP self the minute things get serious near the story climax. This is usually played for laughs, and it works sometimes, but be careful with this approach. Unlike the Superman approach (where the character's secret identity acts as a solid limitation), this fake secret identity approach never rings true because the character could act anytime, they're just choosing not to act because of the plot. It then becomes really tricky for the writer to constantly come up with believable reasons why the main character didn't just take out the bad guys in their first encounter, but waited until the dramatic moment at the end.

MANGA META-GENRES AND PLOTS

GENRES AND META-GENRES

Genres are a way to classify stories based on the emotions (comedy, horror, romance, etc) or themes (action, sports, science fiction, etc) that the story is built around. They're a handy way for audiences to quickly know what to expect from a particular film or book. And, there are many different manga genres and sub-genres (smaller genres inside bigger ones) that readers love, including...

1. Adventure
2. Comedy
3. Cooking
4. Ecchi
5. Fantasy
6. Gag Manga
7. Gambling
8. Gangster
9. Harem
10. Isekai
11. LitRPG
12. Martial Arts
13. Mecha
14. Mystery
15. Romance
16. Science Fiction
17. Slice of Life
18. Sports
19. Superhero
20. Thriller

However, one thing that all of these genres have in common is that they can stand on their own- they're a complete set of ideas surrounding a way to tell a type of story and if you follow the patterns they lay out, then you'll produce that type of story.

But, there are also collections of tropes and story ideas which go together, but don't stand on their own. These collections, called meta-genres, are used to modify other existing genres rather than being a complete story package on their own.

This might sound complicated, but a simple food analogy can easily explain them.

Think of genres as being staple foods- chicken, steak, tomatoes, bread, etc

Think of meta-genres as being spices and condiments- pepper, salt, cinnamon, ketchup, mayonnaise, butter, etc.

You don't eat spices and condiments on their own (you can, but they'll taste bland or overpowering), you use them to make basic foods taste better. Meta-genres are exactly the same- they're used to modify existing story genres to create different flavors and tastes of stories from the usual.

One example of these is the Battle Manga, which is a major meta-genre in shonen comics.

Battle Manga are a meta-genre because while there is a huge number of rules and tropes that go along with them, they don't come with a setting or specific set of themes or characters. Instead they combine with other genres to turn them into Battle Manga stories.

Martial Arts Battle Manga like *Dragonball Z* are their most common form, but you can also find...

- Psychological Thriller Battle Manga (*Death Note*)
- Fantasy Battle Manga (*Black Clover*)
- Harem Battle Manga (*Maho Sensei Negima*)
- Cooking Battle Manga (*Shokugeki no SomaL: Food Wars!*)
- Romance Battle Manga (*Kaguya-san: Love Is War!*)
- Manga Creation Battle Manga (*Bakuman*)
- Sports Battle Manga (*Haikyuu!*)
- Acting Battle Manga (*Glass Mask*)
- Boardgame Battle Manga (*Hikaru no Go*)
- Fishing Battle Manga (*Grander Musashi*)
- Card Collecting Battle Manga (*Yu-Gi-Oh!*)
- Horror Battle Manga (*Rosario and Vampire*)
- Underwater Salvage Battle Manga (*Waga na wa Umishi* – Master of the Ocean)
- And so many more!

Battle Manga aren't a genre, but a meta-genre that covers a way of structuring stories and presenting them to the audience that can be mixed with other genres, sub-genres, and meta-genres to produce different and interesting stories.

In the following chapters, we'll look at Battle Manga, Task Manga, Relationship Manga, Romance Manga, Slice of Life Manga, and many more manga meta-genres to see how they work, so that you can use them to spice up your own stories.

However, before you start, there are three things to consider about using these meta-genres.

First, the important thing to remember here is that these are common approaches to setting up and structuring manga, but they don't tell the writer exactly what the tone or style of the manga itself will be exactly. You can have a Horror Fighting Manga, Horror Activity Manga, Horror Task Manga, or even Horror Relationship Manga. Each of them would feel completely different from the others, and produce a distinctive style and type of story. On top of that, most manga are actually a mix of genre elements, so no two Horror Fighting Manga would be exactly the same, since one might be an Adventure Horror Fighting Manga, while another might be a Psychological Horror Fighting Manga.

Then, depending on which of the big three pillars you focus on (Character, Plot, Setting) you will further still change the resulting type of story. A Character-Driven Horror Psychological Fighting Manga will be different from a Setting-Driven Horror Psychological Fighting Manga, will be different from a Plot-Driven Horror Psychological Fighting Manga. But all of them are still using the Fighting Manga formula, just with different results.

Finally, these meta-genres are combinable, and you can create stories which take elements from different meta-genres and put them together the way you like. (Especially with some of the other types of meta-genres listed after the big four.) However, usually there will always be one meta-genre which is dominant, and the others will just be there to spice it up. That dominant meta-genre will control where the story goes, while the others will influence how it plays out. For example, *One Piece* is a Hunted Hero Fighting Manga, but it is first and foremost a Fighting Manga in its structure and story, with the Hunted Hero elements being used as a way to move the battles from one location to the next.

In any case, don't be afraid to mix and match and try new things! These meta-genres are a tool to let you see stories in different ways, not straight-jackets to lock you into telling a story only one way.

So, have fun and experiment!

In the following chapters we will discuss each of the major meta-genres of manga in turn, going into what makes each tick and discussing the tropes and story structures they use, and then look at the key features of some of the minor less common meta-genres as well.

SHONEN MANGA

Without a doubt, the most popular manga demographic category is shonen manga targeted at boys and teen males. At 2 million copies a week, *Shonen JUMP* is without a doubt the king of manga publications, and it's followed by a series of other shonen-targeted comics. The best-selling girl's comic, *Margaret*, sells about a sixteenth of what *JUMP* does, and on top of that it's estimated that half of *JUMP*'s readership are actually female. (Which means more girls read *JUMP* than any girl's manga there is, despite it being mostly targeted at boys.)

So, it's no surprise that when people think manga, they think shonen manga, and it's the type of manga that most people are interested in writing. Whether they take their inspiration from *Naruto/Boruto, One Piece, Dr. Stone, Black Clover, My Hero Academia*, or *The Promised Neverland*, shonen manga inspire millions of young people to sketch, draw, and imagine stories in their heads and on paper. They dream of creating stories like the ones they read, and want to share them with the world- if they only knew how.

So, let's talk about how!

THE SHONEN PLOT

During the history of shonen manga, there have been stories of every kind- horror, fantasy, comedy, romance, sports, science fiction, post-apocalyptic martial arts, and almost any type of story you could name. However, at some point during the 1990's a formula started to appear that became the default template for shonen storytelling. Maybe it was the success of *Naruto, One Piece, BLEACH!*, or the other epics that followed this pattern, or maybe it was the accumulated wisdom of the editors at the shonen magazines. But whatever it was, a formula was born for successful shonen manga that still rules until this day...

A sympathetic young person with great talent and lofty goals works hard with others to make their dreams into a reality using their own two hands.

Let's break the formula down to make things clearer...

A sympathetic young person...

As covered in the chapters on Manga Characters, the typical shonen hero is going to be between the ages of 12 and 16, and is someone whose life situation is usually pretty rough. The average shonen reader wants to read about protagonists who are like themselves, but usually just a little bit older than they are. Since the target audience is boys, the main characters are typically boys as well (with a growing number of exceptions), and they need to be old enough to go out on their own and be independent from their families- so twelve is a good minimum age. However, they shouldn't be too old or they're not relatable, so sixteen makes a pretty good cutoff. This is as a starting age, of course, they can age up as the story goes on.

As for being sympathetic, it's required that the audience have a character they can connect with, and giving the main character a sympathetic background does it pretty quickly. Manga are filled with characters who are orphans for two reasons- 1) it means instant sympathy from the audience, and 2) it explains how the characters can run around on their own without someone stopping them or getting in the way of them making poor decisions. However, absent and abusive/uncaring parents are also very common ways to achieve the same result without killing them.

...with great talent...

Shonen heroes always have some special strength or great talent that sets them apart from others and makes them the hero of the story. This can be anything from a very good memory to godlike magical powers, but they will have some ability that gives them a huge advantage and thus lets them do what nobody else seems to be able to do. However, to use those abilities to the fullest they will need to nurture them and develop them while overcoming their own personal flaws and weaknesses, which will often be part of the focus of the story. Most often, their special ability is unconscious and not under their control when the story starts, so they need to develop it and bring it out to achieve their potential. This will require a long and hard journey (metaphorically or literally) which will lead to them gaining control of their abilities with the help of the friends they make along the way.

...and lofty goals...

A good character has strong goals and motivations, but a shonen character shoots for the moon and has the motivation to boost them all the way there. A shonen story is driven by a character's desire to accomplish some great deed that looks impossible for them on the surface, and the fun of the story is seeing how they get there. Following the principle of exaggeration, shonen characters never want to just compete- they want to be the best. If they're a police officer, they want to rid the city of crime, and it will be a city overflowing with corruption and vice when the story starts. If they want to be a chef, they want to be a world-class one. If they want to collect stamps, they want a complete set of the rarest stamps there are.

They are always ants challenging elephants to a fight, and finding a way to win.

Similarly, they will have some great motivating force that drives them towards that dream, usually one which is sympathetic to the audience. However, their motivation should never be a selfish one because that won't make the audience like them. It should be a motivation which is directed towards helping other people, and one which benefits the world around them in some way. Even if they seem to be acting selfishly at first, they will eventually give it up and be fighting for something greater than themselves, whether they know it or not.

...works hard...

The audience isn't paying to see a character have an easy life- they're paying to see a character go through hell and come out fighting. Characters who struggle and find their way through adversity are interesting because the audience can learn from them and their actions. This is why the character's goals must be hard, and the challenges between them and meeting those goals are even harder than they could imagine. Audiences want to be inspired by heroes who give it their best, and see what someone who doesn't give up can accomplish.

The challenges the characters face must be ones which force them outside of their comfort zone and to do things they don't want to do, because that's where personal growth happens. They must always be trying their hardest to win, and their opponents should always be the worst possible opponent for them to face in that situation. Only when it's darkest can heroes shine brightest.

...with others...

Shonen lead characters need someone to fight for to bring out their best, and that's usually their friends. Even if they start the story alone, they become part of a larger group who fight together to accomplish something even greater than the lead character could accomplish on their own. Part of the shonen story is finding your place in society, and usually the main character creates that place in society for themselves by bringing together others like them to work for a common goal.

...to make their dreams into a reality...

In the end, as a result of their efforts, a shonen character must accomplish something. Their goal, whatever it was, must be achieved in some way- although not usually how they thought it would be. This will be the result of all the work they put in, all the learning they did, and all the friends they made along the way, coming together into a single event which puts them across the finish line. This victory should not be possible without everything that came before it, and represents their final test to show that they have matured and become who they are destined to be.

...using their own two hands.

And finally, shonen characters should always accomplish their goals through their own efforts. Audiences connect and sympathize better with characters who dig in and get their hands dirty, and the lead characters in shonen stories are always shown doing it the hard way to represent this. This shows up literally in the fact that no matter what great abilities they have, they always finish their fights personally, one-on-one, and fighting face to face. There is nothing distant about shonen fights- they are always up close and personal, because that looks and feels much cooler. It is always a story about them personally giving it their all to do what needs to be done.

Put together, this formula creates an aspirational story that can generate a major hit with audiences because it resonates with their own dreams and is positive and encouraging. The root of this formula is not new, and writers such as Horatio Alger have used it to write successful young adult fiction for a very, very long time. These stories likely are also taking a lot of inspiration from the Chinese story *Journey to the West* (aka *The Monkey King*), and the Japanese story of *Momotaro*. Both of these fantasy tales are about young heroes who go on epic journeys, meet friends along the way, and together change the worlds they live in for the better through their efforts.

As such, this is the formula for an epic story, not a one-shot or a short piece. Stories made using this formula are intended to cover a lot of time and numerous steps as the character matures and has many adventures along the way. If you're writing something shorter, then you might want to take note of it, but scale down some of the epic-ness to something that can fit inside a shorter story. Also, this is for a Battle Manga, Task Story, or other type of epic serial, other stories like Romantic Comedies and Slice-of-Life stories can have their own formulas.

THE THEMES OF SHONEN MANGA

"Friendship, effort, victory." This is the motto of *Shonen JUMP*, the largest and most popular comic magazine in Japan, and it should come as no surprise that every story in *JUMP*'s flagship titles works hard to live up to these guiding ideas. Since 1968, *JUMP* has been experimenting with different kinds of stories aimed at boys 8-12, and each generation of editor has passed along the knowledge and wisdom of the previous generations to their successors.

Using these three guiding ideas, *JUMP* has developed its own style, and every title in *Shonen JUMP* is expected to embody these three ideas in some way. The stories should always be about friends working together with effort to achieve a difficult goal- thus providing a strong positive message to young people that if they work hard then they too can achieve their life dreams.

However, while these three guiding ideas are the foundation of *JUMP*, and shared by most shonen titles from across the Japanese publishing world, that doesn't mean they're the themes of the stories that appear in shonen manga. No, if they were, then every title in *Shonen JUMP* would be identical, which is most certainly not the case. Instead, each title has its own theme which carries it in a different direction from the rest.

- *One Piece*: Following your Dreams
- *Naruto*: Never Giving Up
- *My Hero Academia*: The Value of Hard Work
- *Death Note*: Justice
- *Hunter x Hunter*: Patience
- *Bleach!*: Protecting What you Love
- *Dragonball*: Courage
- **Dr. Stone**: The Power of Science

Looking at that list, you can see a clear overall pattern. All of these are strong positive messages which uphold the values of society and encourage the readers to struggle through the challenges in their own lives. Most of them are also compatible with the ideals of friendship and effort, and explore why the characters in the stories don't easily give up when faced with obstacles in achieving their goals, no matter how hard or lofty they are.

There is also a hidden fourth ideal that runs in shonen manga and goes along with "friendship"- and that is "they sacrifice for others." The main characters in almost all shonen manga are people who selflessly take risks and do things for the benefit of others. They often win their battles and gain friends because they're willing to be the ones to make the first move and take the risk of giving without knowing if they'll get anything back. In fact, usually they give not expecting anything back at all, but because they know and feel it's the right thing to do.

It's human instinct, and good cultural manners, to return the favor when someone helps you. This is the rule of reciprocity, and humans naturally like people who are givers and supporters, and they dislike people who are takers that don't live up to their part of the bargain. Shonen heroes reinforce this rule by being givers and being rewarded for it, while the villains in these stories are almost always takers who reject the social bargain to be selfish.

COMING UP WITH YOUR OWN STORY THEME

If you look at the list of themes from popular shonen manga above, you'll quickly realize that most of them are ones which are clearly compatible with the "friendship" and "effort" parts of the *Shonen JUMP* motto. They are either connected to the idea of working hard, or the idea of what it means to be friends, and these themes work to highlight those concepts in interesting ways.

If you're stuck on a theme for your story, look for a variation on friendship or effort that will best suit your idea of what those words mean and offer to take your story in a new direction. Even if it's the same as one of the ones listed, the story will be a different take on "working hard for what you believe in" or "following your dreams" because you wrote it- and you are unique.

On the other hand, two of the items (the themes for *Death Note* and *Dr. Stone*), don't actually fit in with the themes of friendship or effort. The stories do live up to the JUMP motto if you read them, but the themes of "justice" and the "power of science" are something else entirely.

And, that's okay too!

You can use almost any theme you want when you do your story because it's yours, and by picking a theme outside the usual ones, you'll be making your story all the more unique. A shonen story with a theme about "protecting nature" or "art is a valuable part of society" could be just as interesting as any story about not giving up, and might just offer a breath of fresh air to stale ideas. Art, including manga, is about expressing your ideas and views of the world, and you should be using themes you're passionate about, and have strong feelings towards, to make your story come to life.

However, before you run off writing a story about how "the world would be better off without humanity," or "sixth wave intersectional critical theory is necessary to reflect the post-modern era in which we live," you should probably remember that the simpler and more positive your theme the more likely the audience is going to respond to it. Shonen comics are aspirational, which means they're optimistic by nature, so negative and downbeat themes won't go over very well. Even heavy dramas like *Attack on Titan* (which is technically *seinen*, not *shonen*), still have a strong upbeat theme (survival in the face of odds) which carry them upwards, and not down.

Similarly, complex themes are both harder to express and understand, and will usually work against you when you're writing a story. So, it's much better to just keep your themes simple and straightforward, and if you can't express them in just a few words, they're probably too complex. The more primal the better, since everyone understands the themes of revenge, loyalty, hate, love, trust, and forgiveness and are interested in seeing other takes on those ideas. But, if it's an idea they don't understand to begin with, like historical revisionism, then you've already lost a big part of your audience from the start.

APPLYING THE THREE KEY PRINCIPLES TO THEME

The Three Key Principles of Manga aren't usually applied directly to a theme itself, but come into play when you're developing the story ideas that are going to reflect that theme.

First, when you have your theme, you should sit down and try to think of the most extreme expressions of that theme. So, for example, if your theme was friendship, then you would want to think about the most exaggerated situations that friends can find themselves in. This might be situations like friends who died for each other, friends who have each other's children, friends who raised each other's children, friends who pay each other's debts, friends who save each other's lives, and so on. These aren't normal situations, but that's the point- the most interesting stories about friendship are going to come from the most unusual situations friends find themselves in.

Then, once you have your extreme example, you take that situation and apply a little surprise twist to it. So, if it's a story about friends who die for each other, you might add in a twist about how this story is going to be about two deep sea divers who don't have enough oxygen to reach the surface without running out of air. That's an unusual situation where neither friend can talk to each other, but both know there's only one way one of them can survive- and that's to make the ultimate sacrifice. So, how do you convince the other person to let you die when you can't talk?

Lastly, of course, you want to make it relatable to the audience on primal level, so naturally these two people who have to make this terrible decision are best friends.

They should both be as similar as possible, and both have equal reasons to live or die, because that way the choice is even harder and comes down to subjective little things and the audience's own biases. This makes it deeply personal for the audience, and makes them more emotionally involved as the story goes on.

OTHER KEY CONCEPTS WHEN WRITING SHONEN MANGA

Positivity

Shonen manga, are above all, positive stories. They are about aspirational characters who are trying to make the world a better place, and who aren't easily dissuaded from that goal. Lead characters in Shonen stories are always optimistic people who know in their hearts that they can make a difference if they just try and keep at it. Sometimes they might not be very optimistic at first, but after finding their true path or direction, they will become so.

And their optimism isn't just confined to themselves and their self-confidence, it's also infectious and spreads to the people around them. There are countless examples of other shonen manga and anime characters who have found new ways of seeing the world thanks to the examples of Shonen heroes like Luffy or Naruto. These heroes' unwavering belief in themselves makes others want to improve the world as well, and join them on their journeys.

Always Rising

Linked with Positivity is the idea that the main characters in shonen stories are always advancing upwards in their goals. They might face challenges, or minor setbacks, but no matter how bad it gets they will always bounce back and keep trying until they accomplish what they've set out to do. Even death can't stop some shonen heroes from accomplishing their goals and standing by their friends in times of need.

You might notice that above it says "minor setbacks", and that's because the truth is shonen heroes almost never experience major setbacks. If they did, it would stop their advances, and bring the story to a grinding halt, which must never happen. There must be nothing that keeps the main character out of the action for longer than necessary, and there shouldn't be any introspective long "dark nights of the soul" where the main characters brood and wonder about what their life means. Those are for other kinds of stories like Batman movies.

Individual vs Collective

Most people reading this in English are likely either Western Europeans or North Americans, which means you come from a culture that prizes individual effort and accomplishment. This "Western Culture" is built around the idea that people are all individual people who are responsible for only themselves in their lives. Once they're born, they are free and independent people who should be able to make their own choices, and be accountable for those choices. In North America, the very origin myth of the continent's founding is that of rugged individuals who tamed the savage land and carved out a whole country with the sweat of their brows.

This is reflected in the entertainment as well, which idealizes the lone hero who takes charge and leads his people into victory. The ideal is the self-made man (or woman) who is able to handle themselves in any situation and uses their incredible natural talent and resources to make change and make the world a better place. A hero in Western Culture enters the game at the top of their form (or close to it), and then proceeds to show the world what they can do.

However, the Japanese point of view (and the Asian point of view to one degree or another) is a little different. Instead of seeing people as individuals, Japanese people see everyone as part of a larger group or community. To the Japanese, each person is a part of a larger network of people called a community, and everyone has their part or role to play in that community. In Japan, everyone exists to make the whole stronger, and their duty is to that community.

This collective way of thinking is naturally also reflected in Japanese entertainment. Generally, heroes in Japanese stories are either part of a community, becoming part of a community, or helping to restore a community. Even when you see a lone Japanese hero like Kenshiro from *Fist of the North Star*, or a Kamen Rider superhero, you're looking at a character who is fighting to restore peace and order, not out of some greater goal of freedom or justice. (Like an American superhero would be.) And, in most Battle Manga, characters are either becoming part of a community (joining the ranks of Fighters, Sushi Chefs, Astronauts, etc.) or they're helping to restore order to a community by fighting against people trying to disrupt it. (Aliens, Monsters, Rebels, Pirates, etc.)

Modern shonen Battle Manga tend to reflect this by having lead characters who are teens (or pre-teens) that are just entering new worlds and societies. In other words, they're finding a way to integrate themselves into a larger community and society as a whole. Their story is one of a young person finding their place in society, not venturing out to create a whole new world.

But wait! Some of you might look at the top three Battle Manga of the last decade (Naruto, One Piece, and Bleach) and say that isn't true for those stories. After all, Naruto is fighting to become Hokage, Luffy is trying to become King of the Pirates (Yo-ho!) and Ichigo is trying to protect the world from evil Hollows.

Except Naruto is trying to make himself part of the Hidden Leaf Village and its community to the point where he's its new leader. Luffy is creating a whole new community (his crew and allies), while also becoming part of the greater Pirate culture. And Ichigo finds himself becoming more and more part of the Soul Society as he fights to protect those he loves and is also building a network of his own friends.

So, as you can see, each of them is actually a story about integration and becoming part of something bigger than themselves, whether that's their direct goal or not. This makes them run counter to the Western Culture approach, which is most often about reshaping the world through the hero's efforts and force of will.

Japanese heroes are about Integration, while American heroes are about Revolution.

One final note on this- while the Japanese put emphasis on community in the form of social groups (almost to an extreme), this is not equally true for the Koreans and Chinese. In Korean culture the emphasis is placed on Family, which is why most Korean dramas are actually about family units. In old Chinese culture the emphasis was on family like Koreans, but modern Chinese culture tends to put an emphasis on friendship and personal networks. Yes, these are all different forms of community and reflect a collective culture, but each of them has their own take on it.

Walking to Heaven

The last concept that's important for manga writers to understand might just be the hardest, but it's important you're aware of it. As collective cultures see every member of society as contributing to a greater whole, they tend to rate human behavior in terms of being beneficial or detrimental to society. This can produce interesting conflicts with more European views, as some behaviors that Europeans and Americans would look down on as wastes of time or money are viewed as worthwhile because they are still contributing to greater society in their own way. Scholars, for example, hold much higher places of esteem in Asian culture than they do in Western culture exactly because of their great contributions to society's knowledge base.

Add to that, that in Asian cultures (and especially Japan) mastery of a skill or activity is considered a worthwhile goal in and of itself. So, while a Western point of view would question whether a skill or activity is worth knowing based on its ability to make money or bring value to society, in Asian culture mastery of something is considered its own reward. A lot of this comes from a line of Zen/Taoist philosophy which lurks underneath the surface in Japanese culture. This line of thinking states that one way to achieve Enlightenment (a state of pure spiritual advancement) is through absolute dedication to a task/role to the best of your ability. This translates to the idea that all human activity has value for the people who do it, and even if it only benefits the people who do it, that still means it has worth.

So, in other words, if brewing the best soy sauce, becoming the best UNO player in the world, or traveling to every country on Earth gives people's lives meaning and makes them happy- that's a good thing. As long as the people doing it are getting benefit from it, and not doing harm to themselves or others, their mastery of that thing will only benefit themselves and society as a whole by adding to the pool of human knowledge.

THE RULES OF SHONEN HEROES

The following is a short list of the "rules" which successful Shonen heroes seem to follow, can you add a few more to the list?

Real Shonen Heroes...

1. Dream big or go home
2. Are not bystanders
3. Always fight for someone else. Not themselves.
4. Always believe in their friends
5. Stay positive
6. Have a sense of humor
7. Solve problems with their own hands
8. Thrive in adversity
9. Are clueless about the opposite sex
10. Win by not giving up
11. Lead with their hearts but win with their heads
12. Get their real strength from friends they make along the way
13. ALWAYS SAVE A LITTLE SOMETHING SPECIAL FOR THE END!

BATTLE MANGA

At the heart of shonen manga lies the Battle Manga.

It holds the same place in Japanese pop culture that Superhero comics and pro-wrestling hold in American culture- dramatic and twisty stories about battles between larger than life figures for big and glorious stakes, usually life or death. In many Battle Manga, the characters either win big, or they die, and this constant struggle keeps the audience coming back for the next installment week after week.

In fact, the Battle Manga format has become so popular, that in many ways it IS modern shonen manga. Easily the majority of titles in *Weekly Shonen JUMP* or any of its sister publications or rivals will be Battle Manga, and most of what makes it to animation also uses this format to keep the viewers coming back over the months and years the shows air.

In addition, Battle Manga isn't just *Dragonball*-type fights anymore, and the format has shifted around, with different creators using the structure of Battle Manga to make stories about cooking, fishing, romance, and even writing into page-turning serials. But, before we go into detail about how to build those kinds of stories, let's look at the key elements of what makes a Battle Manga a Battle Manga.

First, a definition.

A Battle Manga is a story focused on a small group of characters in a high stakes situation fighting a series of clearly defined competitive personal duels in a limited space.

If a story meets these requirements, then it can be considered a Battle Manga.

Simple, right?

However, let's unpack that definition and look at each of the elements in detail to make things a bit clearer.

A Story Focused On...

This is a small point, but an important one to remember- Battle Manga stories are about the battle between characters first and foremost. This doesn't mean that they can't be about the characters' lives as well, but it does mean that the focus is always about people with similar goals in direct conflict with each other. This is what makes a Battle Manga different from an adventure story, where the focus is about characters overcoming obstacles and solving problems. Like pro-wrestling, Battle Manga always need to be centered around the competitive element of the story, and all the character's lives revolve around that competitive element as well.

This is what keeps a story like Harry Potter, which meets some of the criteria in the definition, from being a Battle Manga type story- it's about the adventure of growing up in a magical society. For Harry Potter to be a Battle Manga, every story would need to be about him dueling evil wizards in a series of competitions, or would need to revolve around Quidditch, the magical broom sport.

...A Small Group...

Like any good story, the creators of Battle Manga keep their casts relatively small. Yes, stories like *One Piece* and *Naruto* have large supporting casts, but any particular battle story arc will see that cast reduced down to just a few of those characters. Even *One Piece*, with its ever-growing pirate crew as the heroes, constantly splits the crew up in later story arcs with the goal of keeping the number of people involved in any one story manageable.

The first commandment of writing is- "thou shalt not confuse thy audience," and the more characters involved, the greater the chance there is for confusion, so Battle Manga try to keep the number of people involved in any battle to the bare minimum and usually break fights off into manageable paired simultaneous duels.

...Of Characters...

Battle Manga lead heroes are simply-drawn (both literally and figuratively) characters who are goal-oriented, positive people that never give up or surrender to the odds. They are powered by their own internal beliefs in themselves and their goals, and this incredible and unquenchable inner strength allows them to defeat any foe in the long run. Sometimes it will be because they used their own inner power to push their abilities beyond their limits, and sometimes it will be because their positivity let them inspire others to also do their best, but either way their stubborn inability to give up lets them rise above the crowd and go beyond normal limits.

Most often, they are Unchanging heroes, who only rise in power during the story but don't actually change much as people beyond a few superficial traits, but occasionally they will be slightly more realistic types that are affected by the challenges that they overcome.

In the case of Fighting Manga, the main character will generally be limited to hand-to-hand combat because it represents their determination to make their dreams come true with their own hands. As the story goes on, they will slowly develop ranged abilities of some kind, but their strongest attacks will always be ones they deliver with their own hands (or a hand-held weapon) since that represents their inner strength overcoming their foes.

The supporting cast will always include one cynic who doubts the main character's abilities, a fellow cool character who follows a similar path to the main character, a mentor who encourages them, and an innocent character who is learning from the main character. The Main Opponent will always have some personal connection with the lead character which makes their conflict stronger and more bittersweet, although it might not always be an antagonistic one.

....In a High Stakes Situation...

In many Battle Manga, the stakes in any story are life or death, but this doesn't always have to be the case. The important thing is that the stakes in the competition are important to the characters involved, even if the competition itself is for something relatively small. So, this means that even if the competition is over something as minor as who gets to have the first piece of pie, to the characters it needs to be a big deal. The reason it's a big deal can be emotional ("The person who gets the first piece of pie is the most important person at this table, and that needs to be me!"), social ("If I get the first piece, I can give it to Haru-chan and she'll know how much I love her!") or even financial ("I can auction this first piece of this legendary pie off to the highest bidder and make serious cash!"), but to the character it should be significant.

The reason it has to be a big deal to the character is because if the audience sees the character really cares, then they will as well. However, you can have situations where the character doesn't consider it a big deal, but the audience knows that it actually is (just the character is unaware of the stakes involved), and this can also produce tension and drama. Which is the key point, after all, as without high stakes the competition won't mean a whole lot, and that meaningfulness is what generates drama.

...Fighting a Series...

Most Battle Manga are about a "war" which is being fought in a series of smaller battles. Whether it's the main characters fighting minions as they work their way up to the big boss, or a tournament where they're progressing through the levels of a competition. The key is that it shouldn't just be a bunch of individual stand-alone fights in the story, but competitions which are steps on a road to accomplishing a larger goal. The audience needs to feel the main character is making progress towards a goal of some kind, and that these battles are necessary obstacles on the path to making that goal into a reality.

Also, while Battle Manga can be as short or long as needed, they are optimally designed to be serialized and play out over many chapters in a rhythmic series of highs and lows building towards a powerful and surprising finish. Most chapters should end in some kind of Event or dramatic question that compels the reader to jump to the next chapter to find out what happens, and the whole series of chapters in the Story Arc should fit together to form a clear larger story, and perhaps a story within a story.

...Of Clearly Defined...

In order to enjoy a competition of some kind, the audience needs to understand the rules and nature of the game. In the case of physical battles like martial arts duels, this is simple and straightforward, but when it comes to things like card games or sports, the rules get more complicated and the audience must be educated about those rules so they're not left wondering what's going on.

It's not enough for the audience to know what the stakes are, or to like the characters, they must be able to enjoy the flow of the competition and appreciate the strategies that the characters are using to win. While they might not always be able to follow everything in more complicated competitions, they still need to be able to understand most of it, or they'll tune out or get bored.

Just remember, simple is best, and only tell the audience as much as they need to know to understand what's going on, and nothing more, to avoid overloading them.

...Competitive...

Battle Manga are obviously based around competition, and so there needs to be a competitive element to them, but you should remember that the competitive element is really just there to provide some risk and drama to the story. As Battle Manga like *Yi-Gi-Oh!* (the pre-card game version) and *Jojo's Bizarre Adventure* have proven, almost anything can be turned into a competitive battle, even a simple game of rock-paper-scissors or growing flowers. However, the more exciting (and easier to write) stories usually tend to be based around actual physical combat or a directly competitive sport because the audience will know the rules and be more into it.

Also, the main character will almost always win at the end of each fight, often because if they don't then the story will come to a grinding halt. You know this, and the audience knows this, but the thing to keep in mind is that the audience isn't there to see IF the main character(s) win, but HOW the main character wins. Don't become obsessed with trying to reinvent the wheel by having some big dramatic twist ending, which some writers become fixed on, and instead focus on telling the most interesting journey to the ending that the audience wants and knows is coming.

...Personal Duels...

One of the important differences between Battle Manga and typical adventure stories is that the battles in Battle Manga are usually very personal. While in an adventure story the hero will face off against a legion of faceless minions and then face a largely one-dimensional evil boss villain at the end, in Battle Manga most of the opponents the heroes face will also be clearly defined characters with personalities, goals, and usually tragic pasts. This is done to heighten the drama, since watching a battle between two fully developed characters is much more exciting and intense than watching a hero mow down paper cut-outs.

Also, the more the heroes have a personal connection with their opposition, the more story elements the writer has to play with. Conflicted heroes are the best heroes, because they have inner battles raging as well as outer ones, and this interplay between emotions and goals during the battle will really help to take it to the next level. Which is also why the characters with the deepest connections to the heroes are usually the ones they face closest to the end of the story.

And finally, it also gives the writers of Battle Manga an interesting way to fill out their page counts (they're paid by the page, after all) by telling the story of the opposition's dramatic history that brought them into conflict with the heroes.

...In a Limited Space.

Writers of Battle Manga should always follow the Arena Principal (see *Settings*) to make sure that their characters are kept as close together as possible, and not be put in situations where they can easily escape. This not only keeps the tension up, but it also makes it simpler to write and answers the dreaded question of "why don't they just run away?"

Some reason, be it personal, physical, social, emotional or otherwise, must prevent the character(s) from simply avoiding the competitive situation. Usually, the competition stands between the characters and their goals, but there can be other reasons as well. A brilliant example is *One Piece*, where the characters are travelling between islands, which function as arenas the characters must achieve victory in before they can leave and go to the next island. Each island is a limited battle space where characters can't easily avoid enemies and must fight until the situation is resolved in order to complete their goals and move on.

Types of Battle Manga

Any manga which adheres to the above definition can in theory be called a Battle Manga, and this isn't affected by length, genre, style, or the focus of the story. A Battle Manga story can be character focused, plot focused, or even setting focused, but as long as it meets most of the criteria in that definition, it's a Battle Manga.

As a result, creators have used the Battle Manga formula for a wide variety of story types, most of which seem to fall into one of two different categories: Fighting Manga and Activity Dramas. In a lot of ways, these two types of Battle Manga are almost the same, and some manga are actually hybrids of the two, but they are different enough in focus and goals that they're worth looking at separately.

Fighting Manga- These are what people think of when they think of "Battle Manga," and includes legendary titles like *Dragonball Z, Naruto, One Piece, Bleach*, and more. Sometimes also referred to as "Shonen Fight" manga, or other names, these are stories about characters literally battling and fighting each other for some prize.

Activity Dramas- These are non-combat Battle Manga stories where the competitions take other forms, and includes titles like *Liar Game, Hikaru no Go, Haikyuu, Prince of Tennis*, and many more. Stories about collecting cards or monsters and having them fight often fall into this category as well, but not always. The focus of activity dramas is on how competition brings people together, and they usually have a learning/teaching component to them where the audience is being educated about a topic.

In the following sections, we'll look at these two major categories of Battle Manga in detail, but just remember that these are only two of endless possible ways of using the Battle Manga form. A clever writer can use it to tell exciting stories about almost any topic.

BATTLE MANGA CHARACTER PROGRESSION

When planning a story, one of the things writers need to think about is character progression- are the characters going to develop and change as the story goes on? This is a simple question, but the answer to it is both important and complicated.

It is especially important to manga creators because serialized manga are often intended to run for as long as they're popular and make money. However, if the characters change and grow, or worse – reach their goals, then the story and audience will both be done with it. So, manga creators are advised to think deeply about how they're going to progress their stories right from the start.

And this is where things get complicated.

How much progression do you include- if any? And, how fast will things progress? If you promise progression and don't give it, audiences will lose interest. But, even if you're giving it too quickly, you'll run out of story and be forced to come up with new ways to try to keep a story going that probably should have ended already. (Which almost never goes well.)

It's worth mentioning that for a long time, manga creators didn't even bother with character progression, and it wasn't until the 1980s that it started to become common. As a result, you will still see stories which have little to no progression at all (mostly comedies, which don't need it as much), and they can work fine and be quite popular.

In a story with little to no character progression, the story arcs have only minimal connection with each other, and may have none at all. You can almost think of non-progressing stories as a series of self-contained stories linked only by characters (or plot, or theme) that may or may not have any connection to each other at all. A good manga example of this are the manga 4-koma gag strips that run everywhere. The story isn't building to anything at all, and a new reader could read the stories in almost any order and would be fine. Although there is some benefit to reading the different series' in order, it isn't required.

And that's the key, in a non-progressing story, the overall story isn't the point or really that important: the stories themselves are usually about the characters and the setting more than they are some great plot or events. Some writers prefer to write this way, and some choose to do it because it creates lots of jumping on points for new readers. A lot of early 1970s and 1980s shonen comics were structured this way (like

City Hunter, Doctor Slump, and *Mazinger Z*) with the main character often having an overall goal, but only drifting toward it without a clear progression.

That stands in comparison with a progressing story, which became the dominant style for shonen comics after *Dragonball Z* took the world by storm. Writers and editors discovered that fans loved to see the characters clearly moving toward some major goal, and it allowed for stories to be bigger and more engrossing than before. As a result, modern readers are now used to stories where the main character's steps are all interlinked in some way, and building towards a great overall climax that will blow everyone's minds.

While the mind-blowing may or may not occur, progressive stories are now the common way of doing things. Writers give characters a strong and clear goal right from the start, and then the characters march along towards that goal, going up in skill, knowledge, and power level as they progress. How tight the structure is will depend on the writer (and if they're sure they can keep the epic story going for year after year), but generally there will be a clear progression there, and readers enjoy seeing the characters develop and grow.

With this in mind, one way a writer can plan out their character's progression is simply by looking at the procedural steps involved in whatever goal the character is trying to reach and use those as a guide. This is especially useful for Battle Manga, and pretty much required for Task manga stories. It can be broken down into five basic approaches: the step approach, the level approach, the status approach, the cluster approach, and the acquisition approach.

The Step Approach

In an Activity or Task manga, the main character is almost always learning or using a real world set of skills or knowledge and working toward a clear real-world goal. This is a great advantage for the writer, since that means there is already a pre-defined set of steps to learning that skill or gaining that knowledge out there, and the writer can use those as a guide. It doesn't matter whether the topic is playing Poker or becoming a politician, there are guidebooks and videos out there to teach you the steps you need to know to master any activity. The writer just needs to break those steps down into story arcs (or chapters), and use those as a guide for what happens in each of those parts of the story.

In a shonen battle manga which uses the step approach, you're doing much the same thing, but since the story often isn't rooted as deeply in the real-world the writer is free to come up with their own steps instead of using pre-existing ones. That said, there are great advantages to using real-world steps for somewhat related fictional subjects, including that it makes the character's journey much more realistic and relatable for the reader. Not only that, it makes the writer's job easier as well, since they're not forced to re-invent the wheel.

So, for example, if you're writing about a character learning magical combat spells, you could base their learning steps off the steps involved in learning martial arts moves, or maybe coding computers, or perhaps in learning to play an instrument. Each of these has clear steps, and while you might need to add a few more to include magical training or modify the steps, the point is that it makes your progression more natural and adds depth to your story.

The Level Approach

Since the modern world is inundated with video games of all kinds, readers are naturally familiar with the concept of characters having a ranked level at an activity, and this goes back to roleplaying games like *Dungeons and Dragons*, where the characters had numbered levels to represent their advancement in the game world, and it spread from there to computer games and fighting games. Therefore, it's a natural transition for characters in Fighting Manga stories to have levels as well, and you can use these to help rank your characters in their world.

Of course, numbers (or other ranking systems like colors, crystals, metals, etc.) don't actually mean much to you or the reader unless you sit down and quantify them. What can a Rank 5 Magical Fighter do that a Rank 1 Magical Fighter can't? You're best to decide what the range of ranks is (say 1-50, or 1-500) and then decide what the top rank can do and the bottom rank can do, and figure out the steps in between. You don't have to quantify all the steps, but make notes about what happens on the major ones ("When they reach Level 14, they can learn a second magical element.") and what ones will result in the character's change of social status as well. (Rank 1-5 is newbie, Rank 6-10 is Learner, Rank 11-15 is Journeyman, etc.) Also, think about the difficulty and requirements to advance between levels as well because some level based systems become progressively harder to advance in the higher you go (often requiring more time/experience to move up to the next level), and there may be special things the character must do to move between rank categories (You must make your own magical staff to progress from Newbie to Learner, for example.)

Levels in Fighting Manga also serve another purpose- they're instant drama creators. When the audience can clearly see the level difference between a character and their opponent, it's a fast way to create tension. Maybe the main character can overcome a five-level gap, but could they overcome a 10-level gap or a 50-level gap? No way! In those situations, the main character and the audience knows that combat just isn't an option, and it creates instant tension. Just be careful not to overuse this trick too much, or the audience will get tired of it.

Obviously, you might think that the level approach doesn't apply to Activity Manga stories, after all, we don't have ranked levels in real life activities, right? However, this isn't entirely true. In the ancient board game of Go, players have roughly 39 ranked levels (30 learner levels and 9 master ones), and this learner/master level system is also used in East Asian martial arts as well. (They got it from Go.) Also, there are some other activities out there where players or participants have ranked levels, including in games, in education, and in some organizations. So, using levels to measure a character's progress in a story is completely do-able even in some real-life situations.

However, outside of those fairly specific situations, level systems don't work well for Activity Manga overall, and aren't a good way to structure progression. So, most writers aren't advised to use this type of system unless it really fits.

The Status Approach

A third way to structure a character's progression is based on the character's status within the society or culture that surrounds their activity. In this approach, the character must meet certain requirements to move on to the next status rank, which will have a name instead of a number like in the level system. These requirements often come in the form of skills, experience, time, social/political favor, or accomplishments, and as a result sometimes combine with the Step Approach.

For example, maybe the character needs to learn a certain ten skills to go from Dishwasher to Assistant Cook, and so a whole story arc could be constructed around the learning of some of those skills. Or perhaps a character needs to log a certain amount of time on the job to go from Trainee to Rookie, and one or more arcs can be about the character's "Trainee" phase, and then the following one(s) will be about their "Rookie" phase, and so on. A political character might need to win a certain number of elections, or a certain size of constituency to move up in rank, and that would be the structure for their arcs.

And so on.

As you can see, this is often the real-world equivalent of the Level Approach, but tends to work better for Activity Manga type stories because it also includes natural requirements to move between levels. The only downside is that you have to teach the audience what those ranks mean and the requirements that go with them, and then use a system that the audience will remember. But, in an Activity Manga teaching about real-world things is often half the point, so that usually isn't an issue.

Where things get trickier is with Fighting Manga, but even there you can use real-world models to help guide your progressions. For example, you could use an Apprentice> Craftsman> Master progression like the trades of Bakers, Carpenters and Masons traditionally used, but expand it out to include steps like Apprentice> Novice> Learner> High Learner> Journeyman> Master> Grand Master. Or, not expand it at all, and just have the character spend a certain phase of their story as an Apprentice then move to Craftsman at the halfway point, and then become a Master at the end.

The only issue here is that audiences like to see progression, and if you use large steps or have long periods with no progression, the audience may feel like the story isn't advancing, which isn't good for a Battle Manga. Also, if you choose not to use a real-world model, and to create your own terms for the different status ranks, you need to make sure they're ones the reader can easily follow and understand without constantly checking a chart. (One of the advantages of numbered ranks.) One tip here is to use a ranking system that the reader knows and modify it a bit into a status system. For example, audiences know the relative ranked values of common metals (Copper> Silver> Gold> Platinum) and those could be worked into the names. (So, a Copper Apprentice ranks lower than a Silver Apprentice, and that's obvious to almost all readers.)

The Cluster Approach

The second last method for structuring a story around progression is one where the author clusters skills or attributes to be learned based on the needs of the story at that point rather than any real-world progression system. For example, the character is going through a social arc, so they must learn social skills, or a wilderness arc needs survival skills. These may or may not be building toward a greater test of ability at the end of the arcs, but it does allow a grouping of the types of skills needed based on story needs.

Also, the writer can base these clusters of skills off abstract things like stages of life or spiritual enlightenment, or use them to reflect the story's Thematic Statement by working through examples or counter-examples of the greater point they're trying to make. If you're arguing that characters should have self-confidence to be successful in life, for example, you could structure your story arcs around what you think are the steps the character needs to go through to find that self-confidence. (Which may or may not involve some research into human psychology.)

Of course, this method has the dis-advantage that you can't really use it well to rank the character among their peers, or to show clear progression in a quantified way. The audience might vaguely understand the progression, but it likely won't be as exciting or visceral as you might want a Battle Manga to actually be unless you combine it with one of the other methods in some way.

The Acquisition Approach

In shonen manga, the final approach to structuring your story progression is about the main character acquiring or collecting things. At first glance, this could be called the *Pokémon* Approach or *Yu-Gi-Oh!* approach, but it can actually be used in other ways than kids collecting monsters or cards. This is about a story where the main character's goal is to collect objects, people, titles, or anything else that involves a clear progression towards having a complete set. For example, this could be used to structure a story about becoming a pirate king and assembling a crew (*One Piece*), finding magic wishing balls (*Dragonball*), or even assembling a team of skilled surgeons needed to perform a special operation (*Medical Team Dragon*). The key here is that the main character's final goal can only be completed if they have a total set of something, and the progression is represented by completeness of that set.

This approach is especially good for Fighting Manga stories where the main character is often not changing much beyond getting more skilled or powerful, so making the focus on some other exterior kind of progression keeps it simple. In addition, this also naturally creates plots as different things being assembled will have different circumstances that go with each of them. *One Piece* structures itself around how each new member joins the crew of the ship, while *Dragonball* has the characters assembling scattered magic balls which are literally everywhere.

One issue with Acquisition stories that writers should be aware of, though, is that you need to establish the goal right from the start, and if you have too many things you need to assemble the story might end up being too long and run out of energy. Or, on the other hand, if you have too few things to assemble the story might be over faster than you'd like because the audience wants progression, and if you slow down the progression too much it might result in audience frustration.

A simple way to fix this, however, is to combine the Acquisition approach with one of the others, so that the character(s) are progressing in different ways and the audience feels both moving forward. This can allow the audience to accept slower progress on the acquisitions front while enjoying the lead characters gaining strength or ranks. But, as the writer, you will still need to decide which one you're actually structuring the story around from the start, with the other being more there for flavor and audience fun.

In the end, the key to using progression as a guide for story structure is to just remember that everything learned in life involves beginner, intermediate, veteran and mastery phases. The types of stories you'll find in shonen manga are no different, and these make for great guides when planning and plotting your long-term stories.

FIGHTING MANGA

Fighting Manga are stories about direct competition, where the characters face a series of competitive situations and need to find ways to overcome them and normally also advance within their activity of choice. They may or may not involve superpowers or magical elements, and can be built around almost any activity with a strong direct competitive element. (Or which can be made competitive by the attitudes of the characters participating in it, or the stakes involved.)

This structure likely evolved from Japanese and Chinese Martial Arts fiction and other serial fiction of the early 20thcentury, but it definitely came into its own in the late 1980's, after which it became the dominant form of story structure in mainstream shonen titles.

The emphasis in these comics is going to be fighting, levelling, and lots of it! Generally speaking, these stories will follow a talented new fighter who joins the world of duels and then fights an ever-escalating series of opponents to become the top fighter of his type. This type of story is extremely popular, and was perfected by *Dragonball Z*, after which all Fighting Manga began to follow this formula. The audience gets vicarious thrills as they watch their favorite hero fight his way through an endless series of ever more bizarre opponents and learn weird martial arts or fighting techniques that let them become king of the fighters. (Note- these fights can be physical, social, psychological, or take any other form. *Death Note* is also a shonen Fight comic, but it looks nothing like *Dragonball* on the surface.)

FIGHTING MANGA THEMES

As mentioned in the chapter on Manga Audiences, shonen manga are built on three key concepts-*Friendship, Effort, and Victory.* They are about people finding friends, struggling together, and achieving victory through their unity and efforts. This a very Japanese (and Asian) way of looking at the world, as their cultures focus on collective effort and achieving through hard work. This also runs opposite to the North American way of thinking, which is about achievement through individual effort, taking the easiest route to power, and mastering the world around you by virtue of being the best. (Oddly enough, this is the most common Villain perspective in Fighting Manga, which highlights the different worldviews between the two.)

So, what is the core idea of a Fighting Manga?

Through hard work and effort towards <a directly competitive activity>, you can achieve your personal best and become part of a community.

That's it. If you work hard, and become the best you can be at your passion, you will find personal happiness, social respect, and become part of a community.

And some of the ways this argument is supported in Fighting Manga are:

- Those who stand in opposition to our Main Character are always people who have a flawed approach to the competitive element, take the goal half-heartedly, or are trying to do it through shortcuts (like wealth, cheating, crutches, tricks, etc.)
- There are always people who are trying to master the goal, but failing in some way because they're missing something. (Not "pure" or flawed in their thinking or approach to it.)
- There are always people who consider the goal the path to "godhood", which in this case means self-actualization (being all you can be).
- In the stories, the ones who win are always the ones who work the hardest at it and don't quit.
- They find a supportive community through pursuit of their goal of choice. (reward, public esteem)
- Opponents almost always come to see the Main Character's way as the "true" way, and those who come to understand this become allies or at least "reform".
- The love interest (if there is one, as sometimes there isn't in this genre) comes to respect and support the Main Character because of their hard work, acting both as inspiration and reward. (They won't get with the hero until the Main Character has accomplished their goal.) And, occasionally also being inspired by the Main Character to pursue their own goal, often one related to the main goal of the story. (Taking up the Main Character's art, sport or game of choice, for example.)

SUPPORTING ARGUMENTS

There are also supporting arguments in any Fighting Manga which will help to keep the story on track. Here are a few of them:

- Reaching your goal is easier (and more fun) with a community supporting you.
- Practitioners of the competitive element must be good citizens and represent their community well to the greater world.
- People respect those who work hard.
- Quitters never win.
- Hard work trumps talent.
- Talent is needed, but it is only a foundation upon which hard work can build.
- Focusing on just one aspect of the competitive element is not enough, you must be well rounded and flexible. (Usually demonstrated by the Main Character facing an opponent who is massive in one aspect of the competitive element, but not in the other aspects, making them challenging but ultimately still losers.)

Sometimes people mistake the above arguments for the main Core Argument of the story, but if you think about it, you'll see that they only serve to help the real argument of trying to achieve your potential through mastery of an activity.

OVERALL PLOT STRUCTURE

And like any process, there is a clear pattern to how these stories progress, and tightly focused Fighting Manga tend to go through the following stages:

Character Driven Stories

KI- Introduction

- **Gaining Power**– the Main Character is introduced as a normal person living a normal life for their particular setting, then an event occurs where the competitive element (magic, superpowers, ninjutsu, etc.) enters their lives. As the Main Character is usually living an unfulfilled life in some way, they come to believe that the competitive element might be a possible solution to fill that void and begin to pursue it. Sometimes they are reluctant, in which case there will be some character or event which forces them to embrace the competitive element, or sometimes the Main Character starts motivated, in which case there will be a scene where they explain the reason they're already motivated to another character instead. In any case, the audience is presented with the Main Character's reasons for pursuing the competitive element by the end of the opening story.
- **It's Easy!** – the Main Character engages in the competitive element and shows a natural talent or ability for it, allowing them to score their first victory. This gives them the confidence to move forward, and the feeling that this competitive element will bring them pleasure and give them something they've been missing from their lives.

SHO- Development

- **Maybe it's Not So Easy?** – The Main Character encounters their first real hurdle to becoming part of this competitive element - occasionally through an encounter with the Main Opponent. Their early victory was a product of talent, but they quickly learn that talent alone isn't enough, as those who have skill can trump their talent easily. Now they're forced to actually start to learn and explore the competitive element on a basic level.
- **A Whole New World**– The Main Character is introduced to the subculture which exists surrounding the competitive element. Through a guide character (or characters) they discover that there is a whole new world hiding within the community that engages in the competitive element. From this discovery, they begin their first steps into joining that community, and are given basic knowledge about that competitive element.
- **A New Path**– Now combining Talent and Skill, the Main Character starts on their real journey towards becoming a master of the competitive element. They have their first major victory, and get their taste of what it's like to be part of this new community while facing a skilled Opponent (usually the one from **Maybe it's Not So Easy?**) who has a flawed approach to the activity in some basic way. This opponent will seem strong at first, but the lead will realize due to their new skills that this opponent is actually weak because they haven't

mastered the fundamentals. Using those same fundamentals combined with talent, the Main Character will defeat them utterly.

TEN- Activity

- **The Long Road**– Now that they've entered this new world built around the competitive element, the Main Character will begin their path towards mastery. During this stage, they will meet a successive series of Opponents and challenges, make new friends, and learn more and more about the competitive element. This stage is extremely flexible, and can take as long as the story needs it to take, or as long as the steps needed to master the competitive element require. Generally, each "step" along The Long Road is a story arc that will follow the same pattern:

  a) The Main Character encounters a new opponent who is strong in an area where the Main Character is still weak or has knowledge the Main Character lacks. (This can also be a challenge or task which can't be defeated with the Main Character's current skill set.)

  b) The Main Character is defeated by this new opponent/challenge. (Whose ability over the Main Character is often coded by being referred to by a special name)

  c) The Main Character figures out why they were defeated (often by consulting others or through experimentation).

  d) The Main Character seeks and finds a solution to the problem. (Learning new skills/ideas along the way, and possibly a counter-technique.)

  e) While the Main Character is improving, the Main Character's Sidekicks may try to fight the opponent or opponent's allies. If they face the Story Arc Opponent, they will lose but their loss will either gain information or help to inspire the Main Character to act. If they are facing the Opponent's allies, they will fight hard battles but eventually win around the same time the Main Character does.

  f) The Main Character faces the opponent/challenge again, and wins this time because of their new skills/knowledge.

  g) The Main Character is rewarded for their efforts by the praise of others. (If this praise comes from the Opponent, they often become friends or allies after this.)

h) Return to Step a)

- **Rising Competition–** While the Main Character is rising, they may periodically re-encounter the Main Opponent in diverse ways, usually ones that result in indirect competition between them. (Teasing their final conflict and building tension.) This indirect competition is usually through other people who do the competitive element (defeating the people each other have faced or each other's allies) and sometimes by competing in various aspects of the competitive element besides the main one. Also, because of this ongoing rivalry, the Main Opponent will also begin to become stronger as well, overcoming personal hurdles and staying ahead of the Main Character even when it seems like the Main Character is starting to catch up.

- **Social Advancement–** as the Main Character defeats more and more challenges, they also rise up within the sub-culture surrounding the competitive element. They will often find themselves drawn into the politics and deeper aspects of the community and must learn to find their place inside the community. Usually they will learn that the community is bigger than they first imagined, and has far greater depths. They will also make enemies in the community who are threatened by their advancement and/or the changes they represent to the community as it exists now. Those enemies will usually become supporters of the Main Opponent, and help to drive the growing conflict between the Main Character and Main Opponent. Some of them may also try to trap or distract the Main Character through offers of positions of status or profit if they discontinue their journey, but even if tempted, the Main Character will always refuse in the end.

- **Eye of the Tiger–** The Main Character has now mastered/learned all they need to know and become a major figure in their competitive element. They must now face the Main Opponent in a true match to prove their level of competitive element and take their place as a master of the competitive element. Often the Main Character will have a crisis of confidence at this point, thinking they aren't really ready yet, but they'll overcome it and defeat the Main Opponent. Usually the Main Opponent is flawed in some way, often in their thinking or outlook about the competitive element, and the Main Character's victory is due to their purity of outlook, thus showing the audience that their way is the true path to victory in the end.

KETSU- Conclusion

- **Towards the Future–** The Main Character is now a master of the competitive element, and is shown to have a whole new life because of it. They are a happy and fully realized person and member of society who confidently knows their place in the world and is happy within it. The competitive element and subculture around it have benefitted and changed because of the Main Character's entry into it, and they can look back with nostalgia and look forward with anticipation to watching the competitive element grow and flourish under them. Often this is represented by them helping to bring new people into the activity and starting the cycle anew.

Plot Driven Stories

KI- Introduction

- **Our Hero** – The Main Character is a powerful and mysterious figure coming in from outside normal society (a foreign land, isolated village, other world, remote farmhouse, etc.) and is introduced through the eyes of another supporting character (usually a stranger who needs help). Through the eyes of this stranger, we learn what the Main Character is like and what their clear long-term goal is. This Main Character will be highly motivated, usually because of some event in their past we will be shown; however, they will be often viewed as a fool because of their lack of knowledge of the greater world. The lead will proceed to demonstrate their power by defeating a powerful opponent in the opening story, usually to the surprise of the supporting character who underestimated them. Often the supporting character lacked hope or courage, but they gain some by being inspired by the mysterious stranger.

SHO- Development

- **The Journey Begins** -Following the opening encounter, the focus of the story will shift to the Main Character and their journey to accomplish their goals. Often, they will be accompanied by their new ally (the stranger from the opening) and will begin working towards their goal. The Main Character will learn about the world from their new ally, and the new ally will learn about the lead's mysterious powerful abilities from the Main Character. This is where the rules surrounding the Main Character's competitive element (magic, martial arts, ninjutsu, psychic powers, etc.) will be explained to the audience, as well as the setting. Another opponent will be defeated who is slightly more dangerous than the last one, but this opponent usually has connections to some greater enemy.

- **Learning to Trust** – The first story arc (which often includes <u>The Journey Begins</u> in it) will be about the Main Character and their ally learning to trust each other. Usually the ally will have serious flaws or issues, and they find themselves drawing strength from the Main Character. Often, they may doubt the Main Character's intentions or abilities, and as a result be captured or lead astray by the first Arc Opponent the Main Character faces. However, in the end of the first arc, the Main Character will show they are worthy of the ally's trust and their partnership will be solidified. Often the Main Character also learns they have a long way to go to reach their goal, and a long-term opponent may also be hinted at or shown.

TEN- Activity

- **The Long Road**– Now firmly on a road towards their goal, the Main Character will begin to advance in a clear direction towards achieving it. During this stage, they will meet a successive series of Opponents and challenges, make new friends, and learn more and more about their competitive element. This stage is extremely flexible, and can take as long as the story needs it to take, or as long as the steps needed to master the activity require. Generally, each "step" along The Long Road is a story arc that will follow the same pattern:

    a) The Main Character encounters a new opponent who is strong in an area where the Main Character is still weak or has knowledge the Main Character lacks. (This can also be a challenge or task which can't be defeated with the Main Character's current skill set.)

    b) The Main Character is defeated by this new opponent/challenge. (Whose ability over the Main Character is often coded by being referred to by a special name)

    c) The Main Character figures out why they were defeated (often by consulting others or through experimentation).

    d) The Main Character seeks and finds a solution to the problem. (Learning new skills/ideas along the way, and possibly a counter-technique.)

    e) While the Main Character is improving, the Main Character's Sidekicks may try to fight the opponent or opponent's allies. If they face the Story Arc Opponent, they will lose but their loss will either gain information or help to inspire the Main Character to act. If they are facing the Opponent's allies, they will fight hard battles but eventually win around the same time the Main Character does.

f) The Main Character faces the opponent/challenge again, and wins this time because of their new skills/knowledge.

g) The Main Character is rewarded for their efforts by praise of others. (If this praise comes from the Opponent, they often become friends or allies after this.)

h) Return to Step a)

- **Rising Competition–** While the Main Character is rising, they will gain a larger and larger place in the world they live in and so will find themselves facing tougher and tougher opponents and situations. They are moving up a food chain, and with each level the competition becomes more and more fierce. They will often gain more allies as they continue their journey, who will support them in various ways and keep the Main Character's social circle lively. They will also eventually discover a Main Opponent exists– the one who sits at the top of the food chain, and the Main Opponent will also notice the Main Character. If they do clash, the Main Character will usually lose badly, demonstrating how powerful the main opponent is, and making the Main Character redouble their efforts to become stronger.

- **Social Advancement–** as the Main Character defeats more and more challenges, they also rise up within the sub-culture surrounding the competitive element. They will often find themselves drawn into the politics and deeper aspects of the community and must learn to find their place inside the community. Usually they will learn that the community is bigger than they first imagined, and has far greater depths. They will also make enemies in the community who are threatened by their advancement and/or the changes they represent to the community as it exists now. Those enemies will usually become supporters of the Main Opponent, and help to drive the growing conflict between the Main Character and Main Opponent. Some of them may also try to trap or distract the Main Character through offers of positions of status or profit if they discontinue their journey, but even if tempted, the Main Character will always refuse in the end.

- **Eye of the Tiger–** The Main Character has now mastered/learned all they need to know and become a major figure in their competitive element. They must now face the Main Opponent in a true match to prove their level of ability and take their place as a master of the competitive element. Usually the Main Opponent is flawed in some way, often in their thinking or outlook about the competitive element, and the Main Character's victory is due to their purity of outlook, thus showing the audience that their way is the true path to victory in the end.

KETSU- Conclusion

- **Towards the Future**– The Main Character is now a master of the competitive element, and is shown to have a whole new life because of it. They are a happy and fully realized person and member of society who confidently knows their place in the world and is happy within it. The competitive element and subculture around it have benefitted and changed because of the Main Character's entry into it, and they can look back with nostalgia and look forward with anticipation to watching the competitive element grow and flourish under them. Often this is represented by them helping to bring new people into the activity and starting the cycle anew.

Plot Structure Notes

- Fighting Manga are almost always driven more by the events or the emotions of the characters. The setting is usually just there for flavor, and provides only two things– the competitive element of the story and a landscape for the characters to fight on. (Fighting Manga comics are notorious for the lack of detail in their panel backgrounds, partly because the background doesn't really matter to the events and character interplay.)
- Plot based Fighting Manga are usually about exploring new worlds, and are outward facing by nature, so they mesh well with plots about adventure and exploration. Character based Fighting Manga tend to have an inward focus, and so are usually about characters learning about themselves and becoming parts of communities, so they work better with dramatic stories and ones about character interaction.

CHARACTER TROPES

Of course, every genre also has a lot of Tropes that go with it, and the Fighting Manga genre is no different. Here is a list of many of the standard tropes you'll find in almost any Fighting Manga story to one degree or another, which shouldn't be viewed as clichés so much as what's been proven to work by legions of writers producing these types of stories.

- Fighting Manga Main Characters can be Changing or Unchanging leads.
- In plot-driven stories they are usually Unchanging Characters who start the story having already gained some power and with their positive attitudes, goals and beliefs already in place. In these cases, sometimes the Main Character and the Protagonist will be different people, with the "cool" Unchanging lead character as the Protagonist and the "uncool" Main Character being an Innocent character who is Changing and growing in the Protagonist's shadow.
- In character-driven stories, they will usually be Changing leads who have power thrust upon them by circumstances and often don't want it, but must learn to cope with it for the sake of the people around them.
- In plot driven stories, and occasionally character driven ones, the Main Character will be a bit dense and lack knowledge of the greater world, both as a comic aspect, and because it forces the others to explain the details of the setting in simple and diverse ways, thus teaching the audience those details at the same time.
- The Main Character will always have a hidden talent for their competitive element, which gives them an edge over other newbies, but needs to be developed and refined through hard work. If it is a "beast mode" power up that lets them boost their strengths for a short period of time, usually they can't control it at first and must learn to do so over time.
- The Main Character will almost always have some mysterious element to them, usually their origins or the origins of their power(s). This will be a mystery which will run most of the story and usually be revealed near the end, and often be some connection to their Main Opponent.
- The Main Character's outlook on the competitive element will sometimes be flawed in some way, and overcoming this flaw will usually be the final hurdle that lets them overcome the Main Opponent. (Often, it will be linked with some personal flaw or need they have, but not always.)
- The Main Character must make sacrifices to achieve their goal, usually physical and social ones. (Health, relationships, other opportunities, etc.)
- The Main Character always gives 110% to their competitive element, which is what sets them apart from others who do the competitive element.

PLOT TROPES

- There will always be a Main Opponent who acts as the "final boss" for our hero to defeat and who has the same top spot our Main Character wants to occupy. He or she may or may not be evil, and may even have a good relationship with the hero, but they're still the one the Main Character needs to beat to achieve mastery of their activity of choice.
- The Main Opponent will be far ahead of the Main Character at the start (and renowned for their genius at the activity), but their approach is flawed and their development usually plateaued, which lets the Main Character catch up. (Although, interacting with the hero in some way will normally let the Main Opponent start to move forward again once the Main Character starts to catch up.) Although they still don't overcome some central flaw, which is why they lose in the end.
- The Main Character will have to face a series of escalating lesser opponents as they try to make their way to the Main Opponent. Each of these will represent a flawed approach to the competitive element which makes them seem to be winners/powerful, but will be exposed to be weak. (Physically flawed, morally flawed, theoretically flawed, flawed in technique, flawed in outlook, flawed in decorum, flawed in procedure, etc.)
- A tired but common trope in shonen Fight stories with an Unchanging powerful lead is that instead of going through the defeat and learning cycle, the Main Character is instead knocked out of the fight early, leaving their weaker allies to deal with the Story Arc's main Opponent and their allies. This usually results in the Main Character's allies fighting a desperate battle or being chased around by the opponents until the Main Character can be revived and go through the opponents like a hot knife through butter.
- There is some hidden philosophical aspect to the competitive element the Main Character must learn, sometimes several of them.
- If the lead character is Changing, there is often an "Ace" character who is massive at the activity and acts as a cool big brother or sister to the Main Character until the Main Character can finally surpass them.
- There will be mentor characters who recognize the Changing Main Character's talent and help to guide them on their way, but usually this respect must be

earned before they'll help the Main Character. Sometimes they'll even be against the Main Character when they first encounter them.

- The Main Character and the Main Opponent ultimately always have the same goal (or are both trying to be king of the hill), but one has chosen the "wrong" way to reach for it.

SETTING TROPES

- Following the Arena Principal (see chapter on Setting), Fighting Manga are usually structured around characters moving from one "tournament" competition to another. Most stories happen in a specific small location which brings the cast of that story into direct conflict and forces them to interact (fight) to accomplish their goals. These can be literal arenas (*My Hero Academia, Dragonball, Beast Children*), or mission locations (*Fairy Tail, Naruto*), islands (*One Piece*), or anywhere else characters can be locked into conflict and unable to leave until someone has emerged a victor.
- Supernatural elements are not only common in Fighting Manga, they're almost required. It's rare to find a shonen Fighting Manga that doesn't include at least one or more supernatural elements, and sometimes they're built around them.
- There is usually a clear levelling system, mostly used for two reasons: 1) to let us see how far the character has advanced, and how far they need to go, and 2) to create drama by letting the audience see the difference in rank between the Main Character(s) and their opponents. ("He's ten ranks higher! There's no way he can beat that guy!") A lot of stories also spend a great deal of time on the character figuring out how they're going to level and advance as quickly as possible to beat certain opponents.
- The competitive element's rules/aspects will be revealed a little bit at a time, so as not to overwhelm the reader with detailed information dumps and keep the drama moving. The writer will only tell as much as is needed to understand what's currently happening or going to happen, and no more.
- There will be a community of like-minded people who are also passionate about the competitive element, and they will represent other positive aspects and viewpoints of that competitive element.) This serves to remind the audience that there is no one right path to Enlightenment, while also bringing in different skills and approaches for the audience to consider about the competitive element which aren't ones the Main Character's story is exploring.

ACTIVITY MANGA

These comics use the same basic structure as Fighting Manga, but do something different with it. In these comics, the focus is on taking the audience through the journey of someone becoming a master of a sport or other activity. One key difference here is that Activity Dramas are about teaching the audience something useful in the real world. They often replace the more extreme thrills of Fighting Manga comics with actual useful knowledge of some kind, producing a story which is more grounded, but which offers a combination of entertainment and education at the same time. This type of story can also be quite popular, although it usually ranks slightly below Fighting Manga stories, and examples of it range from sports dramas like *Slam Dunk* and *Haikyuu!*, to "Kids collect stuff" dramas like *Pokémon* and *Yu-Gi-Oh!*, or creative activities like *Bakuman*, and many, many other activities and subjects.

ACTIVITY MANGA THEMES

To begin with, here is the Thematic Statement which lies behind Activity Manga:

Through hard work and effort towards <your activity of choice>, you can achieve your personal best and become part of a community.

That's it. If you work hard, and become the best you can be at your passion, you will find personal happiness, social respect, and become part of a community.

Some of the ways this argument is supported in Battle Manga are:

- Those who stand in opposition to our Main Character are always people who have a flawed approach to the Activity, take the goal half-heartedly, or are trying to do it through shortcuts (like wealth, cheating, crutches, tricks, etc.)

- There are always people who are trying to master the goal, but failing in some way because they're missing something. (Not "pure" or flawed in their thinking or approach to it.)
- There are always people who consider the goal the path to "godhood", which in this case means self-actualization (being all you can be).
- In the stories, the ones who win are always the ones who work the hardest at it and don't quit.
- They find a supportive community through pursuit of their goal of choice. (reward, public esteem)
- Opponents almost always come to see the Main Character's way as the "true" way, and those who come to understand this become allies or at least "reform".
- The love interest (if there is one, as sometimes there isn't in this genre) comes to respect and support the main character because of their hard work, acting both as inspiration and reward. (They won't get with the hero until the Main Character has accomplished their goal.) And, occasionally also being inspired by the main character to pursue their own goal, often one related to the main goal of the story. (Taking up the Main Character's sport or game of choice, for example. Or becoming a better artist or businessperson.)

SUPPORTING ARGUMENTS

Supporting arguments in any Battle Manga which will help to keep the story on track. Here are a few of them:

- Activity X is awesome! (i.e. Cricket is Awesome, Baking is Awesome, Skydiving is Awesome, etc.)
- Reaching your goal is easier (and more fun), with a community supporting you.
- No matter what your Activity of choice is, there is a community which will embrace you if you give it your all.
- Practitioners of Activity X must be good citizens and represent their community well to the greater world.
- People respect those who work hard.
- Every Activity has hidden depths if you only look deep enough.
- Quitters never win.
- There is value in hard work for the sake of hard work.
- If you don't take an Activity seriously, you will never really be good at it.

- Hard work trumps talent.
- Talent is needed, but it is only a foundation upon which hard work can build.
- Focusing on just one aspect of the Activity is not enough, you must be well rounded and flexible. (Usually demonstrated by the Main Character facing an opponent who is massive in one aspect of the Activity, but not in the other aspects, making them challenging but ultimately still losers.)

OVERALL PLOT STRUCTURE

And like any process, there is a clear pattern to how these stories progress, and tightly focused Battle Manga tend to go through the following stages:

KI- Introduction
- **Getting Motivated**– The Main Character is given a reason to explore/pursue the activity. Sometimes the Main Character starts motivated, in which case they explain the reason they're already motivated to another character instead. In any case, the audience is presented with the Main Character's reasons for pursuing the activity. The Main Character is usually living an unfulfilled life and comes to believe that the activity might be a possible solution to fill that void.
- **It's Easy!** – The Main Character engages in the activity and shows a natural talent or ability for it, allowing them to score their first victory. This gives them the confidence to move forward, and the feeling that this activity will bring them pleasure and give them something they've been missing from their lives.

SHO- Development
- **Maybe it's Not So Easy?** – The Main Character encounters their first real hurdle to becoming part of this activity- usually through an encounter with the Main Opponent. Their early victory was a product of talent, but they quickly learn that talent alone isn't enough, as those who have skill can trump their talent easily. Now they're forced to actually start to learn and explore the activity on a basic level.
- **A Whole New World**– The Main Character is introduced to the subculture which exists surrounding the activity. Through a guide character (or characters) they discover that there is a whole world they were unaware of hiding within the community that engages in the activity. From this discovery, they begin their first

steps into joining that community, and are given basic knowledge about that activity.

- **A New Path**– Now combining Talent and Skill, the Main Character starts on their real journey towards becoming a master of the activity. They have their first true victory, and get their taste of what it's like to be part of this new community while facing an Opponent (usually the one from Step 3) who has a flawed approach to the activity in some basic way. This opponent will seem strong at first, but they will realize due to their new skills that this opponent is really weak because they haven't mastered the fundamentals. Using those same fundamentals combined with talent, the Main Character will defeat them utterly.

TEN- Activity

- **The Long Road**– Now that they've entered this new world built around the activity, the Main Character will begin their path towards mastery. During this stage, they will meet a successive series of Opponents and challenges, make new friends, and learn more and more about their activity of choice. This stage is extremely flexible, and can take as long as the story needs it to take, or as long as the steps needed to master the activity require. Generally, each "step" along The Long Road is a story arc that will follow the same pattern:

A. The Main Character encounters a new opponent who is strong in an area where the Main Character is still weak or has knowledge the Main Character lacks. (This can also be a challenge or task which can't be defeated with the Main Character's current skill set.)

B. The Main Character is defeated by this new opponent/challenge. (Whose ability over the Main Character is often coded by being referred to by a special name)

C. The Main Character figures out why they were defeated (often by consulting others or through experimentation).

D. The Main Character seeks and finds a solution to the problem. (Learning new skills/ideas along the way, and possibly a counter-technique.)

E. While the Main Character is improving, the Main Character's Sidekicks may try to fight the opponent or opponent's allies. If they face the Arc Opponent, they will lose but their loss will either gain information or help to inspire the Main Character to act. If they are facing the Opponent's allies, they will fight hard battles but eventually win around the same time the Main Character does.

F. The Main Character faces the opponent/challenge again, and wins this time because of their new skills/knowledge.

G. The Main Character is rewarded for their efforts by praise of others. (If this praise comes from the Opponent, they often become friends or allies after this.)

H. Return to Step a)

- **Rising Competition**– While the Main Character is rising, they will periodically re-encounter the Main Opponent in different ways, usually ones which result in indirect competition between them. (Teasing their final conflict and building tension.) This indirect competition is usually through other people who do the Activity (defeating the people each other have faced or each other's allies) and sometimes by competing in different aspects of the Activity besides the main one. Also, as a result of this ongoing rivalry, the Main Opponent will also begin to become stronger as well, overcoming personal hurdles and staying ahead of the Main Character even when it seems like the Main Character is starting to catch up.

- **Social Advancement**– as the Main Character defeats more and more challenges, they also rise up within the sub-culture surrounding the Activity. They will often find themselves drawn into the politics and deeper aspects of the community and must learn to find their place inside the community. Usually they will learn that the community is bigger than they first imagined, and has far greater depths. They will also make enemies in the community who are threatened by their advancement and/or the changes they represent to the community as it exists now. Those enemies will usually become supporters of the Main Opponent, and help to drive the growing conflict between the Main Character and Main Opponent. Some of them may also try to trap or distract the main character through offers of positions of status or profit if they discontinue their journey, but even if tempted, the Main Character will always refuse in the end.

- **Eye of the Tiger**– The Main Character has now mastered/learned all they need to know and become a major figure in their activity. They must now face the Main Opponent in a true match to prove their level of ability and take their place as a master of the activity. Often the Main Character will have a crisis of confidence or suffer from Imposter Syndrome at this point, thinking they aren't really ready yet, but they'll overcome it and defeat the Main Opponent. Usually the Main Opponent is flawed in some way, often in their thinking or outlook about the activity, and the Main Character's victory is due to their purity of outlook, thus showing the audience that their way is the true path to victory in the end.

KETSU- Conclusion

- **Towards the Future–** The Main Character is now a master of the activity they fell in love with, and is shown to have a whole new life because of it. They are a happy and fully realized person and member of society who confidently knows their place in the world and is happy within it. The activity and subculture around it have benefitted and changed because of the Main Character's entry into it, and they can look back with nostalgia and look forward with anticipation to watching the activity grow and flourish under them. Often this is represented by them helping to bring new people into the activity and starting the cycle anew.

Plot Structure Notes

- Activity Manga are usually about the setting, with the setting (which includes the Activity) being the focal point of the story and generating most of the plot events and details. The character is often just there to serve as a window to the setting, and to experience the events (plot) which sweep the character up as they get involved in this new world. As a result, the setting is shaping the character in these stories, not the other way around.
- Magical abilities or Supernatural elements are rare in Activity Manga, except as gimmicks to help set the story or situation.
- There should always be an endpoint planned from the start and shown to the audience right from the start. That endpoint is a physical representation of the main character's goals, and represents to the main character and the audience that the main character has "made it" and achieved what they set out to achieve. Most commonly this is a title or position (King of the Pirates, Ninjas Chefs, etc.) or occasionally it can be relationship. ("We'll marry when I accomplish X!")

CHARACTER TROPES

- The Main Character will often be a bit dense, both as a comedic aspect, and because it forces the others to teach the Main Character the Activity to explain things clearly and slowly in different ways.

- There will almost always be "buddies" who are lesser talents at the activity and are inspired by the Main Character. Usually they will have more knowledge about the activity at the start than the Main Character, but they're all theory and no practice, which is why the Main Character will quickly surpass them.
- The Main Character will always have a hidden talent for this Activity, which gives them an edge over other newbies, but needs to be developed and refined through arduous work.
- The Main Character's outlook on the Activity will always be flawed in some way, and overcoming this flaw will usually be the final hurdle that lets them overcome the Main Opponent. (Often, it will be linked with some personal flaw or need they have, but not always.)
- There will always be a Main Opponent (Main Opponent) who acts as the "final boss" for our hero to defeat and who is aiming for the same top spot our Main Character wants to occupy. He or she may or may not be evil, and may even have a good relationship with the hero, but they're still the one the Main Character needs to beat to achieve mastery of their activity of choice.
- The Main Opponent will be far ahead of the Main Character at the start (and renowned for their genius at the activity), but their approach is flawed and their development usually plateaued, which lets the Main Character catch up. (Although, interacting with the hero in some way will normally let the Main Opponent start to move forward again once the Main Character starts to catch up.) Although they still don't overcome some central flaw, which is why they lose in the end.
- The Main Character will have to face a series of escalating lesser opponents as they try to make their way to the Main Opponent. Each of these will represent a flawed approach to the Activity which makes them seem to be winners/powerful, but will be exposed to be weak. (Physically flawed, morally flawed, theoretically flawed, flawed in technique, flawed in outlook, flawed in decorum, flawed in procedure, etc.)
- The Main Character must make sacrifices to achieve their goal, usually physical and social ones. (Health, relationships, other opportunities, etc.)
- The Main Character always gives 110% to their Activity, which is what sets them apart from others who do the Activity.
- There is often an "Ace" character who is massive at the activity and acts as a cool big brother or sister to the main character until the Main Character can finally surpass them.
- The Main Character and the Main Opponent ultimately always have the same goal, but one has chosen the "wrong" way to reach for it.

PLOT TROPES

- The people around the Main Character will teach the Main Character the Activity's rules/aspects a little bit at a time, so as not to overwhelm the reader with detailed information dumps and keep the drama moving.
- There will be mentor characters who recognize the Main Character's talent and help to guide them on their way, but usually this respect must be earned before they'll help the Main Character. Sometimes they'll even be against the Main Character when they first encounter them.
- There is some hidden philosophical aspect to the Activity the Main Character must learn, sometimes several of them.
- Through mastering the activity, the Main Character becomes "pure" and enlightened about the world.
- The Main Character will usually have no interest in the Activity at the beginning of the story, but will be lured in by the possible rewards of participating in it. (Often as represented by the Main Opponent), who is normally famous for their ability in this Activity.)

SETTING TROPES

- There will be a community of like-minded people who are also passionate about the Activity, and they will represent other positive aspects and viewpoints of that Activity. (In a Writing Drama, there will be characters representing different outlooks on writing (Plotting, Pantsing, Outlining, etc.) and different characters who represent different Genres (Horror, Romance, Westerns, etc.) which will be there to show how those tasks can be done differently (but still equally validly) than the main character might be doing them.) This serves to remind the audience that there is no one right path to enlightenment, while also bringing in different skills and approaches for the audience to consider about the Activity which aren't ones the Main Character's story is exploring.

Extra Notes

While Fighting Manga share many of the same features as Activity Manga (character tropes, similar story structure, progression), there is a key difference between them- Fighting Manga are about the character changing the world they live in, but most Activity Manga are about the world changing the character.

The main character is entering a "new world" (the subculture of the activity) and is being transformed by their experiences in that new world. Each character they meet, and each competition they have brings out the best in the character and slowly reshapes them into a new person until they come out someone new on the other side. So, when planning Activity Manga, think about how the main character will be changed over the course of the story and how they will end up.

Usually the main character will be an unsure, nervous, and almost laughable at the start, but show some hidden talent for the activity. But, by the end of the story they will be a confident, capable master of their ability and the activity itself. This simple progression teaches the idea that the activity is the way to bring out the best in the audience and have fun doing it. If you don't have another theme in mind, just use this one and it will work every time.

ROMANCE MANGA

One of the most basic human needs is the need for love, so it's no surprise that romance manga are one of the most popular manga genres. The best-selling romance manga of all time, *Hana Yori Dango* (*Boys Over Flowers*) by Yoko Kamio, has over 61 million copies in print of its collected volumes, and has been made into 12 different TV series in seven languages. Other popular romance titles like *NANA* and *Skip Beat!* each have over 42 million copies in print, and show that romance manga doesn't lag behind its shonen brothers in popularity.

Not that romance is only for the ladies, male readers enjoy a little romance too, and romantic comedies like *We Never Learn*, *Ranma ½*, *Ah! My Goddess!*, and *Love Hina* have made boys' hearts beat loudly over the years as well. So, there is a market for romance for everyone, and you can always find an audience who enjoy watching a lead couple commit to each other and march off into the future together.

TOP 10 THINGS YOU SHOULD KNOW BEFORE WRITING ROMANCE MANGA

Here are ten important things that anyone who wants to write romance manga should know going into it. This isn't a complete list, but covers the major ideas that any romance manga writer should know before they jump in and start writing their own.

1. Not all shoujo manga are romances.

While the majority of josei and ladies manga are romances, and some shoujo manga are romances, not all manga for girls are romances. Especially with manga for tween girls, the focus is often more on friendship, self-discovery, and adventure instead of romance, which they're still growing into. And, even among manga for older girls and women, there are still many popular series that have romance only as a subplot and instead focus on career building and other interests. Romance may be the queen of women's manga, but it isn't the empress and other popular genres exist as well.

2. Romance is both a genre and a plot at the same time.

While the action, comedy, or horror genres all have many different kinds of plots that go with them, Romance is one of only two genres (the other being mysteries) which are expected to follow the same plot no matter what. In a romance story, two people will meet, are attracted to each other, overcome obstacles, and then unite as a couple in some semi-permanent way. If a story doesn't follow these beats, then that story isn't a romance, it's a drama.

3. The ending to romance stories is written before the story begins.

The audience doesn't want a happy ending to a romance story, they demand it. (And leave bad reviews if they don't get it.) The main character must fall in love, and they must unite with their love interest at the end– full stop, no questions asked. The only dramatic questions that exist in a romance story are **how** they will get together, and **who** they will get together with. (If there is more than one possible romantic partner.)

4. If the romance isn't the focus of the story, it's not a romance.

Many stories have romance in them, but to be considered a romance the romance plot must be front and center in the story. A story about two characters building a school in a slum who fall in love isn't a romance, it's a drama with a romance subplot. A story about two characters who fall in love while building a school in a slum is a romance, because the romance is the focus. It's a small distinction, but it makes a big difference– in the first example the focus of the story is on building the school, but in the second example the focus of the story is on how the couple get together. In a romance story, everything that happens in the main plot is connected to the relationship of the characters, and is developing that relationship.

5. The most popular romance plot is "Beauty and the Beast."

If there is one plot that dominates romance, it's the plot of the powerful and wild alpha male with the broken heart who is healed by the love of the female lead and restored to society. If you look at a list of male love interests in romance stories, you will see a long list of kings, pirate captains, CEOs, werewolves, vampires, billionaires, lawyers, surgeons, presidents, and other powerful high-status men who act like jerks and tyrants when we first meet them. But, of course, every one of them is an emotionally damaged and scared little boy on the inside, and by breaking through their tough exterior and healing their wounds, the female lead wins their love and becomes their partner. It's a tale as old as time, and it still sells well today.

6.   The male lead must always be honest with the female lead.

Even though the male lead might be a jerk, a playboy, a bully, or someone who makes the female lead's life a living hell, the one thing they will never do is lie to the female lead. This is very important to making the end of a romance story work, because if the female lead (and the audience) can't believe it when the male lead professes his love at the end, the whole story will fall apart. The male lead can be a liar who tricks and cheats everyone else in the story, and they may even cheat on the female lead with other women, but their word (when they give it) must be their bond, and they must never break it when she's involved. If they do, the whole house of cards will come down and the audience won't buy the ending.

7.   Romance is all about "balance."

While princes picking up peasant girls and whisking them off to castles to be queens works fine for children, more mature audiences know that real lasting relationships are about communication and respect. If that peasant girl who becomes a queen doesn't show she's worthy of the role, the king is going to get bored of her pretty quickly, and things will sour fast. At the end of a romance, the audience needs to believe this couple will last, and that means that both sides must have shown they're worthy of each other's love. They have to bring equal value to the relationship, and even if a billionaire falls in love with a cleaning lady, she has to prove she's his equal by the end of the story in some way.

8.   In romance stories, the main opponent for the lead is the love interest.

In stories, the main opponent is the person who stands between the main character and achieving their final goals. In a romance story, that person is the lead character's love interest- they are the one who must be convinced to enter into a long-term relationship with the lead character at the end of the story for the ending to happen. This doesn't mean there can't also be rivals and villains in a romance, and there often are, but the main opponent of the story will always be the love interest because it's their heart that is the key to finding love happily ever after.

9. **The rules are the same regardless of the genders of the people involved.**

While most romance stories are about male-female relationships, there are other possibilities as well, and *Yuri* (lesbian) and *Yaoi* (gay) manga are extremely popular. However, even in those same-sex pairings, one character usually has more masculine traits than the other, and one character will have more feminine traits. Thus, a "Beauty and The Beast" plot basically plays out the same whether both the leads are female, or both the leads are male. One will be active and assertive, and the other will be more passive and accepting, because this combination is the most balanced and results in working relationships in fiction and real life.

10. **Men like romance too!**

While surveys done in the last decade by the most popular shoujo manga, *Margaret*, showed that only roughly 4% of their readership was male, that doesn't mean that boys don't love romance manga. They actually like it very much, and at any given time one of the top ten series running in *JUMP* is usually a romance series like *Niseikoi*, *We Never Learn!*, or *Kimagure Orange Road*. The difference is that men like a heavy dose of comedy with their romance, while women tend to prefer more "pure" romantic dramas with just a bit of comedy on the side. Also, the male versions of romance stories tend to have a lot of sexy moments (although no actual sex), and be more about interesting and awkward situations instead of being about feelings.

ROMANCE AUDIENCES

The audience for romance manga is one that changes a lot depending on the age and other demographics of the target audience. Younger audiences like simpler, more chaste and idealized romance, while older audiences prefer something more nuanced and complex with heavier doses of tragedy and sexuality.

However, what all these audiences can agree on is that they see romance stories as a way to escape their daily lives and plunge into a beautiful and exciting fantasy world where true love wins out. In fact, if there's one major rule to romance, it's that true love must always win.

True love has to win in fiction, because if it doesn't win in fiction, how can it win in real life? Romance readers want to be re-assured that "love finds a way," and that "true love is waiting just around the corner." These stories promise them that if they put their hearts into it, and weather the storms of life, they too will find happiness and fulfillment in the arms of the perfect partner. They sell a dreamlike version of reality to audiences whose lives are anything but dreamy, and who want that extra comfort that only a romance story can give.

So, when you're trying to reach a romance audience, always remember that you're selling them a fantasy, and part of that fantasy is keeping them happy and comfortable. That's the winning formula to writing successful romance, and keeping them coming back for more.

ROMANCE THEMES

Romance stories always have a single central theme- "Love conquers all." If they don't have this as their main theme, then they're not a romance story but something else with a romance subplot. This isn't bad, it just means that the story isn't about the romance, but something else.

However, romance stories can and often do have other supporting themes that go along with them and add spice to the story. A "pure" romance story is rare, and most romance manga pair the main romance story with some other theme to give it a more unique flavor and style. For example, common secondary themes in romances include "being true to yourself," "finding the courage to follow your dreams," "love takes courage, but it's worth it," "accepting people for who they are," "love versus family duty," "the power of love to transform your life," and so on.

When planning your romance story, you should always think about what the secondary theme of the story is going to be, and how it will be expressed in your characters, situations, and the ending of the story. If the secondary theme was, "finding courage," then the main character will probably be a fearful person, at least when it comes to relationships, and then the more she opens herself up, the better her relationships will become until finally she takes the biggest step of all with her love interest at the end of the story.

ROMANCE CHARACTERS

Characters in romance stories can be divided into three categories- the female lead, the male love interest, and rivals. Other types of characters exist, like best friends, mentors, wise grandmothers, annoying bosses, and the other people who fill out a character's supporting cast, but they are all dependent on the type of story being told. These three, however, are crucial to the success of a romance story and must be planned with care.

The Female Lead

The main thing you need to remember about the female lead in a romance story is that they're stand-ins for the reader. The reader needs to not only sympathize with them, but connect with them on a deep level, because they're not just a character, they're a mask that the reader puts on to experience the events of the story. The deeper the connection, the more intensely the reader will feel the experiences the main character has, and go through her emotions with her.

So, a lot of the success of a romance story will depend on how well the creator can make the audience connect with their lead character. How to do this has been discussed in other chapters, but one of the main ways that romance manga do this is by having female leads that have positive traits that are traits that the audience either has, wishes they had, or thinks are good to have. On the other hand, the female lead should not have any major negative traits that might distance her from the audience and make it harder to relate to her.

First, female lead characters in romance manga generally have four basic traits in common- they are smart, assertive, tenacious, and good hearted. They are smart because their brain is their greatest asset in the story, and they will need it to overcome the obstacles that get thrown their way. They are assertive because audiences respect assertive characters, and it makes them easier to write because they're doers who actively try to solve their problems. They are tenacious because unless they have a great inner strength and don't give up, they won't be able to achieve their goals and make their dreams into reality. And finally, they are good hearted because it will be their pure heart that makes the male lead trust them deeply and wins the day at the end of the story.

They may have other positive traits, but these are the ones which almost every female lead has and which will end up being crucial to the story's success. It's hard to find a successful romance manga where the lead female character (or feminine character) doesn't have these traits to some degree.

On the other hand, they must not have traits that will make the audience dislike and distance themselves from the lead character. Traits like being dishonest, cheating, stealing, abusing others, or being passive or greedy will turn audiences off if they're a major part of the character's personality and not balanced out in some way by positive traits. Audiences don't want to connect with characters who don't share their values, and they won't root for male love interests to get together with female leads that they don't like.

The Male Love Interest

Just as the audience must empathize with the female lead of the story, they must fall in love with the male lead for a romance story to work. Thus, the male leads in romance stories are idealized alpha-males of some kind who represent the fantasy lover of the female lead and the audience brought to life, and in need of their help.

The key traits that every male lead in a romance story should have are that they should be strong, attractive, trustworthy, and a winner. They need to be strong because they will be called on to show inner strength by not giving up when things get hard, and physically strong when they need to protect the female lead. They need to be attractive because the audience needs to find them as appealing as the main female lead does. They need to be trustworthy (for the female lead) because if their word can't be trusted, how can the main character settle down with them at the end of the story? And finally, they must be a winner at the game of life, or someone who is on their way to becoming a winner, so that they're desirable as a romantic partner. This means they must hold (or have the potential to hold) high social status within the culture they belong to, and be worthy of the female lead's attentions. (Nobody wants to date a loser.)

Also, there are two more important traits a male love interest needs in a romance story- they must be emotionally incomplete, and a reflection of the female lead.

They should be emotionally incomplete because it's the reason why they need the female lead. This emotional incompleteness can be a personal flaw, it can be damage done by previous relationships, or it can be just something missing from their life. Regardless, they are missing something from their life that only the female lead can provide, and through providing it when nobody else can, the female lead is like prince charming showing up with the glass slipper to prove she's miss right.

In addition, the male love interest should be a reflection of the female lead- their balanced opposite who brings out the best in them when they're together. If the female lead is quiet, the male lead is talkative. If the female lead is impulsive, the male lead is thoughtful. If the female lead is fearful, the male lead is brave. He is the one who brings balance to her, and her life, which is how he shows he's the right person for her.

Rivals

In most love stories, there is a rival male or female character (or both, or several) who are trying to get in the way of the lead couple getting together. They are there to add drama, give the audience someone to hate, and add a little uncertainty to how the whole thing will turn out.

The thing to understand about romance rivals is that they're actually funhouse mirror versions of the lead couple. They represent the things that the lead couple are looking for, but in the wrong way, not the right way. For example, the female rivals will be women who are charming and attractive on the surface, but underneath are cold hearted and the worst kinds of women. Similarly, the male rivals are usually alpha males gone bad, who are physically abusive, manipulative, and dishonest. They seem handsome and charming on the surface, and to be mister right, but underneath they're deeply flawed in bad ways that will only break the female lead's heart if she goes with them.

These rivals will tempt the lead couple, and might even get them to lose faith in each other, but will always fail in the end because true love will find a way to get the main couple back on the right path.

ROMANCE PLOTS

The tricky thing about romance stories is that the audience knows the ending (or a version of it), right from the beginning of the story. There are no huge surprises in a romance story (with one exception, see below), because the audience is there for a very specific ending, and if they don't get that ending, they're going to be very, very unhappy.

For a story to be a romance story, the ending is already written before the writer even begins- the main couple gets together and commits to each other for the long term, forsaking all others. It doesn't have to be marriage, it doesn't even have to be forever (sometimes, "for now" is good enough), but the key is that the story will end with the leads pledging their hearts to each other in a way which makes it clear that this is going to last.

If the ending is anything else, then that isn't a romance story, it's a romantic drama, which is another kind of story. A romance is about finding love, accepting love, and gaining love- it's that simple.

That doesn't mean other kinds of stories can't also include romance (most do), but a story which **is** a romance, and where the romance is the point, is a very particular kind of story. So, if you're planning to write one, you should always remember that your ending is already written for you, and your readers will riot (and write bad reviews) if you don't give it to them. (Because it breaks the fantasy that they too will find love and happiness with that perfect person someday.)

Some people might think this puts the writer in a difficult position- after all, how do you write an interesting story when the audience already knows how it's going to end? But, the truth is romance stories aren't about the ending, they're about the journey and how those two characters get across that finish line. The audience is there to find out how the characters get together, not whether they do.

The audience's interest in romance stories is in seeing how the characters overcome challenges to get together. The bigger the challenges, the more the audience is interested in seeing how the main characters overcome them. These challenges can come from within the couple and outside the couple, and most stories have a series of these obstacles that stand in the way of the couple getting together.

Challenges from Within the Couple

There are two types of challenges that come from inside the couple- personal flaws and couple flaws.

Personal flaws are issues that one member of the couple has and which affect their relationship. These can include the following:

- Addictions
- An overdeveloped sense of duty
- Attachment to a parent or relative
- Bad habits
- Being a devout believer in an ideology
- Being a devout follower of a religion
- Being a ninja
- Being a workaholic
- Being physically or mentally disabled
- Being too attached to fictional characters
- Being uneducated
- Doubts about themselves or others
- Emotional scars from previous relationships
- Fears
- Goals they're unable to give up which interfere with the relationship

- Having a mental illness
- Having a serious illness
- Loving manga or anime too much
- No sense of fashion/style
- One side has no interest in personal improvement
- Poor personal hygiene
- Pride
- Stubbornness
- The inability to adapt to new environments
- The inability to admit they're wrong
- The inability to change
- The inability to choose the best partner
- The inability to commit
- The inability to communicate with others
- The inability to forgive
- The inability to give up standards of living/lifestyles they are used to
- The inability to have children
- The inability to hold steady employment
- The inability to keep pets
- The inability to let go of past events
- The inability to let go of past relationships
- The inability to perform sexually
- The inability to trust
- The inability to use technology

Any of these can seriously affect one or both people in a relationship by making it hard for the other person to have a relationship with them. However, these are not the only issues– there are also couple flaws which specifically affect their ability to have or maintain a relationship with each other. These include the following:

- Different hobbies or interests
- Different relationship goals
- Different relationship styles
- Different sexual tastes
- Different styles of fashion
- Different styles of living
- Different styles of work
- Different tastes in food
- Differing sex drives

- Habits that drive each other crazy
- One person being overly critical of the other
- One person just isn't interested in the other as a romantic partner
- One person not liking children/pets
- The couple are unable to use the same language to communicate
- The inability to communicate well
- The inability to satisfy each other sexually
- The side they bring out of each other when they're together
- They have conflicting worldviews about politics, social change, religion, or pizza toppings

Any of which can affect their ability to be together as a pair, or to interact with each other well. Not a few of these have been deal breakers in many relationships, and all of them offer potential as reasons why a couple is unable to get together in a story.

Challenges from Outside the Couple

Being in a relationship and bonding with another person is hard enough, but on top of that there are many external forces which prevent, harm, and even destroy relationships. These outside challenges keep couples from being together, and a few of them includes the following:

- **Biology** - there is some external biological reason they can't be together, such as drug treatments, surgical procedures, infectious diseases, or genetic manipulation
- **Chance** - one side never gets the opportunity to get close with the other
- **Custom** - cultural or family traditions keep them apart
- **Duty** -having to perform a task, fulfill a promise, take care of someone, do a job
- **Education** - one side's education level keeps them from getting together with the other
- **Emotion**- they are surrounded by people who hate one side or the other, or are afraid of one side or the other

- **Family** - their families stand between them getting together, usually by not liking the partner or their family members
- **Geography** - distance, borders, walls
- **History** - their personal, cultural, or family history keeps them apart, for example their families fought on opposite sides of a conflict, or relatives harmed each other
- **Honor** - a vow or promise which prevents them from getting together with the other person
- **Intent**- one or both people is being forced to harm or take advantage of the other person in some way
- **Law** - laws keep them apart, for example one of them is a fugitive or criminal, one is already married, their relationship is illegal, one person is a slave, etc
- **Money** - one side needs money to get together with the other, for example dowries, buying the other person's freedom, having enough money to meet some standard or requirement
- **Optics** - not being able to be seen together without facing censure or creating a false impression
- **Other Lovers** - one or both of the main couple are being pursued by other people, or in love with other people.
- **Politics** - gang, tribal, local, or national politics prevent them from getting together with the other person, for example wars, revolutions, belonging to rival organizations, belonging to different political parties, belonging to an underclass
- **Race** - their racial backgrounds keep them apart
- **Reputation** - the poor reputation of one side (deserved or not) keeps the other one from getting together with them
- **Rules** - one or both people are bound by some external rules which prevent them from accepting the other person
- **Status**- there is a large gap in status between the two which prevent them from getting together
- **Work**- their jobs keep them emotionally, physically, or socially apart in some way

These outside pressures put a lot of strain on relationships, and make a couple finding happiness with each other an even bigger challenge than it might normally be. Just remember that these, like the flaws listed above, should be used in ways which are consistent and reflect the themes of the story.

Also, if you're looking for excuses to shove a couple together who wouldn't want to be together, and keep them there, then the above list can be used for that too! Every one of those above reasons can push a couple together as much as it can pull them apart, and keep them together until they figure out how to love each other the way you want them to.

However, if these long lists leave you confused and unsure of which challenges you want to put between your poor star-crossed lovers, then you can always fall back on the big five:

<u>**Top Five Relationship Challenges!**</u>
1. **Doubt in themselves or each other**
2. **Family troubles**
3. **Other lovers**
4. **One person just isn't interested**
5. **The inability to change**

This quintet is so popular you will find them everywhere in romance stories, especially Asian ones.

However, there is one other way which creators keep audiences interested in romance stories besides the normal challenges of getting and staying together-competition.

Who Will they End Up With?

While it's clear that the main character will get their happily ever after ending in a romance story, what isn't so clear is who they'll be spending that ever after with! This is the one thing that the writer is actually allowed to play with about the ending, and in fact is something that can keep audiences interested and guessing until the very end.

Love triangles, squares, hexagons, and do-decahedrons are as common in romance manga as stars in the sky, and they're an important tool in a romance serial writer's toolbox. Audiences can get antsy very quickly if they feel an author is just stalling a couple getting together to stretch a story out for time, but if there are several different suitors then sometimes it isn't so clear in whose arms the main character belongs. This lets the story go on for some time without worrying about dragging because the main character is reasonably exploring possibilities with different partners and trying to determine the best one.

It also turns the story into a bit of a contest, as each suitor tries to prove they're the best partner for the lead character, and the audience is left to judge with whom the main character really belongs. This was the classic formula that propelled *Boys Over Flowers* into its top spot, and has made harem manga (one boy pursued by many girls), and reverse-harem manga (one girl pursued by many men) into industry standards.

Thus, between how the couple gets together, and who they end up with, a creator keeps the audience interested and turning pages.

ROMANCE MANGA STORY STRUCTURES

Like other serialized entertainment, romance manga function on two levels- the overall story and the individual stories. The overall story is the story of how a particular pair of people end up together, while the individual stories represent the smaller steps the couple takes in their slow dance towards leaving the story together.

The structure of most romances is a natural and universal one- boy meets girl, they overcome problems, and they end up together. This is how real (successful) relationships tend to work, and the audience knows and expects it to go this way. However, writing a good relationship story isn't quite this simple because if the story is just about the author coming up with random reasons to keep the main pair apart in an effort to make the story last as long as possible, then the reader is going to feel like they're in a relationship where the other side is never going to commit. They'll be bored, restless, and eventually they're going to be the ones to head for the exit.

This is why it's important to plan and write the romance story in such a way that the audience can feel there is actual progression happening, and it's a natural progression which is playing out the way they'd expect based on the situation and circumstances. That doesn't mean there can't be twists, reversals, and exciting turns, but it does mean those should be used sparingly, and preferably set up or foreshadowed long before they actually happen.

The best way to structure a relationship story is to set it up so that each story (or story arc) of the tale is centered around the characters dealing with one of the obstacles or problems which are keeping them apart, and growing closer together through the experience. The Overall Story of the relationship is built around the steps the characters must go through to go from being apart to being together, and each smaller story inside that greater story represents the actual steps of that journey from A to Z.

Thus, a typical Overall Story structure for a romance serial will look something like this:

KI - Introduction
- The lead characters and their situation are introduced and we're shown that they're right for each other. Typically, the audience (and sometimes the leads) know they're meant to be together from the start.

SHO - Development
- The first story arc is about introducing these people who belong together, and then showing why they can't be together.
- The second story arc happens, expanding the world the characters live in, their supporting casts, and detailing the magnitude of the problems which stand between them.
- They usually confront one of the less major problems and overcome it, showing that they have the potential to be together if they work at it.
- Usually one of them admits their feelings to themselves, and sometimes the other person (but is rejected).

TEN - Activity
- A series of escalating challenges appear, each one representing a reason the couple can't be together, and each one is (at least partly) overcome at the end of the arc, bringing them closer together.

KETSU - Conclusion
- They overcome the final challenge, usually one which forces them to either get together or forever be apart, and walk into the future together.

This gives you, as the writer, three clear story arcs which need to be told (Introduction, Development, Conclusion) and then a more flexible number of story arcs which play out between them (Activity). Each of the Activity story arcs being about a particular problem that stands between the pair and how it's resolved, thus keeping the plot moving forward. So, say there are three things keeping them apart - family, emotional baggage, and work - one arc is about the family issue, one arc is about the emotional baggage issues, and one arc is about the work issue, and each one of the problems is solved in some way which brings them closer together. This is a simple approach which gives the story a clear and finite structure and progression that the audience can feel and see.

Often, each of the individual Story Arcs will look something like this:

KI - Introduction
- Set up the leads, the current situation, and controlling ideas.
- A situation, problem or task which will provide the spine of action for the story is introduced.

SHO - Development
- The characters become involved in the main plot and begin working toward resolving it.

- Complications are introduced which will affect the story as it plays out.
- Something happens that either separates them or pushes the main characters together.

TEN - Activity

- In the process of dealing with the situation, the leads are forced to deal with the problems and their feelings about each other at the same time.
- Escalating Events happen which make them confront their feelings for each other or the factors which keep them apart.
- The leads deal with the situation and solve it, often in a way which brings out their feelings for each other.

KETSU – Conclusion

- The main characters either grow closer or farther apart- almost always growing a bit closer.

For example:

KI - Introduction

Bob and Sue are high school students caught in a complicated school romance where Bob likes Sue, but Sue isn't sure about how she feels about Bob. The two of them are ordered by their teacher to work on a presentation project with some other team classmates, including the attractive Tiffany.

SHO - Development

Tiffany starts flirting heavily with Bob, which makes Sue jealous, but she doesn't want to admit her feelings and simply starts to avoid Bob instead. The project also involves some interviews, which Bob says he can get because his father has connections.

TEN – Activity

- Sue leaves a project meeting when Bob seems to respond to Tiffany's advances.
- Bob tries to explain to Sue he didn't mean anything by his behavior, but she won't listen to him.
- Tiffany uses the chance to get closer with Bob, who appreciates the support, but he still cares for Sue. Sue sees them together and gets even more jealous.
- Bob tries to get the interviews they need for the project, but discovers he's made a mistake as his father's friend will be out of town. Now they have nobody to interview.
- Sue finds Bob worrying and confronts him about the situation. When she discovers he can't get the interview she says she can help, and the two go together to the police station where her father works, getting a useable interview.

- In the process, they have to travel together on the bus, and start to talk, opening up about their feelings, and Bob apologizes for trying to bite off more than he could handle. Sue apologizes too, confessing she was jealous when she saw him with Tiffany, when it's none of her business.

KETSU – Conclusion

The two finish the project together with their group, and in the process move their relationship a step forward.

As you can see, the "problem" of the story is there to provide a situation which forces the characters to confront their own personal problems and each other, usually by either keeping them together or pushing them apart. Meanwhile, they deal with their feelings in a way which ends with them communicating and bonding (or not), and in the end the relationship moves a step forward. Usually the problem isn't directly about the relationship, or them, because that can only happen when the relationship is going to take a big step forward. (Which is something that is usually saved for beginning, the end, or really important story arc.)

ROMANTIC COMEDY

Another popular type of romance is stories where there is a large dose of comedy to go alongside the romance. These stories are popular for many reasons, not the least of which is that they appeal more to both sexes, but mainly because they lighten the story and present a happy, positive world the audience can escape to for a few hours a day.

Romantic comedies are largely driven by their casts and the interactions of those casts, often drawing heavily from the slice-of-life genre. They are also usually linked more heavily with a setting, exploring the ins and outs of that setting while at the same time serving up a heaping helping of love and comedy. So, for example, a school romantic comedy might be about the odd members of an astronomy club and the situations and relationships which come from those people interacting together as they try to explore the heavens. (And spend a lot of times out in the dark countryside huddled together in blankets waiting for celestial phenomena.)

A typical romantic comedy will usually have a lead couple, but also a few other couples in the supporting cast, and will alternate between focusing on the leads and the secondaries as it plays out to extend the story. The supporting cast, of course, represents the good and bad sides of the main couple, and their relationships will make the main couple reflect on themselves and their own connection. In the end, of course, the main couple finally admit their love for each other, but not before the rest of the cast and the setting are as familiar to the reader as their own lives.

See the Romantic Comedy Plot under *Common Plots* for more on this type of story.

ROMANCE SETTINGS

Because romance stories are so hyper-focused on characters, the setting in romance stories is mostly just there to provide an interesting backdrop for the drama to play out in front of. Or, when it does become involved, the setting is there to either push the characters together or keep them apart.

The most common places for romance manga to happen are schools and workplaces because those are both familiar environments for the audience. Using familiar environments has two big advantages- first, since the audience also lives in those environments, it makes the characters and situations feel more familiar to them, encouraging sympathy. And second, it lets the creator skip a lot of the worldbuilding and go straight to the important parts that make the characters' little world special or unique and reflect the themes of the story.

Here are a few places romance manga are often set, and notes about them.

School Romance

Since most manga characters are young, a large amount of romantic manga is set in schools, mostly high schools with the occasional middle school, college, or university. The school in these stories provides a place where the students need to meet on a regular basis (forcing them together), but also acts as a miniature society with its own rules and customs. (Which can keep them apart.) The school also provides a rhythm to the story, as the characters progress through the school system and deal with the recurring stresses and challenges that come with school life. And finally, the school can even pull the characters apart, as graduation looms, creating a natural deadline for their time together.

Common Obstacles to getting together at school include rivalries, school social politics, school policies, different social status, poor reputations, the need to study, part-time jobs, gangs, family, competing romantic partners, and school officials.

Workplace Romance

These are stories about finding love at the workplace, or through work. This work can be anything from cake decorating, to making films, to working on the international space station. The job in this story acts as the thing that brings the leads together and then pushes and pulls on their lives as they try to find a new balance with each other. The workplace is also the arena where the story will play out, and will prevent the leads from avoiding each other- forcing them to confront their feelings.

Common Obstacles to getting together include differing workloads, jealousy, rivalries, ambition, different levels of status within the company, different levels of social status, personal finances, personal goals, and office politics.

Palace Romance

Romances of this kind are almost always between an emperor, king, prince, or other high court official and a female character of lower nobility, or peasant birth. Typically, the female lead enters the palace with some purpose, sometimes as a concubine, nurse, or maid (for peasants), or as a teacher, doctor, or cook (for low nobility) and catches the eye of the male lead. They then begin a romance where everything and everyone says they shouldn't be together, but the female lead overcomes the challenges and, in the process, proves her worth to the king and his court. Typically, he has to make a large sacrifice for her at some point near the end, but this helps to convince everyone of his sincerity, and she becomes his first lady.

Common Obstacles to getting together usually include status differences, social politics, national politics, war, vows and promises, finances, promised marriages, family objections, cultural traditions, rivals, attitudes towards women, infertility, and legal restrictions.

ROMANCE NOTES

While they are simple at heart, romance stories have more than a few things creators should think about.

Chemistry

It isn't enough to just assume the leads need to be together because they're the main characters in a relationship story. You have to give both the characters and the audience reasons to believe that these two people belong together forever. Whether you want to call it chemistry, a spark, or resonance, the two leads need to bring out something in each other that they don't have with any other characters in the story.

This can be different sides of their personalities, this can be vulnerabilities, this can be forgotten memories, or even old habits, but there needs to be some special connection between them that the audience can see and feel.

Also, being attracted to each other is nice, and being compatible in their life goals is good, but the real connection happens on a much more subtle level. It's the little things the characters do as they interact that will indicate whether they belong together or not. Things like considering the other person's feelings when they don't need to, putting the other person first, and showing extra care for the people and things that the other person considers important. Sometimes these things are subconscious, especially at the start of the relationship, but characters taking actions like this show their inner feelings about the other person and what that person means to them.

Finally, good verbal chemistry is important as well. People in love not only listen to each other, they mirror and echo the words and ideas the other person expresses. There is a dynamic energy to their conversations because each side can't wait to express their thoughts and help the other person express theirs as they work as a team. When they're together, they aren't two separate people talking, but two parts of a single mind working in natural synchronicity.

Vulnerability

"The best way to find out if you can trust somebody is to trust them," Ernest Hemingway once said, but for many people this isn't so easy. Trusting others means letting your barriers down and being vulnerable, but that means also risking being hurt, not such a simple thing for people who have been hurt in the past or have their own emotional issues. But unless both sides let their defenses down and trust each other enough to let themselves be open and risk being hurt by the other person, true deep love can't actually develop. If one side doesn't open up, then the relationship is unbalanced, and is likely going to fail because of that unstable nature.

For writers, this means that a big part of writing relationship stories is often about the characters lowering their barriers to each other, which is often a slow and difficult process. Trust comes with time and understanding each other, and these personal barriers are something that the characters will often need to work through as part of the story.

Going it Alone

Not everything in a story can be solved by the main couple together, and sometimes one member of the couple (usually the lead) will need to take time off from the relationship to solve their own problems. Especially with deep, personal problems, one of them will sometimes have to go and deal with it on their own before they come back ready to be part of the relationship again. In this case, the story/arc will be one which forces them to confront their problem and either solve it, or give them the key to working toward solving it. Not everything can be fixed overnight, and sometimes a little personal space might be needed.

In cases like this, the writer should generally not be afraid of time-jumps. If a character needs six months, then wrap the other time-sensitive stories up (or tell them during that period), and then jump the story into the future to when the characters are ready to be part of the relationship story again. Always remember that this is the story of the relationship, not the people, so if there are gaps in the people's lives where nothing important happens that's fine, because we're there to read about the interesting parts of the relationship. Just do it as smoothly as possible, and not too often, as the audience will get annoyed with regular unscheduled time-jumps that feel like the writer is skipping past what could be interesting stories just because they don't know how to tell them.

Ending it All

All good things must come to an end, and the lead couple need to get together at some point (or permanently go their separate ways) or the audience is going to be pretty unhappy. They started this journey to see the story of how these two people got together in an interesting way, and if the author doesn't deliver, or takes too long to finish what they started, the audience is going to get tired and restless. This is why it's important to know from the start where the endpoint will roughly be so that you can work towards it in a natural way.

Remember there are three criteria for a good ending- it must be reasonable based on what happened, earned by the protagonist, and surprising in some way to the audience – and when the time comes to deliver those three things, the writer must be willing to finish the story and walk away. Don't keep a story going for the sake of keeping it going, but instead finish it and write a new story that the audience will enjoy just as much, maybe better.

This is why it's important to know how long you plan the story to run, and the steps the characters will need to go through right from the beginning. By setting everything up, the audience will be able to feel the progression, not just hope for it or guess at it, and the whole thing will feel much more satisfying. In addition, it will also feel earned, because the characters really did the work, and the writer will have time to plan an ending that the audience didn't quite expect, but still works out happily in the end.

A perfect place to close the curtains and call it a night.

EXPLORATORY MANGA

When you read the words "Exploratory Manga" you might think about stories like *Star Trek*, *Indiana Jones*, *Uncharted*, or other adventure stories where the hero is going into strange new worlds. However, while those do have elements of exploration, they are much more adventuring stories where the characters are the stars.

Instead, Exploratory Manga (and anime, and light novels) are a type of milieu story where the whole purpose of the story is to explore a setting and the characters are basically just guides leading the audience through that setting. They might be knowledgeable guides who know the setting well, or they might be characters who have entered this setting at the start of the story and now explore it along with the audience, but their function is to be a guide for exploring the setting.

So, for example, maybe the main character is exploring the world of food. In that case, they might explore the world of deserts (*Kantaro: The Sweet Tooth Salaryman*), or wine tasting (*Drops of God*), restaurant culture (*Oishinbo*), or any of a host of other food-related topics. All of which are stories where the focus is mainly on a character working their way through the cultures, sub-cultures and wisdom that surround food culture in Japan and abroad.

In these stories, there is (often) no real overplot or goal for the main character beyond gaining knowledge and understanding of their chosen topic. Maybe they want to improve their skills in their chosen area, or maybe they have someone they want to surpass, but either way, the real star of the show is the setting they're exploring. The character is just a vehicle for going though that setting like a car in a theme park ride.

These lead characters usually have little to no character arc beyond maybe going from inexperienced in the ways of the setting to experienced, and maybe not even that in some stories. This is because the character is not the point and is only there to be a viewpoint for the audience to come to understand the world around the character.

Because of this, these stories are usually fairly low impact, and often (but not always) have little to no conflict in them. These aren't Hero's Journeys, but stories where a character is simply learning and exploring a world the creator finds fascinating and wants to share with the audience. The conflict in the stories (if any) is often speed bumps instead of obstacles, and is there to add a light touch of drama at most.

A good example of this is the manga *Heterogeneous Linguistics*, which also demonstrates that these kinds of stories don't even have to be set in the real world. In this story, a young graduate student from a human-dominated continent in a fantasy setting travels to a continent dominated by primitive monster races in order to continue his professor's work of studying their languages. The whole story is about him and his young wolf-girl assistant living among primitive peoples of the continent and figuring out how each communicates. There are no battles, no action, no romance, and little to no conflicts except for the occasional linguistic challenge or miscommunication.

And yet, the story itself is unique and fascinating.

Heterogeneous Linguistics also demonstrates one of the two main patterns these stories tend to follow – the learning lead, or the observing lead.

As with *Heterogeneous Linguistics* (the learning lead), the main character is encountering and learning from a series of other characters who are part of that world. In these stories (and in Exploratory Manga, it's often about a series of short stories, not long epics – they're almost anthologies), each new part of the setting the character explores has a guide character (or characters) for the main character to interact with. The main character learns from each of them, and then moves on with more understanding than they had before they met the "guide."

Other examples of this pattern are *Laid Back Camp*, *Yotsuba&!*, and *Super Cub*.

The other variation is the "observing lead" stories. In these stories, the main character really is just an observer, and the real story is about the other characters they meet and encounter. One example of this is *Wandering Witch: The Journey of Elaina*, where the main character is a young witch on a journey to explore the fantasy world they live in. Elaina is just there to meet other characters who represent the different aspects of the setting world and the stories are really their stories, not hers. But, through each of their stories, we learn something about the setting they all live in.

If this sounds familiar, it's because this is also the pattern for old American cowboy westerns (and Japanese samurai movies) about the action hero who wanders from town-to-town meeting new people and finding trouble. However, in this case, there's usually little to no "trouble" and the focus of the story is more on slice of life and daily life.

To give a comparison, in an action/adventure cowboy western story about a town well, the lead character would wander into a town where the local well has run dry and a local rancher is using the only remaining other water source as an excuse to rule the town with an iron fist. The lead character would get to know the local suffering townsfolk and their problems. And then, when the tyrant tries to kidnap and marry the local saloon owner's daughter, the lead would jump into action and work his way through the tyrant's men with his six-shooter until the tyrant was dead and order was restored. (Before riding off into the sunset, to the next town.)

However, in an exploratory story about a town well in the old west, the lead character would wander into town looking for work and find the local well had run dry. Then he'd meet the local doctor, who thinks he can solve the town's water problem through finding new underground water sources and end up getting hired to help the doctor. As they work to solve the problem, he would learn about the doctor's motivations and the doctor would talk about the relationship the townspeople have with water. Finally, after some effort, the doctor would find a way to use their theories to tap the water and return the town to normal. The lead would then go on, having learned about the relationship between life and water in the old west.

As you can see, these are very different stories, despite the same premise. One is about the lead restoring order through action and violence, and the other is about the lead meeting a character who acts as a guide through a piece of the world they live in, before themselves moving on to explore another piece of the setting.

This type of story is largely possible because the Japanese use the Ki-Sho-Ten-Ketsu story structure which doesn't require conflict to work, but only requires that progressively interesting things happen. Then, following the Japanese approach of watching interesting things interact, the author only needs to bring the main character in contact with the characters or parts of the setting they find interesting, and the story naturally flows from their interactions. There can be conflict, but it isn't needed, and most often the story is built on learning rather than drama.

Which brings up the question – what makes these stories work?

Well, as was mentioned in the section on *Joy* from *Making the Audience Feel*, there are five things readers get from stories, which can be remembered from the mnemonic SPICE – Skills, Perspective, Information, Creativity, and Emotion. And, even without conflict, these stories can offer pretty much all of those things to audiences to keep them hooked.

Skills: In some exploratory manga, they're literally teaching the audience how to do things, like cooking or camping.

Perspective: Often these stories offer a new perspective to the audience about some aspect of the setting or the real world. For example, why do people love stamps so much? Or why are some people obsessed with fishing? These stories give us a glimpse into parts of our world we don't normally interact with, or parts of other worlds which can give us new reflections on our own.

Information: Exploratory Manga are all about sharing information. Usually, they're sharing some combination of Information and Perspective as their main driver. The audience is learning as they're being entertained.

Creativity: Through offering Skills, Perspective, and Information, these stories let the audience explore a new world they haven't seen before and come to know more about the world they live in. These stories are trying hard to evoke a sense of wonder in the everyday and mundane, and often use their art to bring that wonder to life.

Emotion: Sometimes these stories have drama, especially if they're about the characters the lead meets as they travel/explore, but most often these stories evoke positive emotions like curiosity, fulfillment, happiness, and humor. They're about the joy of learning about the world, a joy which many people have often forgotten as they have aged. Or, they might be mono no aware stories where the audience is brought in touch with complex and melancholy emotions connected with the passing of time.

Using these ways, and often paired with appealing art and characters, the creators delve deep into the setting of their stories and teach us about those worlds while expanding our own.

Notes on writing these stories:

Most often, these stories tend to be written by and for older and more mature audiences. This makes sense because you normally have to have some life experience to write one of these stories well, and most younger creators (and audiences) don't have the time or patience for these stories. They want something with a stronger emotional impact and prefer more visceral works. That's why many of these stories would be classified as Gekiga (dramatic pictures) not Manga (foolish pictures) and are usually found in publications for older audiences. (See the works of Jiro Taniguchi for examples.)

That isn't to say that these can't be appealing to younger audiences, and in fact you could easily make the argument that a number of Miyazaki's films are actually Exploratory Anime, like *Kiki's Delivery Service*, for example. However, it takes a light touch to make them work well for a younger audience, so even there the creators are usually older and more experiences artists.

Instead, for younger audiences, you usually see elements of Exploratory Manga incorporated into other manga genres like Battle Manga or Romance. Where they take the exploratory elements and use them to help build and flesh out the world of the characters. A good example of this would be *Yowamushi Pedal* ("Weakling Pedal") which is primarily a sports manga about cycling, but delves deep into different aspects of the amateur cycling world in Japan. In fact, many Sports Manga make heavy use of Exploratory Manga approaches to teach their audiences about the sport in between the competitions. The main difference being that at the end of the day the sports manga are about the characters, battles, and competitions, while their exploratory manga counterparts are about the setting first and foremost.

The other way these types of stories are often made to appeal to younger audiences is by making them funny or humorous. Everyone likes to laugh, and humor is a natural way to bring out the appeal of the story events and setting. Thus, commonly these are written like slice-of-life stories where the character ends up in some humorous situation by the end of the story, or has a series of amusing (but rarely laugh out loud) events happen to them. This isn't a sitcom, but a gentle and fun reflection of reality that is often (but not always) bathed in sunshine.

You also see this type of story in hobbyist and profession-related magazines in Japan, where they often function as basically a serialized "for dummies" guide for people new to the hobby. In this case, they're usually built around appealingly designed characters having amusing slice-of-life experiences related to pursuing the hobby or profession in some form. This can be as simple as playing collectable card games or model kit building, or full-on professional activities like voice acting or being a country veterinarian.

Lastly, it should be mentioned that these stories are largely possible because the Japanese are producing them in comic book form. The comic book form allows images and pictures to make complex or sometimes dull subjects lively and interesting in ways that text struggles to. Yes, there are Exploratory Light Novels that exist, like *Kino's Journey* but it can be argued they're possible because the audience is already used to these types of stories from manga. Also, Kino's Journey is still mostly about the characters the lead meets and their dramatic lives, as opposed to a story about the intricacies of stamp collecting which would be dull as dishwater without visuals to help prop it up.

This isn't to say that you couldn't do this type of story as a prose novel or story collection, but it would take a lot of skill to do well.

Final Notes

When North Americans write about stories exploring setting, they almost always turn it into a mystery or literary fiction of some kind. Most often, it's a character trying to uncover the truth about some event, and to do so they must come to understand a new environment or world they (and the audience) weren't familiar with before. This is a good way to do it because the mystery frames the exploration and gives the writer a conflict-based reason to examine a setting that often doesn't want to be examined by the lead character.

Exploratory Manga bypass this approach and instead throw open the doors of the hidden world and invite the character and audience in for tea. The reader isn't an intruder uncovering dark secrets (although that's not off the table), but instead a welcome guest invited in like a beloved grandchild to experience the hidden corners of their grandparent's ancient home. The joy of exploratory manga comes from discovery and learning, not from violently ripping back the curtains to expose the truth to sunlight.

Exploratory stories are driven by love, not fear or hate, and a sense of curiosity that often takes the reader back to their youth. They reflect on the human condition, and gently make readers consider their own lives in a non-confrontational way or expand their horizons to understand our world a little better. They are about the joy of interacting with the world around us, and reminding us that we are part of a vast web of connections. Never alone, and always linked to the greater world we live in.

A very Japanese way of seeing the world.

SLICE-OF-LIFE STORIES

Someone once described life as "long periods of boredom punctuated by exciting moments of screaming terror," and while most stories are built around those "exciting moments," there is a place for stories built around "long periods of boredom" as well. Those so-called periods of boredom are where the small realities of people's lives occur, and they make up the bulk of time we spend as living beings. They aren't empty, but instead filled with trivial moments and a constant stream of choices being made, just ones that aren't epic or life changing, so they're ignored or forgotten.

But, where there are choices, there is story.

The term "slice-of-life" was first coined by 19th century French playwright Jean Jullien to describe a type of theatre where we see random pieces of the lives of characters without plot, story development or conflict, like we're looking at random "orange slices" without seeing the whole "fruit." The idea was to capture the lives of the characters in a pure and natural way by removing them from the structure of plot and just showing them living as pure individuals uninfluenced by ideas of story.

However, in the last hundred or so years since Jullien's time, the term has shifted to mean not the separation of character from plot, but instead stories about characters living everyday, mundane lives just like the rest of humanity. Slice-of-life now refers to a meta-genre of stories where characters are freed from adventures, mysteries, quests, and other great dramatic genre plots, but instead are doing what normal people do- work, sleep, study, relax, play games, commute, shop, fight, cook, and the hundreds of other small and large activities that make up people's daily lives.

Slice-of-life stories are about the common, the mundane, the ordinary, and the routine.

But, that doesn't mean they're boring- not at all.

The slice-of-life story looks at the mundane aspects of life, and then lets us see them in new and interesting ways. Usually by sticking interesting characters into ordinary situations, or by putting ordinary characters into extraordinary situations, it helps the audience to see life from a different angle and get another, often amusing, view of the world we might not normally see.

A typical slice-of-life story might be structured like this:

- **KI- Introduction** – Characters and situations are introduced.
- **SHO- Development** - Interesting characters are presented with a mundane task, or mundane characters are presented with an interesting task.
- **TEN- Activity** – Interesting and unusual things (to the audience, at least) happen while the character tries to do that task, either because the person or the task itself is interesting.
- **KETSU- Conclusion** – The character(s) accomplish their task, and we see how the whole thing works out.

This isn't the only slice-of-life story structure, but it is a common one, and works because the fundamentals of story (action + results) are still present. A character has a goal, and then sets out to accomplish that goal, even if the goal is extremely mundane or vague. For example, a character is bored and decides to go to the store to buy something to drink. The character is trying to relieve their boredom and buying something to drink is a method to solving that issue because it gives them something to do. Along the way, they see some interesting things, and so when they reach the store they're no longer feeling bored. They were bored and solved it by going out (achieving a result).

This story structure will still work if characters decide to be inactive. Even when characters are passive and do "nothing," they are still doing something by making the choice to do nothing. Not taking action is still an active choice, and therefore can produce results as well. By not taking out the garbage, garbage piles up, and a result is produced (a stinky place filled with garbage), or by choosing to just sit there and not move, other things they need to do (cook, clean, call their mother) will still affect them sooner or later (again, the results of inaction). Whatever they choose to do, or not do, produces a result, and that can be used for producing story.

Slice-of-life, then, comes from using the activities of life to produce story, no matter how simple or vague that story may be. And this may be why the Japanese have been so drawn to it, because it falls right in line with the *Ki-Sho-Ten-Ketsu* (KSTK) structure that they use to conceive of story- a structure not built on conflict but on invoking reader interest. Slice-of-life stories often don't involve conflict, which puts them at odds with the normally used conflict-based American Three-Act Structure that's become the fundamental story form in the West.

On the other hand, Japanese KSTK stories don't require conflict, and therefore slice-of-life approaches fit right into their concepts of story. You can find slice-of-life story approaches everywhere in Japanese fiction, from their anime to their manga. In fact, their use of the slice-of-life approach in manga is one of the things that makes their work feel unique or different from other types of stories. It isn't unusual to find manga where the entire story structure is a slice-of-life approach, often mixing normal people with interesting situations or interesting people with mundane situations to produce stories.

Comedy manga using a slice-of-life approach are especially common, where a normal, average person suddenly finds themselves surrounded by a collection of weird and eccentric characters making their life miserable. Each of these eccentric characters brings with them complications, dramatic questions, and situations that make their interactions with the lead character and others interesting, and the story runs off the interest this generates. Whether it be that the weird characters are fish out of water in this setting, or have personality issues, or needs and goals that conflict with those of the lead, it creates situations that the reader will find fascinating and/or amusing. This juxtaposition of interesting characters and mundane situations keeps readers' attention, and the story in motion until the end.

And, each time the comedy starts to run out of energy, the writer just needs to introduce another character to spice things back up, using the new arrival to keep things lively. Of course, this has its drawbacks, as there are only so many cast members you can add before it gets too crowded, and so pure slice-of-life comedy stories done in this way have a limited lifespan unless the writer is very clever or the characters very interesting.

As a result, most manga combine some element of slice-of-life with another kind of genre or meta-genre to keep the story interesting. For example, many manga use the approach of having a grand overall story like a quest or situation to be resolved, but then use a series of slice-of-life stories to advance that greater plot instead of having each story be about the overall story. Each individual story is a slice-of-life story about the characters and situations, but taken as a whole they tell a greater non-slice-of-life story about how the character(s) accomplish something. For example, say the story was about characters trying to build up an interstellar transport business (Mundane Characters + Interesting Situation), and each story is a slice-of-life tale about daily life in the space freighter trade. The overall story might be about them going from nobodies to successful business owners, but that's a story playing out in the background of the slice-of-life pieces of their daily lives.

Not that a writer MUST be stuck with any particular kind of story structure (you could alternate between slice-of-life and High Adventure stories, and that would be fine too), but that's something that needs to be planned and set up from the start. The characters in a Mundane Characters + Interesting Situation type story aren't likely to be as suited to situations of high adventure as the characters in a Interesting Characters + Mundane Situation story are. The leads in *The Devil is a Part-Timer* are all exiled warriors and powerful figures from a fantasy world, and despite working at McRonalds, if called upon they do have a skill set for dealing with fantastical situations. On the other hand, if you put characters who work at a real McRonalds into a fantasy world (Mundane Characters + Interesting Situation) they'd be monster chow pretty fast unless the author gives them a little help.

That said, can slice-of-life stories be built around Interesting Characters and Interesting Situations paired together? The answer is yes they can, but the problem is that slice-of-life is about the mundane, and unless there are mundane elements to the story it isn't a slice-of-life story. So, a heroic space fleet admiral who lives the life of a glorious military officer overseeing a million worlds can still be a character and situation you can tell a slice-of-life story about, but it will mean finding the tiny mundane details in their life to focus on. (Like them trying to sneak out to get fast food when their ship's doctor has put them on a diet.) In addition, the more "interesting" the character and situation are, the less mundane and normal they are, and slice-of-life stories are built around the normal, which makes them more challenging to write.

At the other extreme, we have stories about normal people in normal situations, which are also perfectly good fodder for slice-of-life stories, but have much the same problems. If the character and situation are both very ordinary and not especially interesting, then you have lots of mundane, but not much to build a story on that will keep the reader's attention. This too will require a lot of skill as a writer, as the interest in the story will come from adding little twists and turns of setting and circumstance to the character's otherwise dull lives. (Like two middle aged women who meet for tea every day at a coffee shop, but one day their waiter is a gorgeous man who the two very normal women begin trying to out-flirt each other with. Leading to a fight that ends when the waiter's boyfriend shows up to pick him up.) There are always situations which can turn normal people into interesting ones by bringing out their hidden sides, and normal situations can be made abnormal when the quirks of human behavior become involved.

However, the easiest type of slice-of-life setup, especially for longer stories like serialized manga, is an equal mix of the unusual and mundane, which by its nature generates stories that are going to hold the reader's interest and offer a lot of material for the writer to work with. Writing is already hard enough without making your life more difficult by choosing a hard to work with set of controlling ideas. Unless you're a dramatic or comedic writer who is an expert at finding the interesting in the everyday, trying to work with mundane characters and settings for the long haul might not be the best choice for you.

Which brings us to the final, significant topic to consider when writing slice-of-life stories- humor.

While slice-of-life stories don't have to be humorous in any way, humor and slice-of-life go together like icing and cake. Whether the story itself is meant to be humorous, or just the situations and the reactions of the characters involved makes the reader laugh, most slice-of-life stories use some element of humor to keep their audience interested. In shorter slice-of-life stories, this is often a comedic twist at the end, and the story effectively plays out as a joke leading up to that twist. In longer slice-of-life stories, the humour will often come from the character interactions and situations which appear, and there may not be any twist at all, just a resolution as the characters realize the nature of the situation they've found themselves in. Or, the twist may still be there, but serve as a reminder to the characters (and audience) about some flaw of human nature. (see the above story about the tea friends)

Many American Situation Comedies (SitComs) you see on television are similar to slice-of-life stories, although they've turned up the level of humour to an extreme and are very plot and joke driven. This generally makes them funny in short bursts, but they lose much of the relatability that comes with a real slice-of-life story. In a slice-of-life story, the closer the story is to mundane reality, the better it works, but comedies like SitComs take it to another level and become another type of story altogether. Real people don't talk like that and aren't that witty. Ironically, however, the most popular SitComs of all time (*Leave it to Beaver, All in the Family, M*A*S*H, Different Strokes, FRIENDS, Seinfeld, Big Bang Theory,* etc.) have tended to be closer to slice-of-life stories than their joke-driven counterparts, and this focus on the natural humor of those characters and situations was largely responsible for their success. (As opposed to the many joke-driven shows that appear each year and are cancelled and forgotten with equal frequency.)

Final Notes on slice-of-life:
- Slice-of-life stories get their energy from interesting characters and interesting twists on daily events.
- Sometimes used for relationship stories where the romantic leads have a series of slice-of-life experiences together and these represent the evolution of their relationship.
- Mundane means that the story element or character is everyday in our real world. Something like Monster Hunting might be mundane in a fantasy setting, but it isn't mundane in our world so it's not going to be slice-of-life. However, if you could present the job of Monster Hunting in a way which makes it seem just like a job in our world (say being a Pest Control Expert), then it can still come across as slice-of-life.
- Slice-of-life stories often have a lead character, but they don't have to, and can be about groups or themes instead.
- This form works very well for Four-Koma comic strips.
- Japanese slice-of-life stories are often built around routine tasks, procedures, festivals and seasons.

FOUR-KOMA MANGA

As you have probably noticed, Japanese comic strips (called four-koma manga) are a little bit different from American ones. First, they have four panels (*koma* in Japanese), instead of the usual American three, and second they are read from top to bottom instead of left to right. This second difference is because they were created near the start of the 20th century, when Japanese still read from top to bottom, so that was normal at the time.

The fact they use four panels, however, is much more important.

As you can probably guess by now, the four panels correspond roughly to the standard *Ki-Sho-Ten-Ketsu* pattern you've seen referenced throughout this book. And, in fact four-koma manga are actually a much closer interpretation to the original KSTK poetry pattern of *Meng Haoren* than regular manga use in their stories. Like the original four-line poems that inspired the pattern, the four panels of the four-koma comic strip each represent the different phases of the KSTK pattern and tell the writer clearly what goes where.

This actually makes the four-koma pattern extremely easy to use and once you get the hang of it, they're very easy to write. (Although, as always with manga, starting is easy, mastering is a different thing entirely.) Let's take a look at the basic pattern:

- **Ki (Setup)** – a situation is presented, usually one which the audience is familiar with
- **Sho (Development)** – the situation is explained in more detail, and a character is presented as doing something normal in this situation
- **Ten (Twist)** – something unexpected happens, such as the character finding or doing something strange
- **Ketsu (Reaction)** – the characters/audience react to what happened

So, for example:
- **Ki (Setup)** – a man is shown drinking water
- **Sho (Development)** – he looks at the camera and says "The doctor says you need to drink 6 glasses of water every day to stay healthy. But I want to be extra healthy, like Popeye!"
- **Ten (Twist)**- he continues "So, I drink spinach water!"

- **Ketsu (Reaction)** – the man smiles at us and we see he has green teeth- "But all it did was make my teeth green…"

As you can see, the first two panels are about creating audience expectations, the third one puts a spin on what the audience expects, and the fourth panel shows the result of that twist. The goal is to make the audience react, usually either in laughter or horror at the silly result or expressions which the characters in the last panel make.

Speaking of characters, because these stories are so short, they usually only have one or two speaking characters in them. Typically, there is one main character who is the one being weird, and another character who is there to ask questions and react to the twist. There can be other characters, but they're usually silent and in the background, and sometimes there is only one character who is either talking to the audience or whose thoughts the audience can "hear."

The most common form is the "two-hander," where it's like a comedy routine where one character sets things up and the other character provides the entertaining twist or reaction.

- **Ki (Setup)** – A young man and a woman are having a romantic evening stroll in the park. The woman thinks to herself, "Now's my chance to get him to propose!"
- **Sho (Development)** – The woman says, "It's so beautiful, just the two of us here alone. Does looking at the stars make you think of anything, darling?"
- **Ten (Twist)** – "It sure does," replies the man. "We're just like a couple in a horror movie about to be abducted by aliens!"
- **Ketsu (Reaction)** – "C'mon, we'd better get someplace safe. They don't like crowds!" Says the man as he leads the unhappy woman out of the park by the hand.

People and situations which don't go as the audience expects are the bread and butter of the four-koma pattern, and you can get a lot of different situations from them, especially if the audience comes to know these characters. That's why the best four-koma strips aren't one-off jokes, but actually help to build a small world that the audience gets to know. This might be why the most common genre for four-koma stories is slice-of-life comedies, which are a natural fit for the form.

Each single strip represents a small entertaining piece of the character's lives that together form a greater story and characters the audiences relate to and enjoys reading about. Not to mention that writing a series makes the whole thing easier because the audience comes to know the characters and develops expectations on their behavior that you can play with instead of constantly having to come up with new situations. Even whole scenes can be broken down into a series of smaller four-koma strips that build on each other and show the lighter sides of these characters. Just by thinking through the unexpected twists that could happen in everyday interactions, a whole series of strips can naturally come to mind.

Of course, the four-koma KSTK pattern can be used for other kinds of stories, and even in other mediums. You could use this pattern to develop short films, flash-fiction, or even poetry. It's all about playing with the form.

Have fun!

Four Koma Tips:
- Before you try writing four-koma, make sure you read the Slice-of-Life genre section, as that will help give you more ideas for characters and situations you can use to create your own little four-koma world.
- Another common four-koma pattern you'll see is the "double sho" pattern where both the middle panels are Development, and both the Twist and Reaction to the twist come in the final panel. This allows for slightly more complex jokes, and shows that you don't need to be a slave to the form- it's just a guide.
- Some four-koma strips are built on making the audience feel gross or uncomfortable, and these will end with a final panel designed to shock the audience rather than a character reacting. As long as the final panel makes the audience react, it's doing its job, though!

OTHER META GENRES

SPORTS STORIES

Sports manga are a classic example of stories about an individual becoming part of a group. In sports manga, the main character is almost always a new player who either dreams of joining the sport or is forced into it, but either way has incredible talent for the sport. This rookie usually knows little or nothing about the actual sport (putting them in the same position as the audience), and the story of the manga will be about them learning the ins and outs of the sport while they work to master it.

Through the eyes of the main character, the audience will come to know the rest of the team or (if it's an individual sport or pair sport) the allies and rivals who also do this sport. This will almost always include a mentor character of some kind (usually the team captain) who has dedicated their life to this sport and can be a bit brutal. Also, there will be at least one rival character on the team who motivates the main character to do better in order to defeat them, and a wise buddy who is there to offer emotional support and advice. Finally, most teams have a wise coach there to moderate the captain and keep the team going. They rarely interfere, and mostly act as a foil to the main character- not letting them do what they might want to do because they're not ready (or because it's better dramatically to hold them back until the last minute).

The rest of the team will be a collection of people who reflect the themes of the story or sport in different ways, often being alternate versions of the main character. For example, if the theme of the story is working together to become stronger (a common theme), then the various team members will be people who have different ideas about working together. Some might see the team as something they're just using to achieve glory, others might not believe in teamwork, while still another character might be overdoing it and their life is falling apart because they're trying too hard at the sport. In any case, the members of the team usually become a collection of rivals and advisors to the lead, but at the same time also act as comic relief with them doing some weird or crazy antics. If the team is large, not all the members might be named characters with only the characters who are important to the main character's story being actual named characters.

In terms of writing and presentation, sports manga are actually just another type of Battle Manga. They play out largely like a typical Battle Manga, but with a twist because of the larger cast. The duels in sports manga actually happen inside the larger games themselves, with the bigger game acting as an arena where the various characters face off against rivals in smaller matches that contribute towards the bigger game. Or, to put it another way, the larger sporting event is presented as a series of important moments from the game where two or three players faced off against each other and either won or lost their smaller matches.

If you read sporting manga like *Slam Dunk*, you'll see that each chapter or two during a game is usually about how one player on the main character's team has to face off against a character on the team they're playing and defeat that character's talents or abilities. Maybe the rival has a special move, or maybe they're just really skilled at one aspect of the game, but either way that rival team character is a threat that the main character (or their teammate) must overcome. Once they defeat that person, the next chapter the focus will usually shift to another teammate, and another rival or situation that character is facing. This jumping from challenge to challenge will continue until the end of the game, not unlike what you see in Fighting Manga where the main character and their friends fight against a rival group.

Since there is rarely time to focus on everyone (if the team is large, and there's two teams involved), then the story will usually only be about a few of the players on each side per game. In a quick game, it might be about just two or three people on each side, even if each team is fielding groups of a dozen players. This focus is also necessary because during the game the story will often give the backstories of the players involved as flashbacks or asides, helping the audience to get to know and understand them and upping the emotional element of the story. If the story tried to give a full backstory for everyone involved in the game it might take years to present a single two-hour competition!

A few other notes about sports manga:
- An advantage of team sports is that the team can be winning while the main character is losing. Thus, the team all together follows the "always rising" rule by going up in ranks, but the main character can stumble, fall, and pick themselves back up during or between games.
- If the sport is an individual sport, the story will generally play out like a typical Battle Manga, with each story being about facing a new opponent and the challenges that come with them.
- Sports manga often make heavy use of fools and commentators in the audience to control the flow of the story, jumping back and forth between the

action and the audience. The audience also serves to act as comic relief and to explain what's happening in the game to the readers.

- The hardest part of writing sports manga is presenting it in a way which doesn't overwhelm the audience who are new to the sport and learning about it through the manga. A good sports manga is enjoyable even by people who have never watched the sport, and never will, but still find the manga accessible and fun to read.
- Almost every sports manga main character has a crisis of confidence, plan yours carefully.
- Coming up with interesting training methods is half the fun of writing sports manga.
- Examples include *Slam Dunk, Aim for the Ace, Haikyuu!, Beast Children, Captain Tsubasa, Ace of Diamonds, Inazuma Eleven, Giant Killing, Eyeshield 21, The Prince of Tennis, Yawamushi Pedal, MAJOR,* and *Initial D.*

HAREM STORIES

This type of story is about a male lead character who ends up surrounded by a collection of women who are all in love with him and want to be his number one. This is also usually played as a comedy rather than a drama, and runs on the message of "helping others can transform your life and theirs." In terms of story structure, it will depend on whether the Harem part of the story is the focus or just a running secondary element. If the Harem is the focus, then it's a Procedural Manga where each story arc will be about how a new "wife" enters the harem of the male lead and how he wins her over. If the harem element is background, then it can be any story structure but as the male lead helps various girls he meets during his adventures they join him and stick around in hopes of becoming his future love interest.

- In a "pure" Harem drama, the first "wife" introduced will almost always be the true Love Interest for the lead character, but there will be something which keeps them from just getting together as a couple. Subsequent "wives" will then start to appear and then join the pair's life, much to the distress of the Love Interest who will then slowly come to accept the others as a mix of rivals and sisters.
- In some "pure" Harem dramas, the main male lead is pretty bland and almost a plot device to get the girls together and bind them to each other, and once

the harem is formed the girls and their lives often become the focus of the story.

- Each "wife" in a pure Harem drama will have an extreme personality, and there will usually be a theme to the girls that unify them.
- The members of the Harem will end up living together with the male lead under the same roof, and sometimes all sleep in the same room.
- The members of the Harem will eventually form a family unit that makes all of them stronger and better people.
- The story will end with the male lead and the Love Interest from the beginning (the "first wife") committing to each other as a couple but deciding to continue to live together with their "new family" in a happy communal relationship.
- Examples of pure Harem stories are *Monster Musume, Urusei Yatsura, Ah! My Goddess!, Love Hina,* and others.
- Examples of partial Harem stories includes *Magic Teacher Negima!* (Which is a Transformative Teacher Harem Story!), *Gate - Thus the JSDF Fought There!, Overlord,* and many, many, many others. (Many non-harem stories take on a harem element in an effort to keep popular female characters in the spotlight after being introduced, and to pad out the dramatic elements of the story.)

HUNTED HERO STORIES

Hunted Hero stories are tales where a small group of heroes are being pursued by a large and powerful enemy, and travel from place to place until they get strong enough to face their larger foe in some sort of showdown. This is another type of meta-genre which was more popular in the past than it is now, and mostly shows up in Anime form rather than comic form. The message behind these stories is usually "through working together we can overcome any foe" or something similar. The most common genre for these stories is science fiction (classic Japanese examples being *Space Cruiser Yamato, Macross,* and the first *Mobile Suit Gundam*); however, these stories can be set anywhere or anywhen, and be of any genre. (The first "hunted hero" story being the semi-legendary story of the mighty Japanese warrior Yoshitsune chronicled in Kurosawa's *The Men Who Tread the Tiger's Tail.*)

- These stories almost always take place in a setting ruled by an Evil Empire which is directly or indirectly oppressing the common people.

- The main characters will be a team, but there will be one main lead character who will have some special ability or piece of technology that makes them very powerful, but not powerful enough to defeat the vastly larger foe.
- The heroes will travel from place to place, usually aboard their own special vehicle, and meet new friends and enemies, all while the Main Opponent's army dogs their heels.
- The lead character can be Changing or Unchanging, but will always be progressing in skill and ability as the story goes on. They will need this skill and ability to face the seemingly unbeatable foe at the end.
- If the lead character is Changing, there will almost always be a Mentor character who teaches and leads the hero until they are ready to stand on their own, which is usually when the mentor dies or is imprisoned by the enemy. (Or both)
- Sometimes the main characters are uniting and inspiring the common people as they go, in which case the peoples they helped will come back to help them in the final showdown.
- Within the Evil Empire, there will be different factions which are vying for control of the Empire, and which want to use the heroes to help them achieve their goals. Some of them see the Empire as evil and want to take it down, and some of them want to become the new ruler.
- Most commonly, the rulers of the Empire don't see themselves as evil, but as bringers of peace, order and stability.
- Often, these stories play out as a type of Battle Manga with the characters facing a series of new and ever more powerful foes as they work their way to the top.
- Other examples of this story are *Star Wars* (Starting with the fourth movie, and the TV Series *REBELS*), *One Piece*, *Captain Harlock*, most *Gundam* TV series (and their many, many mecha anime clones), *Jojo's Bizarre Adventures: Stardust Crusaders*, *Samurai Jack*, and *Voltron: Legendary Defender*.

TRANSFORMATIVE TEACHER STORIES

This type of story will center on a dedicated but unusual teacher who comes to a school and then proceeds to transform the troubled lives of the students in their class through their passion and wisdom. Often played for comedy, the message here is the simple "if you have problems, your teacher is there to help" or something similar. In terms of story structure, these function as a type of procedural mystery where each troubled student is a puzzle to be solved by the teacher.

- Sometimes the story will be told from a troubled student's point of view, who ends up playing the Watson to the teacher's Holmes, and in the process learning to fix themselves and their own problems.
- The troubled students are often all introduced in the opening story, and then their different life issues become the foundation of the overall story structure as each of them gets their own story arc. When the class is all fixed, the teacher will leave.
- Each student will have a problem that could be solved if they only reached out for help, but were too ashamed (or unable) to do so.
- Most of the students will reject the teacher as an idiot or stupid because of their unusual methods, but by the end they will all love and adore this teacher who changed their lives for the better.
- Examples of this genre are *Great Teacher Onizuka*, *Gokusen*, *Hell Teacher Nube*, and *Assassination Classroom*

WEIRD APOCALYPSE STORIES

This type of story is a relatively recent invention, but has its roots in mid-twentieth century apocalyptic fiction. In this meta-genre, a young person or group of young people (most often people going to the same high school) are thrown into a survival situation when society suddenly collapses one day due to something strange happening. The message of these stories is usually something like "by working together we can overcome any challenge" or "the power of the human spirit in the face of odds." Structurally, these stories start a short time before the apocalyptic event, which happens during the first story. The main character(s) usually have to escape their school first, search for their loved ones, encounter lots of other humans being selfish jerks, avoid whatever it is that is causing the apocalypse, and try to survive. Very often, there's a "mystery" element as to why this apocalypse is happening, and the characters end up being the ones who solve that mystery and may even stop it.

- This genre was kickstarted by the huge success of *High School of the Dead*, but has since blossomed to include apocalypses which were caused by giant insects, magical girls, demons, dolls, and even giant chickens. Commonly, there is some element of people turning into monsters, animals transforming or acting monstrous, people acting crazy, people vanishing, monsters appearing, or technology rebelling,

- Usually, someone close to the main character or in the group is connected to the apocalypse in some way. Maybe they made a wish that started it, their blood holds the key to solving it, or some action they did triggered it. There is often some original sin that starts the weird apocalypse and only a sacrifice can bring things back in balance to end it. The story is about how the main characters end up in a position to stop the apocalypse, or at least survive it.
- There will always be rules which the enemy act under, and the main characters figure out those rules, which is why they survive.
- The main characters will always encounter other survivors who are using the wrong way to survive- usually reverting to acting like selfish animals. In many ways, other humans are usually the biggest threat to their survival, not the monsters.
- Examples include *Green Worldz, Dolly Kill Kill, 51 Ways to Save Her, I Am A Hero, School-Live!, Cagaster of an Insect Cage, Magical Girl Apocalypse, HIVE,* etc.

COMMON MANGA PLOTS

Manga use a wide variety of plots for their stories, but there are a few very common ones which are worth breaking down into more detail. The Duel Plot is the foundation of the Battle Manga, and many shonen stories use The Righteous Avenger Plot and Investigation Plot on a regular basis. On the other hand, the Romantic Comedy plot will work for stories which are neither totally a romance or a comedy, and is a good generic plot to know.

THE DUEL PLOT

Summary: The Duel Plot is one of the most common types of Battle Manga plots, as the majority of stories in a Battle Manga are based around it. In its simplest form, it is two characters dueling against each other, usually for some (to them) high stakes prize.

Required Characters:
- A main character
- An opponent
- Commentators on the duel (optional, but useful, see below)

Plot Structure
KI- Introduction
- The main character(s), the situation (place/time), and their abilities are introduced. Any strengths and weaknesses which are relevant to the story will also be introduced here.
- The reasons for the main character to be involved in the duel plot are introduced, usually in the form of their story goal and motivations.

SHO- Development

- The main character(s) may (or may not) take an action which triggers the duel while trying to accomplish their goals. (Sometimes they're just minding their own business when the duel is thrust upon them.)
- An opponent is introduced for the main character(s) to duel against. (They may also be introduced during the Introduction phase, depending on the story.)
- The stakes are introduced.
- The key rules (official or unofficial) that the audience needs to know to understand the competition (and any twists in it) are introduced (or re-introduced if part of a larger series of duels.)
- The reason the main character doesn't run away is introduced.
- The duel will play out in a series of "rounds", which may be official rounds/turns/phases, or it may be simply a series of back and forth plays built into a single duel. Typically, there will be three rounds to any duel, with a maximum of five rounds depending on the story length. (Any more than five rounds will start to bore the audience.)
- The first round will generally go well for the main character to show that they are capable and to give the audience a sense of hope that they can win.
- In between rounds, there will often be a "break" in the form of timeouts, dialog, flashbacks, commentary, or other cut-aways from the action to balance out the duel's intense moments with slower and more emotional material. This both acts to inject tension and emotion into the fight while extending it to meet the author's pacing needs.
- The second round will go against the main character, thus putting everything at risk, and making things even again. Usually the opponent will also display overwhelming and unexpected power/ability at this point, making the main character's victory look highly unlikely.

TEN- Activity

- There will often also be an additional twist at this point, which might be an unexpected upping of the stakes, or the main character(s) developing a weakness that will make things even more difficult. (Equipment starts to fail, weapons run low on ammo, the main character's loved one is revealed to be held hostage, focus/concentration is lost, extra penalties come into play, etc.) This is often the result of something the main character did during the Introduction or Development phase coming back to haunt them, but not always, it can be pure Murphy's Law or sabotage coming into effect for drama's sake.
- In the final round, the main character will gather all of their cleverness, courage, skill, or strength and find a way to win despite the odds. This will

usually be accomplished in the most dramatic way possible, and will normally involve a display of cleverness or a surprise sacrifice on their part to achieve the greater goal. If possible, this ending should be set up or foreshadowed in some subtle way during the Introduction or Development phases.

KETSU- Conclusion

- The main character will receive the rewards that come with victory, while the Opponent will pay for any underhanded or treacherous means they used during the competition.

Notes:

- Duel Plots almost always use the Negative TEN KSTK pattern.
- You can do a longer-form version of this plot where there are multiple duels happening simultaneously in different or similar locations and the action jumps between them, thus extending the fight.
- There is a variant of this plot where the main character loses the first round, makes a comeback in the second round, and then the additional twist at the start of the third round increases the stakes as the duel plunges into the final round. In this case, the Opponent will generally have the upper hand for the first part of the third round, and then the main character will pull the fat from the fire at the end to win.
- There is another variation of this plot where the first cycle is told from the main character's point of view, the second cycle is from the opponent's point of view, and the last cycle is told from the main character's point of view again. (See the manga/anime *Kagyua-san: Love is War* for a brilliant version of this in action.) This version is useful for creating purely dramatic battles which largely take place internally as opposed to externally.
- There are often other characters present to serve the role of Commentators-people who are commenting on the duel as it happens. These Commentators can be allies, enemies, or neutral third parties, but they serve three important and useful purposes. First, they act as a dialog based way to convey information about the events unfolding to the audience (extremely useful in visual mediums like comics and film). They can inform the audience about rules, background information, and anything else the writer needs the readers to know. Second, their reactions act as emotional cues for the audience, making the duel feel more exciting and letting the audience know how they should be feeling about what's occurring. (Hopeful, worried, scared, shocked, etc. The audience will feel what the Commentators tell them to feel in their reactions.) And third, Commentators can help to control pacing, as every time we cut away to the Commentators it slows the action

down and makes the audience wait to find out what happens next, building dramatic *Sho* tension. (Or relieving dramatic tension if things get too intense, with a little comic relief!) See the short YouTube video titled "What if UNO was an Anime" to see an almost perfect use of Commentators in action doing all three roles.

- The Opponent can also act as a commentator, and so can the main character. This is often done in the form of internal monologs and used to add commentary to a one on one fight with no-one else present.
- In duels which are heavily rules based, and the rules will be part of the plot, there will often be a judge or referee. They will normally act to make sure the rules are enforced, but can also be acting against the main character in support of their opponent in the case of corrupt judges or biased ones. To maintain the judge's appearance of neutrality, they will often not be Commentators on the duel unless things get so dramatic even they can't help it.
- In order to heighten the tension of a duel plot, the presenter often relies on extreme visuals and reactions from the characters to make the audience more excited as the story goes on. This can easily fall into self-parody levels if they overdo it, but how much the creator can push it will depend on the style and tone of the story and art. (More cartoonish stories allow for more extreme expressions of emotion.)
- The "God of The Duel Plot" is Hirohiko Araki, the creator of the manga *Jojo's Bizarre Adventure*, and the classic *Stardust Crusaders* arc and later arcs of that series are a collection of non-stop variants of the duel plot in action that have yet to be beaten. However, almost all Battle Manga lean heavily on duel plots and you can find them everywhere in manga and anime.

Examples: *Dragonball Z, My Hero Academia, Naruto, One Piece, Death Note, Shokugeki no Souma, Pokémon, Hikaru no Go*, and most shonen comics in general.

THE RIGHTEOUS AVENGER PLOT

Summary: The Righteous Avenger plot is an extremely common plot in manga and anime, and appears from time to time in Western media as well. In short- it's a story where a powerful hero saves a noble innocent from a true villain.

Required Characters:
- A powerful hero (the "righteous avenger")
- A virtuous Innocent
- An irredeemable villain

Plot Structure

KI- Introduction
- The powerful hero and the virtuous Innocent are introduced. The hero is shown to be strong and capable in some way, or is shown to represent some powerful force like the police or government. The innocent is introduced as the main character of this story, and as someone who is trying to accomplish a goal the audience will find strongly sympathetic. (Generally helping others selflessly, trying to protect loved ones, or standing up for a noble cause.)
- The hero and the innocent encounter each other, and the hero may stay around to help the innocent or may leave, but will be shown to be close by.

SHO- Development
- The innocent will be shown working to try to accomplish their goal, and we'll be shown why that goal is so important to them (or at least it will be hinted at).
- The villain will be introduced and shown to be working at cross purposes to the innocent. They will also be shown to be much stronger than the innocent.
- If the hero and innocent are together, they will become separated early on in the development phase, usually after a falling out or under some other circumstances which make it unlikely that they will return. If the hero is not working with the Innocent, the audience will be reminded that they are around, but in a way which doesn't put them in a position to help the Innocent. Usually they are investigating the situation on a separate line from the innocent's story.

TEN- Activity
- Once the hero is gone, the villain will close in and begin to prey upon the innocent like a cat toying with a mouse. They will torment the innocent and use the most underhanded methods to make their life miserable.
- As the villain is torturing the innocent, the innocent will be given the opportunity to submit and give up their noble goal. This is the villain trying to break the Innocent and prove to themselves that the Innocent isn't special or better than them, or perhaps it's just for fun because they're that sadistic. Regardless, the innocent won't break, and will refuse to surrender despite their position of weakness.
- The villain will see that they aren't going to win, or perhaps the innocent finally succumbs to the torture and passes out, in any case, they decide to

deliver a blow that will physically, mentally or emotionally destroy the innocent...

- The hero appears, having been brought there just in time by some reasonable explanation, and stops the final blow from being delivered. They then proceed to deliver righteous vengeance upon the evil doer. It might be a long battle, or a single act like arresting them, but will be done in a fashion which makes it clear the villain suffers for everything they've put the innocent through.

KETSU- Conclusion

- The villain defeated, the innocent is rewarded for their unyielding efforts to achieve their noble goal, and the hero helps them enjoy their new situation, the innocent having gone through a trial by fire and succeeded.

Notes:

- This pattern always uses the Negative TEN KSTK pattern.
- Almost all anime and manga series do a version of this plot sooner or later because it's so powerful when properly executed and creates great drama. Watching a powerful avenging figure save the innocent and crush evil speaks to the human psyche on a primal level and creates a mix of hope and bloodlust in the audience.
- This is a great plot to use with very powerful heroes, because it takes the focus off the hero and just makes them into an agent of justice. This is especially useful for heroes who can't be challenged otherwise because they're too powerful, or because the writer is keeping them a little mysterious.
- The key is that the main character is actually the innocent, not the hero, who is just there to provide support and save the day. The innocent is the one going through the trial by fire and having to decide whether to stand by their beliefs or give in to weakness.
- Often the story starts with the hero introduced first and acting as an initial viewpoint character, but then shifts quickly to the Innocent who becomes the main viewpoint for the rest of the story.
- This plot works well for short stories and story arcs/single stories, but not so well for whole series. A common version of it used in story arcs/single stories will involve the main Hero taken out of action early in the story and their allies left to fight the powerful villains without them for a large part of the story until the hero returns at a key moment to unleash justice.
- Sometimes the hero and innocent never meet until the end, when their separate plotlines intersect at the crucial moment. For example, a woman being stalked by a killer and a police officer who is simultaneously hunting

that killer. This creates a situation where the audience doesn't know when, or if, the hero will arrive in time.

- In darker versions of this plot, the villain often kills the Innocent (or delivers permanent damage to them) and the hero is truly avenging them as opposed to rescuing them. In these stories, the hero will almost always kill the villain or give them a horrible fate to balance the scales of justice.
- Also, in darker versions of this plot, the "Hero" might be anything but heroic, and even be another villainous character, just so long as they deliver a form of justice on the villain, they qualify as a "hero" in this story.
- The trick with these plots is to time the length of the "torture" so that it doesn't go on so long the audience gets bored or uncomfortable, but goes on just long enough that they really hate the villain and are screaming inside for justice to be delivered.
- Examples of this plot in action are abundant, but *Onepunch-man*, *Overlord*, and *One Piece* often use versions of it.

THE INVESTIGATION PLOT

Summary: The Investigation Plot is basically a standard detective/mystery procedural story but with a Japanese twist to heighten the drama. A standard of Japanese TV and manga storytelling for decades, it harkens back to the pulp detective stories of the American 1920s and 30s, but can be found everywhere from 1980s Samurai and Ninja episodic period dramas like *Yagyu Conspiracy* and *Kage no Gundan*, Anime like *Gatchaman* and *Sailor Moon*, and Tokusatsu shows like Sentai (Power Rangers) and *Kamen Rider*.

Required Characters:
- A "detective"
- A virtuous Innocent
- A villain

Plot Structure
KI- Introduction
- The detective is introduced along with their motivation for getting involved in investigations. (Usually that they are a detective or law enforcer of some kind, but they can be anyone, really.)

SHO- Development

- The detective's talents/abilities are introduced along with their strengths and weaknesses relevant to plot. (They can see ghosts, have superpowers, are a keen investigator, etc)
- The detective is put in a situation where they become involved in the story, often because of an Innocent who is caught up in some plot outside of their control.
- The detective discovers the villain's plot already in motion, usually through the Innocent caught up in it, but at best only has a vague sense that something is going on.
- The detective encounters their first obstacle to finding the truth and overcomes it, but is left feeling no further ahead in their investigation, only having gained some small potential clues.
- The detective encounters their second obstacle, which makes the plot seem to have a simple explanation after all.
- The detective is thrown off the scent, sometimes thinking they found the truth they were looking for, sometimes having chosen the wrong suspect, sometimes having been imprisoned/trapped, and sometimes thinking they've won and given up.

TEN- Activity

- A twist occurs, usually the innocent discovering that the detective was wrong and the true villain is revealed.
- The villain torments the innocent.
- The detective realizes their mistake and rushes to find the innocent. (Optional)
- The detective arrives in time to prevent the villain from finishing off the innocent.
- The detective defeats/captures/arrests the villain

KETSU- Conclusion

- The detective is rewarded and the villain receives punishment.

Notes

- The main difference between this story structure and the one Americans typically use is the revelation of the "true" villain near the start of the Ten phase, there often having been a false or red-herring villain prior who was just an underling. This is done to heighten the drama by setting up a situation where the hero is "gone," the Innocent is in jeopardy, and the villain is triumphant. Which is naturally followed by the Detective showing up just in time to prevent the villain from succeeding and save the day.

- In many ways, this is the Righteous Avenger Plot from the hero's point of view, whereas that plot follows the innocent instead.
- Often, in this plot, it is usually a race for the hero to solve the mystery in time to save the innocent. Can the hero uncover the truth in time?
- In superhero stories for younger children, the innocent will be in danger of something bad happening to them when the hero shows up just in time to save them. In stories for teens and older children, the innocent has often already been used by the villain and turned into a monster (which the hero will have to fight) or is seemingly about to die due to injuries unless they receive immediate medical attention.
- The detective's realization of their mistake is sometimes done as a flashback after they arrive to help, or they explain how they got there as they confront the villain. This lets the hero's arrival seem even more uncertain, since the audience thinks the hero is on the wrong track and doesn't know where they're needed. In this case, there always needs to be some clue or event that allowed the hero to figure out the truth in time.
- Sometimes the detective pretends to fail at the second obstacle to lure the villain out.

THE ROMANTIC COMEDY PLOT

Summary: The Romantic Comedy (RomCom) plot is the standard plot used in romance and comedy manga where the goal is to present the slow development of a relationship between two leads- each side moving a tiny bit closer to admitting their feelings for the other through shared experiences.

Required Characters:
- A main character
- A love interest
- Friends (optional)

Plot Structure:
KI- Introduction
- Characters and situations are introduced.

SHO (1)- Development

- The main character of the episode has a problem... (pick one from the list)
  - They try to recruit others to help them solve it, and they do.
  - They try to solve it themselves with some success.
  - They try to solve it themselves and fail, but others notice they need help and offer it.

SHO (2)- Development

- A larger obstacle appears... (pick one from the list)
  - Something unexpected happens that complicates the situation.
  - They try to solve it and make things worse. Now must dig themselves out.
  - They try to solve it and succeed, but then the unexpected happens and they must deal with it.

TEN- Activity

- The main character and allies try their best to solve the problem by using clever and creative solutions... (pick one from the list)
  - By working together, they accomplish what the main character couldn't on their own.
  - They end up digging deep and finding the solution to the problem inside themselves by overcoming or accepting something they didn't before. (Unlocking their special strength.)
  - They have a series of experiences which make them see things in a new light and provide a solution to their problem.
  - By other characters opening up emotionally, they give the lead the strength/wisdom to overcome their own issues.
  - By helping to solve another character's problems, they solve their own.

KETSU- Conclusion

- The main character's overall situation improves a tiny bit as a result of this experience, and... (pick one from the list)
  - They grow closer to their love interest emotionally.
  - They grow as a person, making them more ready to be in a relationship with others.
  - They understand their love interest better, making them better suited to be their partner.
  - The audience feels more strongly that these two belong together.
  - Their relationship becomes more balanced.

   ○ On rare occasions, their relationship becomes worse, but in a way that will eventually lead to their relationship improving through later story happenings.

Notes:
- This plot is used for individual episodes of a RomCom story and can be used for story arcs as well. It doesn't work so well for the Overall Story of a relationship because the goal here is limited/slow change to give the feeling the relationship is moving forward while still keeping the main characters from admitting their feelings for as long as possible.
- The main character of the episode doesn't always have to be the main character of the series, in fact it's good to switch it up and offer different perspectives on the situation. Sometimes it's the series lead, sometimes it's the series love interest, sometimes it can be a rival character, and sometimes it can be one of their friends. This can really pad out an episode count.
- Usually each character has at least one major personal flaw that prevents them from truly bonding with the other character or admitting their feelings. Through shared experience they get to know each other and by doing so move closer together. It's about trust, and the endgame is being able to admit your feelings because you feel the other side has the same feelings.
- At the end of most episodes, they will feel closer to their love interest. This may be consciously or unconsciously, and if they are young teens they may not really understand these feelings and it will lead to them being confused and more unsure.
- Unless it's near the end, something will always keep them from confessing. Usually their own fears or being rejected or insecurities.
- Usually the problem of the story is emotional/personal, not an enemy or opponent. There is something they're not willing to do but they must do it or overcome it to succeed in this situation. The problem of the episode is there to make them confront their personal flaw and force them into facing it. The way they overcome the problem should always reflect the theme of the story.
- The opponent in these stories is usually the situation which forces them to do difficult things, or their own friends/allies who work to keep the main character on track in an effort to help them overcome the problem.
- When a main character is faced with a problem in this plot, they will often try to solve it in a way which is linked to their personal flaws. The comedy part comes from them trying to solve it the wrong way, and then finally accepting they need to use the right way to solve it at the end. (A way which they knew all along, but weren't willing to do because it requires more effort than they want to put in.) An example of this is a lazy character who tries to

solve the problem in a lazy way, which seems to work, but really makes things worse, and then they actually end up having to work harder than they would have if they'd done it right in the first place. (Used this way, it's basically the same as a typical American Situation Comedy (SitCom) plot.)

- One difference between this plot and the American SitCom version is that in a SitCom the goal is no change at all, while in a RomCom plot the goal is small change with the feeling that it was more change than it really was.

- This plot works equally well for conflict and non-conflict based stories. In a non-conflict based version, the main character usually solves their problem themselves by hearing the thoughts or seeing the experiences of others. Inspiration from others leads to them to a solution, and no direct opponent is needed or other characters to conflict with.

- Since the goal of the story is minimal change and maximum interest, stories using this pattern will generally used the Positive TEN KSTK pattern. They avoid the Negative TEN pattern because the bigger the conflict at the end, the more change is required for the audience to feel satisfied with the outcome. Small stakes allow for small changes, but bigger stakes require bigger changes for a good ending. Negative TEN patterns should only be used for stories where there is real change happening, like one-shot stories that are complete, or major turning point episodes of a larger story.

- The feeling of change at the end comes from change happening to a particular character, but not necessarily a change in the situation. Maybe the character is a little more confident, or wiser, or has learned something about themselves. These kinds of changes lead up to a major change, and changes in the situation, and feel like real change, but don't change the real status quo of the story.

- For larger story arcs, you can do a series of these types of episodes which are linked together by characters, situations, time or location. These arcs usually culminate in some small, but real change in the situation or character's feelings to feel satisfying. In typical teen RomCom manga stories, these arcs are usually built around a school trip, a club outing, a school festival, the classic group summer vacation trip to the mountains, or (everyone's favorite) the beach.

- A common variation of this story is the Harem story, which will rotate the main character's interactions with a group of cuties. Each story will be about a problem they solve along with a new or previously introduced cutie, leading to positive feelings between them, then jump to another member of the harem for the next story. Usually the main character is solving the cuties' problems, which leads to them bonding with them.

Example Series: *We Never Learn, Toradora, Niseikoi, Rascal Does Not Dream of Bunny Girls, Kimagure Orange Road, etc. (Many Shoujo comics use this plot as well.)*

PUBLISHING YOUR WORK

MANGA SCRIPT FORMAT AND WRITING TIPS

If you're reading this and planning to write prose fiction, and not comics, then you can probably skip this section. You can write your prose using anything that lets you put words in front of other people's eyes: screens, paper, skin, or whatever your medium of choice is.

As for the rest of you, come close and let's reveal a dirty little secret about the comic book industry.

Are you listening? Good.

The truth is, unlike screenwriting for movies and TV, the comic book industry has no standard format for writing scripts for comics in.

So, unless you're writing for a specific client or artist who wants it done a certain way, then as long as you write it in a way that works- you're doing it right! Congratulations!

You can use any word processor and any program you like, and as long as the artist understands what you're trying to say and convey, technically there's no problem. So, feel free to use whatever you choose to write your stories, and do it proudly.

That said, there are a few common approaches that you'll generally see.

American comic book writers tend to write in script form with the story broken down into pages, panels, descriptions, and dialog. So, you'll get something like this:

Mulligan's Alley: Page 4

Panel 1: Inside a warehouse, moonlight shines down and illuminates a man sitting on a box. This is Tom, a balding gangster in his forties, who's looking right at the reader. He's wearing an expensive looking gray suit and half his face and body are in shadow while the other half are visible in the light. The box is a wooden shipping container, and the rest of the warehouse is shrouded in darkness, so we can only see a bit of the grungy floor and silhouettes of other boxes.

TOM

Good evening, Rick. I didn't think you'd come.

RICK

(Off panel.) Hey man, you call. I come. Right?

Panel 2: Same as above, but now a medium shot of Tom's face. He looks sinister and threatening, almost like a demon. To emphasize this, we can see the eye in the shadows as well, as though it has its own inner light.

TOM

You did indeed. Now, let's have a talk about loyalty.

And so on...

You can use any program for writing your scripts, but using a scriptwriting program will make your life easier because it will take care of all the formatting for you, and let you just focus on the creative side of things. There isn't a best program for comic book scriptwriting out there yet, but one that works pretty well (and is free!) is *CELTX*, which is a universal scriptwriting program that comes with comic book templates built in. *Scrivener*, also has comic book templates built into it, although they require a little more work to use than CELTX does. (They involve some extra key commands.) Some writers also use *Final Draft* and *Movie Magic Screenwriter* (which are the programs the entertainment industry writes movies on), but those require finding templates or playing with them to get the results you want.

More software is being developed all the time, so do a search and find something you feel comfortable using, even if it's Notepad on your PC or phone. As long as it works, it's all good.

Overall, how you do it is up to you and whoever you happen to working with. Although, if you're submitting your work for professional review, you might want to make your work look as standard and organized as possible to impress them and hopefully get work.

Also, while this book doesn't cover the visual art side of creating manga, there are a few important ideas that even the writer of manga stories must know in order to make the jump from text to art as easy as possible. Knowing them and keeping them in mind will make the artist like you more, and can only help to produce better manga in the end.

- Know whether your artist is going to be working in the traditional paged style of comic art, or the modern vertical strip (Korean webcomic) style designed for phone reading. Whichever type you choose, make sure you study the way it flows deeply. Try taking some of your favorite comic stories and breaking them down into script form to study how the creators put them together.

- The job of the writer is to inspire the artist, not to tell them what to do. Limit your descriptions to what happens in each panel and try to make the artist feel what should be in the panel. Don't describe it in extreme detail unless you're working with a new artist who doesn't understand visual comic composition and layout.
- Don't forget comics are a visual medium. The story should be told through visuals first, text and captions second. Try to write so that your story could be followed even if all the captions disappeared one day.
- Remember that each comic page should end on some visual or dramatic hook to get the reader to turn to the next page. If you can't think of a dramatic (story) hook, then use something simple like a character asking a question, or the results of an action to get the reader to turn the page.
- A typical comic page is 4-6 panels, and when in doubt, shoot for five as your target number. This will leave enough room for art and balloons/captions so the page isn't overcrowded. It also leaves enough room for the artist to add, subtract or re-arrange panels as needed if they get inspired.
- Word balloons and captions should have a maximum of 25 words in them to keep them from crowding out the art. This can vary depending on the size of the panels, and a single panel should have no more than three large balloons.
- Once you've established something in the first panels, you don't need to keep describing what's in each new panel if the location doesn't change. Only describe what's different.
- Avoid using too many captions, and try to use visuals (and dialog) to convey needed information except when really necessary. This is mostly about style, but captions slow the reading experience down, whereas dialog is interesting and quick. (Unless there's too much of it.) Things like signs and in-setting text convey both setting and information, whereas captions only convey information.
- Remember that while it might take you a few seconds to write something, it might take a poor artist days to actually draw it. Write as though the detail of every panel costs you money (which it might), and the more complicated the panel the more expensive it is. That way you'll save the really beautiful shots for when they're needed and will make the most impact.
- Consider doing a separate profile reference sheet for each major character, including their descriptions and any other information the artist needs to know. You can do a similar reference sheet for any major locations where the action of the story will be occurring. This way you can avoid cluttering up your script with overly long panel descriptions (letting it flow better), and also give the artist quick reference materials to work with they don't have to dig for. These

don't have to be books, just a page or two containing the important information the artist needs to know.

- Don't be afraid to include hyperlinks with the panel descriptions to online resources the artists might need.

- Google the "Comic Book Script Archive" and read some of the sample scripts professionals have donated to it. If possible, compare them to the actual comics, and see how the writers put their scripts together. Sadly, it's very difficult to find Japanese manga scripts translated into English, so unless you can read Japanese you're better off using American ones as your models.

Each writer/artist team has their own way of working together. It will be awkward at first, but with time you'll get to know and trust each other, making things go more smoothly. Be patient with yourselves and your partners. Learn to let the other person use their strengths and when to do a little extra to help them with their weaknesses. Communication is the key to making great comics!

R.A. Paterson

THE JAPANESE MANGA
INDUSTRY

In many ways, the Japanese comic book industry and the American one were born out of the same circumstances. In America, the comic industry exploded out of the Great Depression at the end of the 1920's as young people sought a cheap and light form of fantastic entertainment in a harsh world of poverty and struggle. Similarly, the modern Japanese *manga* (manga means "foolish pictures") industry was born in the economic devastation of the post-World War II Japan era when, again, people wanted something cheap and entertaining to distract them from hardships of the day.

However, while they both came from similar beginnings, both industries took very different paths. The American comic industry bloomed brightly until being declared a threat to American youth in 1954 and being forced to limit itself to becoming a form of children's entertainment to escape the wrath of concerned parents. Under the watchful eye of the Comics Code, American comics would stay neutered and harmless fun for decades, and develop a reputation as something only children and nerds would enjoy.

The Japanese manga industry, however, wouldn't face the challenges of concerned parent's groups until well into the 1970's, and by then it was too late- the horse had long left the barn. While early manga of the 1950's were indeed targeted at a young audience, thanks to the *gekiga* (dramatic pictures) movement of the 1960's and artists who wanted to push the limits of the medium, the manga industry quickly became a mass form of entertainment enjoyed by people of all ages, backgrounds, and interests. From comics for girls, to comics for adult male office workers, and from comics about sports, to comics about gambling and fishing, from comics about romance, to ones about gothic horror, the Japanese manga industry has comics for all people of all tastes.

So, with that in mind, let's look at a few key features of this very Japanese, yet somehow still global and universal art form.

Format

As many readers likely know, Japanese manga initially come out in chapters published in weekly, bi-weekly, or monthly magazine anthologies. *Weekly Shonen JUMP*, for example, has roughly 23 titles running in it at any given time, each of them

260

publishing a new 15-20-page chapter each week. There will also be one-shot stories and other shorter features like gag comic strips and articles in each issue, all of it printed in a black and white pulp paper book that looks a bit like an oversized paperback novel. Other manga magazines may be shorter and have less titles and different features, but most will follow this same format in one way or the other. Chapters in monthly magazines tend to be 45-50 pages to make up for their slower release schedules, and accordingly monthly magazines will have fewer titles. A slow shift has also begun to publishing manga as webcomics, but the Japanese publishing industry is highly resistant to change (like the American comics industry) and they are still working out format and distribution methods.

Once a manga title has reached 8-10 chapters in length (or equivalent), it is then collected as a *tankobon*- a paperback collected volume which is sold in bookstores, specialty shops, and many other locations. The *tankobon* of popular series can sell millions of volumes by themselves upon their releases, and then go on to sell further millions of copies over years and decades as new generations of readers who never touched a magazine find them and collect them. Some series like *Naruto, Bleach,* and *One Piece* can have fifty or more collected volumes. This has also created a rhythm to manga publication where manga creators often think in terms of where and when story arcs will start and end in relation to the collected volumes they will be released in. (Trying to end each *tankobon* on a high note that makes the reader eagerly want to buy the following one to find out what happens next.)

Production

Manga production works roughly as follows:

1. The manga creator (who is usually both the writer and artist, but sometimes these are different people) comes up with a few chapters for a story and does very rough storyboards (simple sketched comics called NAMEs) of them.

2. They take these to the editor their publisher assigned to them, and the editor tells them what works and what doesn't until they both agree on the changes that need to be made.

3. Once the storyboards are finalized, the creator then sits down and draws the important parts of the pages in pencil and sometimes inks them as well.

4. As the creator finishes pages, they hand those incomplete pages off to a team of assistants who specialize in things like backgrounds, text, and other parts of comic art. Those assistants quickly take care of the things that still need to be done before handing them back to the creator.

5. The creator then checks over each page, and when satisfied, they give them to their editor, and if the editor is satisfied they go for publication while the creator shows the editor their ideas for the next chapters and the cycle begins again.

This is an extremely repetitive assembly-line process and goes on week after week, and year after year, which is why some manga creators get burned out or take long breaks. It is a grueling method which also acts as an informal apprenticeship system, where new artists become assistants to published ones, and then with experience and connections in the industry leave when they're ready to strike out on their own.

Reader Response Cards

Manga publishers pay close attention to their readerships through reader response cards which are inserted into every issue of the magazine. These simple to fill-in cards have allowed publishers to keep the pulse of their reader for decades, and they are considered key to keeping magazines like *Weekly Shonen* Jump alive and vital. The editors and publishers of a magazine watch new titles like hawks, always checking to see if a title is maintaining, losing, or gaining popularity and the possible reasons for the reader reactions.

As a result, most manga creators only work a few weeks ahead of their publication date at most. This is to enable them to react and change the story depending on the reactions of the readership to the currently running chapters. Depending on reader reactions, a storyline may be extended, cut short, or even changed completely in an effort to keep ratings up, and if a series falls below a certain threshold it can even face a creator's worst nightmare- cancellation.

A manga creator must always be ready to try every trick in their disposal and draw on their experience to create stories that keep readers enthralled. If they don't, there's always a new creator ready to take their place (and their income) and a team of assistants they will have to lay off due to their own personal failure to keep the series running. It is a hard job, and one that favors young creators who have the energy to pull regular all-nighters to get the work done over older creators who can't draw for as long as they once could.

GETTING PUBLISHED

When it comes to getting your work published, there's good news and bad news.

The good news is that you have decided to put your work out into the world at a time of transition, when the old models of top-down publishing are falling away and there has never been more opportunity to get your work out there for people to see. Your audience is now potentially global, which means your work can also be seen and enjoyed by roughly 3.2 billion people. Also, there are now more markets than ever, with various websites in different languages ready to promote work they think their audience wants to see, and even share the profits with creators.

The bad news is that any of those 3.2 billion people who have internet access can also publish just like you, and quite a few of them have, and so it's created a flooded market where even the best work is hard to find in a sea of really bad stuff. At the same time, the big publishers are slowly dying, and the whole ecosystem for promoting, selling and marketing comic books in English is slowly falling apart.

Comics have never had it worse, but even in the bad times, there are always opportunities. So, let's look at the available markets for getting your work out there.

THE AMERICAN COMIC MARKET

The United States has the biggest English comic book market in the world, but it's not in good condition right now. Much of the American market was built on superhero comics, and while superheroes are flourishing in other media like movies and TV, sales of comic books have been on a steady decline for years. Not so long ago, a top Marvel book could sell half a million copies a month, but now the biggest Marvel comics only sell around 50,000 copies- a 90% drop. With so much competition from other media, the physical monthly comic book is becoming a relic of the past, and its future doesn't look good.

As a result, the industry is working hard to survive. They're trying different types of comic book genres, and even different takes on superheroes, but so far nothing has really caught on with a larger audience. They've also shifted to selling graphic novels, which is proving more successful, but those are mostly collections of older comics from the glory days of the American industry. This makes it a hard slog for new material to get out there into the bookstores and get noticed, even in graphic novel format.

But, there is a little bit of hope on the digital horizon.

First Marvel and now DC are trying to use the Netflix model to create their own online comic book platforms by offering subscription services that give readers access to their vast back catalogues and new material as well. If these catch on, this might mean they will start looking for more content that they can publish to attract new readers, and the most popular of that material will end up being published as graphic novels. This is similar as to what's happening in the Asian webfiction markets already, where the online platforms have become a way for the big publishers to profit-share with new talent and promote the best of that new talent to star status.

But, whether it works out that way remains to be seen.

How to get in: The best way to enter the American Comics Market is to do a Web comic (see below) and then use that as a way to get experience and attention. Then use that as a showcase for your work to approach the publishers and show them what you can do. Alternately, you can try to network and get to know editors and people in the industry at conventions and online, but if you don't have good work to show them to prove your ability, they're not likely to trust or hire you, so you still need to get work out there in some form first.

WEB COMICS

Web comics are currently the best entry point into the comics industry.

All they take is for you to draw them, stick them up on your own website (or a hosting site), and then list it on one of many web comic directories. After that, it's all about two things: 1) producing quality work on a regular basis and 2) finding an audience.

Number one is entirely up to you, and will probably take a while to get right. Nobody starts amazing, and everyone has to slowly work their way up the quality ladder through sheer sweat and hard work. Also, you need to have a regular schedule, because humans are creatures of habit- if they like your work and you tell them there will be new pages up every Monday and Wednesday, then they'll keep coming back on those days. If you break that schedule, they'll break the habit of reading your work, and your audience won't grow. Even the best work released on a poor schedule won't build an audience, while average work coming out steadily can build a big one fast.

Number two is about a good schedule, as was just mentioned, but it's also about plain old marketing. While the web comics market isn't as flooded as the ebook market is (because not everyone can draw, there's less competition), there are still a lot of web comics out there. So, if you want to get a big audience for yours, you'll need to find ways to get the word out and get noticed. You can list it on web comic directories, you can participate in web comic forums, and go on sites like Reddit which have groups you can use to promote/list new releases. However, don't expect any of this to produce a result overnight. Just stay active and keep trying, and your audience will either come or it won't.

Now, what do you get for all of this work?

Well, beyond the experience, exposure for your work, and networking with fellow creators and audience members, web comics can also be profitable. Some web comic hosts share the advertising money they make from your comic with you, so that can help, and you can also set up a Patreon page where your audience members can support your work through regular donations or subscriptions. Also, once you get enough pages done, you can collect them into a graphic novel or collection and stick them up on websites for sale in digital or print forms.

However, the real money, as George Lucas discovered after he made a small film called *Star Wars*, is in the merchandising. Web comics are a visual medium, so you have art you can turn into t-shirts, cups, or whatever else you and *Café Press* and *Zazzle.com* can come up with. If you can build a big fandom, they will support you by buying your related merchandise, so even a free web comic can be very profitable for the creator down the line.

You can also publish any kind of comic you like as a web comic, rather than being limited to any particular genre or format. Of course, like anything, the more different your project is from the norm, the harder it will be to get people to give it a shot. So, it's often best to stick to the more familiar genres and styles at first and then experiment over time, but as a smart man once said- you're not being paid, so do whatever you want!

THE (ACTUAL) JAPANESE MANGA INDUSTRY

Unless you're Japanese (or at least grew up in Japan), forget it.

Not only is it extremely difficult to even gain entry into the comics industry in Japan due to language and cultural barriers, but working as part of it is a nightmare. Manga artists literally work themselves to death on a schedule that involves drawing 16-18 pages of quality comic art a week, and then doing the same the next week, and the week after that, and the week after that, for years or decades. By comparison, an American comic artist does 20 pages a month, and they still come in late sometimes because it's hard to get it done on time.

Even if you do get in, the competition is fierce and you're locked into a constant ratings battle with whoever else is published in the same magazine, and if your ratings drop below a certain point you're cancelled in favor of new up and comers. You also have to collaborate with an editor, and in any disagreement, the editor wins because he has the money backing him, so forget having the freedom to write what you like.

Now, on the plus side, yes, you can get paid reasonably well, and there is always the potential for an anime series if your manga is a hit. However, you have to share that money with the assistants that you need to actually pull off the insane production schedule, and your odds of getting an anime are only slightly better than getting a winning lottery ticket unless you're in *Weekly Shonen JUMP*. (And even then, go look at the current issue of *JUMP* and count how many manga series in there actually have anime adaptations and you'll see the numbers aren't in your favor.)

Finally, if you're really determined, at least read the manga *Bakuman* before you try, since it will give you a good view of the Japanese process. However, keep in mind that *Bakuman* is a highly romanticized Activity Manga story, and the main character **still almost dies from overwork** at more than one point in the story. The real process is nowhere near as fun.

THE KOREAN/CHINESE WEB COMIC INDUSTRIES

If you can fluently read/write Korean or Chinese, both of them have flourishing web comic industries that you can try to become a part of. There are several big portals like Naver in Korea and Fengxuan.net in China you can submit your work to, and potentially receive money for it from their profit-sharing systems. Just make sure you read the submission rules carefully, or else you might end up giving up a lot more rights to your work than you'd like.

Also, there are unique challenges to working in the Chinese and Korean markets, as they both have different art styles they prefer and Koreans even use an entirely different webcomic format than almost anyone else. Add to this that they have genres that are unique to their cultures and dissimilar tastes to Americans as well, and it can be quite a challenge for someone from outside the market to get in.

WEBFICTION

Leaving the comic book format, you might want to try writing webfiction as a way to practice your writing craft. Big sites like *Wattpad*, *Webnovel.com*, and *Fictionhub* offer the potential of huge audiences for original work, and they also let you network with other writers and fans to build up your own personal reputations. Some of these sites will also do profit sharing on the more popular stories, sharing ad revenue with the authors, and will help to promote the works they see as worthy. They also don't usually lock you in (read contracts carefully), so once your story is done you can turn around and also publish it as an ebook (see below) and find new audiences and sources of revenue.

On the downside, as usual it's hard to get noticed on these sites unless you're really good, and each hosting site has its own audiences. Wattpad, for example, started out as a fanfiction site, and as a result has a huge audience of female teen readers, and a much smaller one of males and non-teen readers. This is great if they're your target audience, but if they're not your target audience you might find trying to get an audience for your story there more difficult. So, if that suits your style, you're set, but if it doesn't then you might find it harder to build an audience. Finally, there isn't much money in webfiction unless you illustrate your works and can then turn those illustrations into merchandise.

To learn more about writing webfiction read *How to Write Light Novels and Webnovels*, by R.A. Paterson.

THE EBOOK MARKET

At the moment, roughly 40% of online book sales are of ebooks, and so naturally any writer should consider self-publishing their work as ebooks as an option. There is a huge wealth of wisdom regarding this subject online, and David Gaughran and Chris Fox are two names you should look up if you want to enter the ebook market. Both of them have written books to walk you through the process, and you can find more information about self-publishing on forums like kBoards and Absolutewrite.com, and the Creative Penn podcast.

However, the ebook market is not a place for the faint of heart. Yes, it's easy to get in, but because of that the competition is massive, and writers need to also be skilled marketers if they want to get any success. If you're a new and unknown writer, don't expect any attention, feedback, or sales unless you get very lucky or have an amazing product with an amazing cover (sad to say, it seems like most ebook sales are due to their covers, not their content). This is a little easier if you're publishing ebook versions of graphic novels, since there's less of them, but even then, it will be a hard battle to get noticed.

If you do decide to brave the vast ebook seas in search of treasure, here are a few tips:

- Get the best cover you can afford.
- Get the best editing you can afford.
- Pick a genre and build your reputation in it, don't jump around between genres.
- Write a series, not stand-alone books.
- Write fast, publish often.
- Research the market, it literally changes every few months.
- Expect to write at least three books before you get any real audience.
- View every book you write as a lottery ticket- it might yield nothing, or it might be a hit. You never know until you put it out there.

CONVENTIONAL PUBLISHING

Finally, if you want to publish fiction and your dream is to have a publisher do the marketing while you just write and bask in book tours, there's something you should know- that kind of author/publisher relationship doesn't exist anymore. Even if you sign with a big publisher, at best you'll get a US$5000 advance (down from US$20,000 over two decades ago) and still be expected to do your own marketing and all the work you'd have to do if you self-published. In return, you'll get around 7% of the profit of each book sold in the almost extinct bookstore market, as opposed to the up to 70% you get from self-publishing.

All this, after potentially years of waiting to hear whether your book was accepted by the big publishers, when it could have been out there making you money and building your career as a self-published book.

However, the big publishers aren't the only ones in the game anymore. There are now a number of small-press publishers who offer good terms, help with marketing, and even help with editing and covers. So, if you want to see your work in bookstores, but don't want to give up all your rights to a big publisher, do some research into small-press publishers and see if you can find one which might work for you.

FINAL ADVICE

When you first start to write, there are generally two views new writers have:

1) I've got this. This writing stuff is easy.

2) OMG! Where do I start?

Now, you might think the second person is the one who's going to have a hard time while the first person is going to breeze through things. This, however, isn't always the case.

Writing is hard work, and people who think they've got it right at the start are usually underestimating just how much work is involved in writing not just a story, but a good story. All too often they have a few areas where they're ahead of the curve, but they're mostly doing it from instinct based on having already read a lot by their favorite writers. Instinct and talent is a great thing to have, but it's only a start, and hard work will trump talent every time.

Meanwhile, the second writer, the one who is intimidated by the whole thing, is actually the one looking at it realistically. There is a lot to being a writer, and if you don't believe me go on a writer's forum and ask people who have two, three, five, ten, twenty, forty or more books to their name if they think they've mastered it. Very few of them will tell you that have, and most will say they're still learning and still struggle with X, Y, and Z in their writing.

So yeah, writing is a hard, never ending journey, just like any art.

But, the good news is that the basics you need to know to start that journey aren't actually all that difficult to learn. With a little knowledge, and a lot of practice, most people can be solidly decent writers in terms of technique, and start to put out work they can be proud of.

With what you've learned in this book, you should be among them. That is, if you keep practicing, and keep putting your work out there.

Science Fiction Writer Robert. A. Heinlein in his essay "On the Writing of Speculative Fiction" once gave his rules of writing as follows:

1) You must write.

2) You must finish what you start.

3) You must put it on the market.

He said that if you accomplished these things, you would be a writer.

He wrote those rules in 1947, but the truth is that they're just as relevant today, and perhaps even moreso. To be writer you need to write (not talk about it or think about it, but actually DO it), you need to finish what you start (starting stories easy, finishing is what's hard and takes skill), and you need to get it out there so other people can give you feedback (good and bad). If you can't do these three things, you can't be a writer.

But they're not hard things to do.

They just take time.

And work.

And not giving up.

But if you follow them, like Heinlein, I will promise you one thing- you will be a writer.

You might not be rich, famous, or even successful (whatever that means), but you will be someone who can call themselves a writer and be able to point to a body of work that shows your writer's journey to date. You'll be able to hold your head up high when asked what you do and say- "I write".

And that, is perhaps one of the best feelings in the world.

Good luck in your writing. Keep learning, and keep pounding those keys.

Rob

DID YOU ENJOY THIS BOOK?

If you want to know more about me, you can check out my blog at Robynpaterson.com where I post about my stories, writing, art, podcasting, culture, history, and whatever I think is interesting. You can also subscribe to my blog, which will let you hear about the latest posts.

Also, sign up for my newsletter on my website to get access to special offers, writing tips, and worksheets to use when crafting your masterpiece.

You can also find my author page on Facebook.

Thanks for reading!

ISEKAI FANTASY AND MORE!

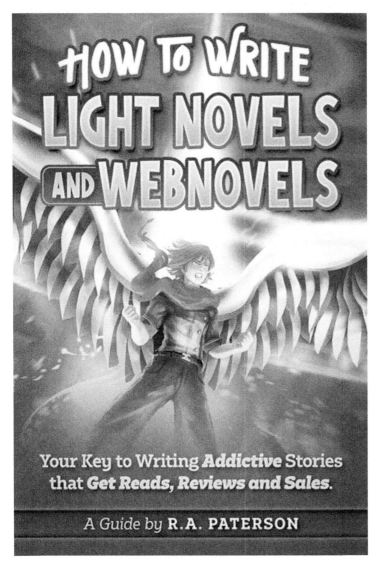

R.A. Paterson

R.A. Paterson

Printed in Great Britain
by Amazon

82574073R00161